# Beginning Zend Framework

**Armando Padilla**

**Beginning Zend Framework**

ISBN-13 (pbk): 978-1-4302-1825-8

ISBN-13 (electronic): 978-1-4302-1826-5

Printed and bound in the United States of America 9 8 7 6 5 4 3 2 1

Trademarked names may appear in this book. Rather than use a trademark symbol with every occurrence of a trademarked name, we use the names only in an editorial fashion and to the benefit of the trademark owner, with no intention of infringement of the trademark.

Lead Editors: Steve Anglin and Matthew Moodie

Technical Reviewer: Adam DeFields

Editorial Board: Clay Andres, Steve Anglin, Mark Beckner, Ewan Buckingham, Tony Campbell, Gary Cornell, Jonathan Gennick, Michelle Lowman, Matthew Moodie, Jeffrey Pepper, Frank Pohlmann, Ben Renow-Clarke, Dominic Shakeshaft, Matt Wade, Tom Welsh

Project Managers: Beth Christmas and Debra Kelly

Copy Editor: Nancy Sixsmith, ConText Editorial Services

Associate Production Director: Kari Brooks-Copony

Production Editor: Ellie Fountain

Compositor: Tricia Bronkella

Indexer: BIM Indexing

Cover Designer: Kurt Krames

Manufacturing Director: Tom Debolski

Distributed to the book trade worldwide by Springer-Verlag New York, Inc., 233 Spring Street, 6th Floor, New York, NY 10013. Phone 1-800-SPRINGER, fax 201-348-4505, e-mail orders-ny@springer-sbm.com, or visit http://www.springeronline.com.

For information on translations, please e-mail info@apress.com, or visit http://www.apress.com.

Apress and friends of ED books may be purchased in bulk for academic, corporate, or promotional use. eBook versions and licenses are also available for most titles. For more information, reference our Special Bulk Sales–eBook Licensing web page at http://www.apress.com/info/bulksales.

The information in this book is distributed on an "as is" basis, without warranty. Although every precaution has been taken in the preparation of this work, neither the author(s) nor Apress shall have any liability to any person or entity with respect to any loss or damage caused or alleged to be caused directly or indirectly by the information contained in this work.

The source code for this book is available to readers at http://www.apress.com.

*To my parents, Guillermo Padilla and Francisca Osuna. To my friend Susannah Halweg. You have shaped the person that I am today. Thank you.*

# Contents at a Glance

# Contents

x

# About the Author

Armando Padilla has spent the last 3.5 years working on Zend Framework projects such as http://www.dundermifflininfinity.com (NBC/Universal) as well as personal projects. His PHP experience began in 1998, when he created small PHP web pages for Thomas Jefferson High School (Los Angeles). Armando's most recent work was for NBC/Universal, where he built medium- to large-scale applications.

Armando now spends much of his time working for Shine (Yahoo!), reading the Zend Framework API, creating extensions for the Framework, and expanding his skill set by pursuing a master's degree in computer science.

# About the Technical Reviewer

Adam DeFields is a consultant specializing in web application development, project management, technical writing/editing, and instructional design. He lives in Grand Rapids, Michigan, where he runs Emanation Systems, LLC (www.emanationsystemsllc.com), an IT services company he founded in 2002. Adam has coauthored or reviewed more than a dozen books on various technologies, including Java, PHP, Apache, MySQL, and Zend Framework.

# Acknowledgments

There were times that I felt I could not write this book. I think all first-time authors must feel this way, no matter how knowledgeable they might be in a certain field. It's a very humbling feeling.

I know I wouldn't have grown from this experience without the Apress team. I want to thank all of them. Thanks especially to Beth Christmas for putting up with my "deadline malfunctions" and having the patience to work with me. Thanks to Steve Anglin for taking a chance and giving me the opportunity to write this book, and a big thank you to Matthew Moodie for taking the time to lend a hand.

# Introduction

Welcome to *Beginning Zend Framework*! The primary goal of this book is to set the foundation for your journey into Zend Framework. You can be a beginner or a seasoned developer—this book includes something for everyone. For the Zend Framework beginner, this book covers everything from the basic setup to answering questions about what a controller is. For the seasoned developer, it includes chapters on the caching and the search component of Zend Framework.

What the book doesn't include is a how-to of PHP. Because the book is entirely focused on using PHP, you need at least a basic understanding of the language.

## Overview

Following is a chapter-by-chapter breakdown—the road map.

## Chapter 1: "Getting Started with Zend Framework"

You need a starting point, and there is nothing better than setting up a working development environment to get off on the right foot. This chapter covers all the tools you need to get a simple and complex application powered by Zend Framework up and running. It furnishes step-by-step instructions on how to install and test each component, and finishes up by showing you how to create a small application using Zend Framework's Zend_Tool.

## Chapter 2: "The Application"

If you're reading this book chapter by chapter, here you will create a small application called Loudbite, which is a small music mashup site. The application leaves plenty of room for you to expand on and is only used for the examples. This chapter provides not only the background but also the database ERD and overall architecture of the application.

## Chapter 3: "Writing Controllers Using Zend_Controller"

Zend Framework has a unique way of controlling user requests, and this chapter covers the basic building blocks of this process. The chapter describes the URL structure as well as how Zend Framework treats each piece of the URL to route the user to the appropriate controller-action of the application.

## Chapter 4: "Views, Forms, Filters, and Validators"

What would a Framework book be without a chapter on the crucial elements web developers create everyday on a project? Forms! This chapter covers how Zend Framework eases the grueling tasks of creating, validating, and filtering forms.

## Chapter 5: "Database Communication, Manipulation, and Display"

Because most web applications require a persistent storage unit such as a database, this chapter looks at the database support that Zend Framework provides. This chapter covers using PDO, creating statements, executing statements, retrieving information, using object-oriented statements, and working with built-in pagination support.

## Chapter 6: "Sending and Receiving E-mail"

E-mail! Zend Framework did not stop at database and typical web layer functions; it also created a solid e-mail component for sending and retrieving e-mail. This chapter shows you how to create e-mail, how to send e-mail using text and HTML, and how to send attachments.

## Chapter 7: "Web Services and Feeds"

For today's developers, REST and RSS feeds are part of the standard vernacular. So it's no surprise that Zend Framework has included support for these services and has gone one step further by providing wrappers for your favorite open APIs. This chapter covers how Zend Framework works with the current web service alphabet soup: REST. It also shows you how to create web services, call web services, and create and consume feeds.

## Chapter 8: "Creating a Search Engine Using Zend_Search_Lucene"

This chapter discusses search engines and how Zend Framework has packaged a proven search engine such as Lucene. It takes you step by step into creating each of the building blocks of the search engine: from creating an index to adding content using the built-in wrappers for Word, HTML documents, and Excel files.

## Chapter 9: "Caching with Zend Framework"

The last chapter discusses how you can get that extra juice by speeding up applications using cache. You will learn how to successfully implement the Zend Caching component for standard HTML to database records.

# Contacting the Author

As a reader of technical manuals, I tend to have more questions about topics covered in the book after each chapter. If you encounter any questions, I'm here to help. You can reach me directly at armando_padilla_81@yahoo.com or you can find me posting Zend Framework–related items as well as answering any questions you may have with this book on this site: www.beginningzendframework.com.

All source code for this book can be found on the Apress web site as well as on http://www.loudbite.com and http://www.beginningzendframework.com. Enjoy!

# CHAPTER 1

■ ■ ■

# Getting Started with Zend Framework

Regardless of your programming skills, you have decided to make your way into the Zend Framework world. Some of you might be new to programming; others might be seasoned developers heading a large team. Regardless of your status or reasons why you want to enter the Zend Framework world, everyone starts on the same page. Yes, stop your groaning; that means setting up the environment and dealing with the technology that will get you up and running toward building your application powered by Zend Framework.

You might be wondering why you need to go through this process. That's fair; when I started developing PHP applications, I asked the same question—but I continued to follow the steps to set up the environment. Looking back to my experience, I can say that setting up the environment will give you a few things right away. For new developers, it will introduce the technology Zend Framework needs to successfully start developing applications. Think about it like this: if I gave you a box of tools and asked you to build a house, how on earth would you go about accomplishing that task if you didn't know how to use each of the tools in the box? So you also need to learn which tools you need to build your figurative house: a Zend Framework application.

If you know which tools are needed to run applications, you will understand the limitations of those applications. If your boss came up to you, stared into your eyes, and (besides telling you that you rock) said, "I need a Zend Framework application that will handle ten million users per month, a few hundred thousand hits per minute and have a response time of less than a second. Can you do it?" You should be able to tell him, "Yeah, I rock. What's new?" You can also say, "Yes! You'll have it in a month, with all the bells and whistles you asked for." I can't promise that Zend Framework will handle 1,000 hits per second because that's for your load balancer to handle, but I do promise that Zend Framework will make it fun for you to deliver the product on time.

The goal of this chapter is to set up a development environment with all the free tools available:

- Apache 2.2
- MySQL 5.1 or later
- PHP 5.2.4 or later.
- Zend Framework 1.8

You will also create your first Hello World application powered by Zend Framework and review the basic components required to power all Zend Framework applications efficiently.

## The Tools

Let's open up that toolbox now and see what's in there. You see a hammer, some nails, and a blow torch, enough to start a house. Don't worry; installing your tools will be an easy process. If you're a senior developer, take a look at the list of software and determine whether you need to read this section or not. If you feel comfortable installing the tools on your own, or if you already have a development environment that will run the required PHP version, skip these few sections and start with the "Installing Zend Framework" section later in this chapter.

Regardless of your experience, take the time to read through the installation and setup process of Zend Framework and create the small Hello World application outlined in this chapter. Trust me; it will prove invaluable to read the section and create the test application.

Let's begin installing the development environment step by step.

---

■ **Note** Windows users should continue reading; Mac users can skip to the section called "Installing a Mac Development Environment." We don't cover Linux/Unix installation because your distribution will have its own way of installing Apache, MySQL, and PHP (although we do discuss installing Zend Framework). Refer to your distribution's documentation if you are unsure or need more help.

---

# Apache

You will start with the base software that most web applications need: Apache. Without Apache, most web applications installed on computers could not communicate with the world.

## Installing Apache on Windows

As of this writing, Apache has released version 2.2.x of its free web server. If you have a hosted web server you can use it; depending on your setup you might need to skip this section and head toward the "Installing Zend Framework" section. For everyone else, let's start the process of installing Apache on your computer.

Pull up the Apache web site (http://httpd.apache.org), click the "Download! from a mirror" link on the left side, and select from one of the mirror sites shown on the following page. Windows users: download the Windows installer file apache_2.2.x-win32-x86-no_ssl-r2.msi.

After the file has completely downloaded, open the installer. The initial window will be a security warning (see Figure 1-1). Depending on your version of Windows, ignore it and click Run to get into the installation.

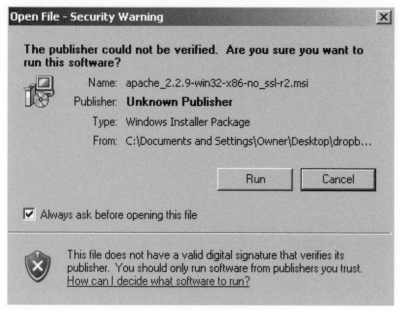

**Figure 1-1.** Windows installation security warning

The next window is the Apache setup window. If you have a previous version of Apache installed, you might see another pop-up window that asks you to remove the previous installation before you begin the new one.

---

■ **Note** If you don't want to upgrade, skip the steps dealing with Apache.

---

Click Next on the initial window (see Figure 1-2).

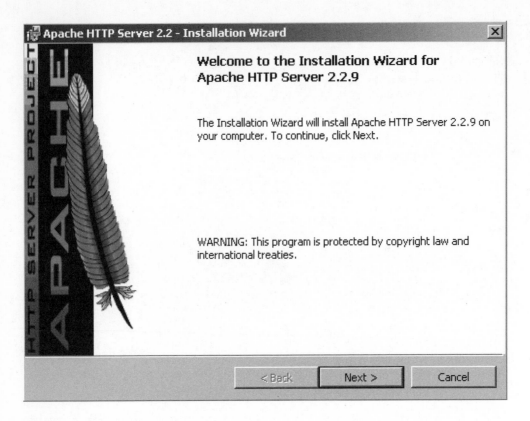

*Figure 1-2.* *Apache installation welcome window*

In the License Agreement window that displays, select "I accept the terms in the license agreement" and click Next (see Figure 1-3). Click Next in the following window.

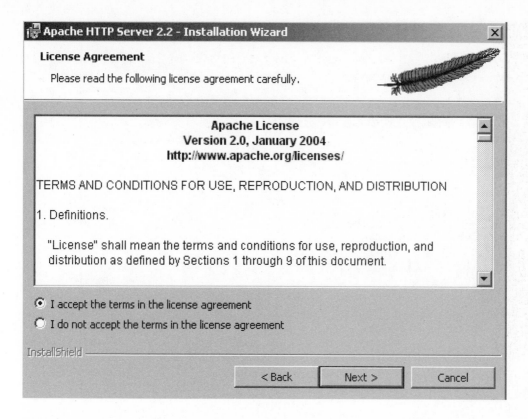

**Figure 1-3.** *Apache server terms and conditions window*

The Server Information window displays (see Figure 1-4). You need to fill in all the fields. Because this will be a web server operating on your desktop, you can add any domain name and network name into the Network Domain and Server Name fields, respectively. I chose to enter **localhost** for both of those fields. Enter your e-mail address in the Administrator's Email Address field and then click Next.

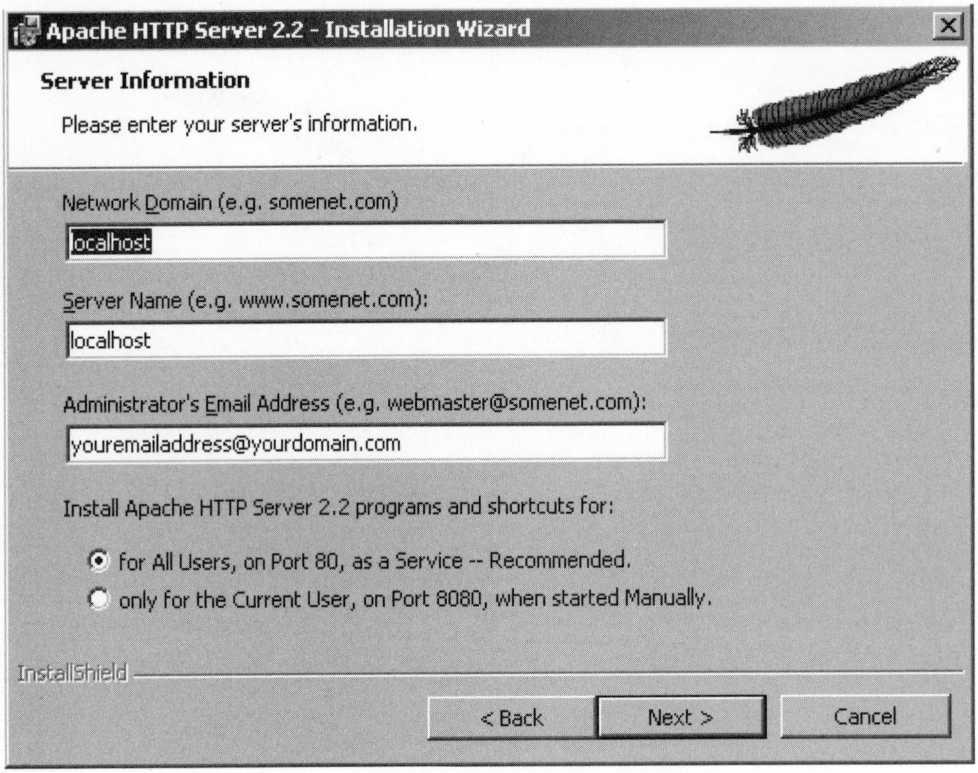

*Figure 1-4. Apache Server Information window*

Next, start installing the software. You need to tell the Apache Installation Wizard where to install it. The window shown in Figure 1-5 allows you to do just that. Click Custom and then click Next.

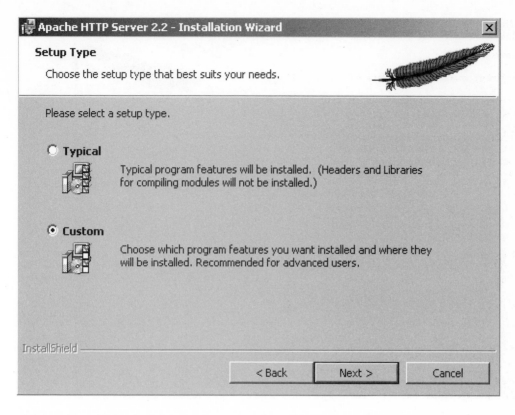

***Figure 1-5.*** *Apache Setup Type window*

In the Custom Setup window shown in Figure 1-6, click Change.

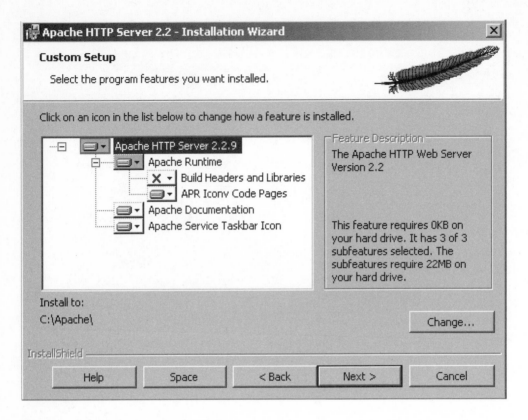

***Figure 1-6.*** *Apache Custom Setup window*

For ease of use throughout this book, I recommend that you change the location of the installation directory in the Change Current Destination Folder window to C:\Apache (if you want to save Apache in an alternative location, that's fine, too).

---

■ **Note** For future reference, remember that C:\Apache will be referred to as APACHE_HOME from here on out.

---

Click OK and then click Next.

Finally you're at the last window. Click Install and watch it go. That's all there is to it. You have successfully installed a web serveron your computer.

## Installing a Mac Development Environment

Mac users, you're in luck. Installing a complete development environment with Apache, MySQL, and PHP requires you to download only one all-in-one package, MAMP (Macintosh, Apache, MySQL, and

PHP). The package can be found here: http://www.mamp.info. Go ahead and load the URL in your browser as you continue reading.

After the page loads, click the Downloads link. You'll see two available versions of the package at this point. For your environment, you'll be okay with the basic MAMP version, not the MAMP & MAMP Pro version. Click the Download link and wait for it to download.

As soon MAMP completely downloads, double-click the .dmg file saved to your computer and install MAMP into the Applications folder.

---

■ **Caution** It's critical that you do not install MAMP in a subfolder; it will not work properly if this is done.

---

Open the Applications directory, click the MAMP directory, and click the MAMP manager, as shown in Figure 1-7.

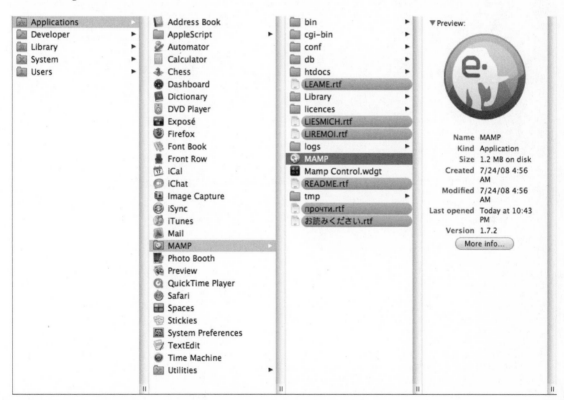

**Figure 1-7.** *MAMP executable in the Applications directory*

The manager will appear. If everything worked as expected, you should see the MAMP manager display a green indicator on both the Apache Server status and the MySQL Server status (see Figure 1-8).

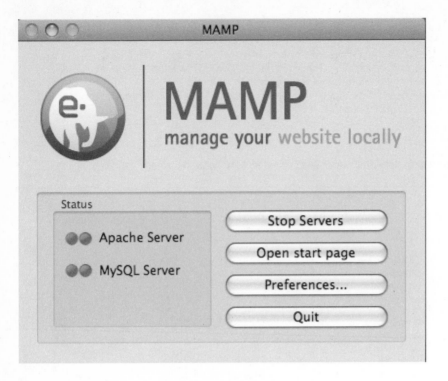

*Figure 1-8.* *MAMP Manager servers running OK*

You're almost done. Click Preferences, and you'll be presented with a window much like Figure 1-9.

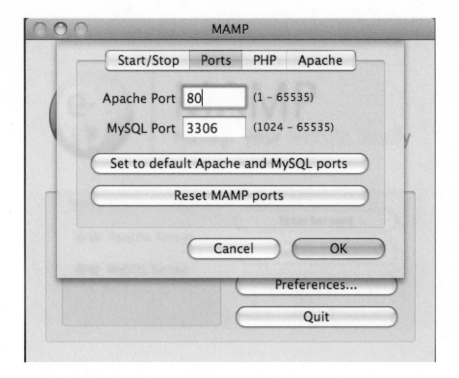

*Figure 1-9. MAMP Preference Manager*

Click "Set to default Apache and MySQL ports" and then click OK. This will allow you to disregard the port number when loading a URL on your browser. You now have installed not only a web server but also a database server.

---

■ **Note** The default installation of MAMP sets the MySQL and HTTP port number to X and X, respectively. The port numbers, though effective, are not the standard for both services. By default, MySQL should operate under port number 3306; Apache should operate under port number 80.

---

## Post-Apache Installation

If there were no errors during the installation of Apache on Windows, you should see the Apache Monitor icon in the task bar (see Figure 1-10). Right-click it and then click Open Apache Monitor, which is the tool that allows you to start and stop the web server. Mac users open the MAMP manager and verify that the status indicators on both Apache and MySQL are green.

■ **Tip** For easier access to the manager, I suggest you install the MAMP widget included in the installation bundle.

■ **Note** During this process, you might have to go back to this tool to restart Apache, so remember where this icon is located.

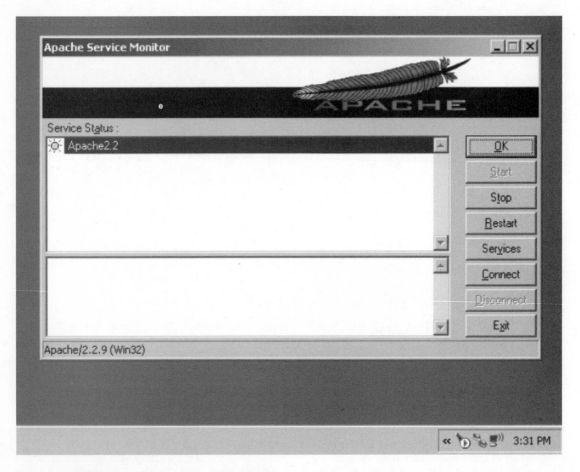

*Figure 1-10. Windows task icon for Apache Monitor*

Now make sure that Apache is running on the computer. To do this, you need to call Apache from the web browser. Pull up your favorite web browser and type in the following URL: http://localhost. You should now see the result, as shown in Figure 1-11.

# It works!

**Figure 1-11.** *Apache index success page*

---

■ **Tip** If you have any issues and can't see the page, look in the Apache error logs located at APACHE_HOME/logs/error.log. The problem can often be found here and easily taken care of by simply reading the errors saved to these files.

---

## MySQL

You have turned your computer into a nice web server in which you can begin creating your application. Great! The next piece of the puzzle is installing a database to store user-entered data for the application. By doing this, you can ask customers to enter data such as favorite bands, favorite songs, and usernames they want to use. You can then save this data for later use so you don't have to ask them every time they visit the site.

There are many database software packages available, but here's one that works well with PHP: MySQL. You will now turn your computer not only into a web server but also into a database server.

---

■ **Note** Mac users: you should skip to the "Post-MySQL Installation" section. You should already have MySQL installed if you've been following along.

---

## Installing MySQL on Windows

Installing MySQL 5.1 or later is very straightforward. Head to the web site http://www.mysql.com and download the latest software by clicking the Downloads link on the top menu bar. After you reach the new page, click the Download button under MySQL Community Server and scroll down until you reach a portion of the page containing the different download options.

Like Apache, MySQL gives you the option to install the software in either Windows or Linux. Windows users should download the Windows MSI installer (x86) ; Linux users should download the appropriate installer for the Linux flavor by clicking any of the installers under the specific distribution you have. Once you select a package (by clicking "Pick a mirror"), you are asked to log into your account. Click "No thanks, just take me to the downloads!", and a list of mirror links displays. Select one of the mirror links and start downloading.

As soon as the download is complete, run the setup file to start installing MySQL. On the initial welcome window, click Next.

In the Setup Type window, you're presented with the option of setting up a typical installation or a custom installation (see Figure 1-12). Click Custom and then click Next. This process enables you to install MySQL in a directory of your choice.

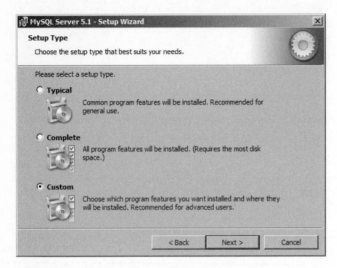

*Figure 1-12.* *MySQL installer Setup Type window*

As soon as the Custom Setup window displays, click Change. The Change Current Destination Folder displays. For simplicity, install your MySQL files in the location C:\mysql (see Figure 1-13).

---

■ **Note** In subsequent chapters, I will refer to this path as MYSQL_HOME.

---

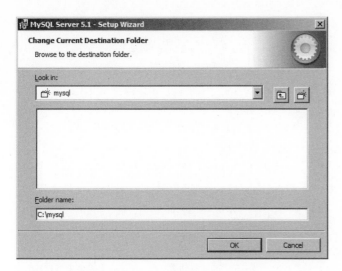

**Figure 1-13.** *MySQL installer Change Current Destination window*

Click OK and then click Next. The Ready to Install the Program window displays (see Figure 1-14). Click Install and watch MySQL install. If you're prompted with additional screens, click Next.

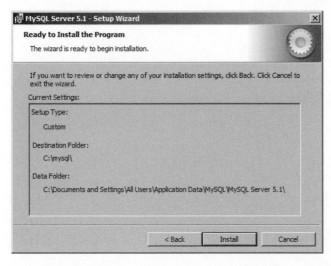

**Figure 1-14.** *MySQL installer Ready to Install the Program window*

If there were no errors during the MySQL installation process, MySQL has been installed on your computer, and a configuration window will pop up.

Let's now go through the steps of configuring yourinstance of MySQL.

## Configuring MySQL

Configuring MySQL takes only a minute. In the first window that displays, click Next to start the configuration process (see Figure 1-15).

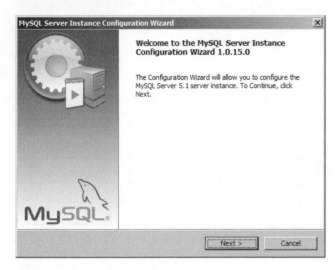

**Figure 1-15.** *MySQL Configuration Wizard* welcome *window*

In the MySQL Server Instance Configuration window shown in Figure 1-16, click the Standard Configuration button to speed up the process of configuration and then click Next to continue.

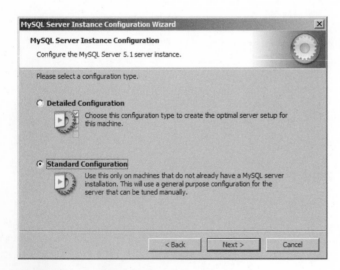

**Figure 1-16.** *Choosing standard configuration*

In the screen shown in Figure 1-17, choose the default Install As Windows Service option and click Next.

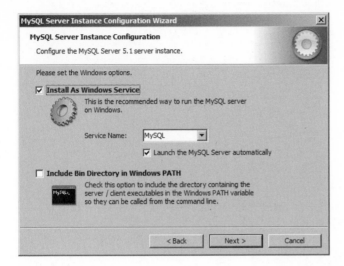

***Figure 1-17.*** *MySQL configuration Windows options*

Almost done. In the window shown in Figure 1-18, you need to set up a password. Enter a password for all the fields, leaving Modify Security Settings checked, and then click Next.

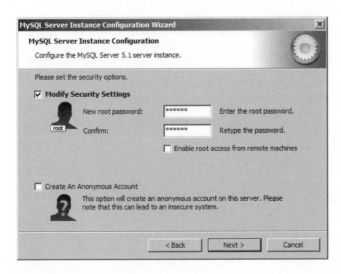

***Figure 1-18.*** *Choosing security options*

Finally, click Execute and watch the check marks come up. If the installation and configuration completed successfully, you'll see four check marks that indicate no errors (see Figure 1-19). Congratulations! You finished the setup. Click Finish and relax.

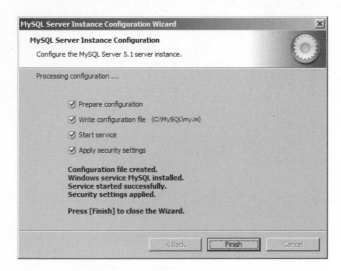

**Figure 1-19.** *Finishing the configuration*

## Installing MySQL GUI Tools

At this point, all basic tools are on your workstation. To make things easier for you as a Windows user, download and install a free MySQL GUI tool: MySQL Query Browser. The tool allows you to connect to the newly installed database server, view table schemas on the fly by simply clicking a button, and (most importantly) run SQL queries on the data.

Head back to the MySQL home page, located at http://www.mysql.com, and click the Downloads link. After the Downloads page loads, click the GUI Tools link located on the left navigation bar. The MySQL GUI Tools Downloads page displays.

---

■ **Note** At the time of writing, the MySQL GUI tools target version 5.0, but are compatible with 5.1. You'll notice that the following figures mention MySQL version 5.0 for this reason.

---

There are two types of installers: a Windows version and a Linux version. Windows users can download the Windows (x86) installer; Linux users should select the appropriate installer by clicking the "Pick a mirror" option next to the specific Linux distribution you have installed. When the next window comes up, it prompts you to log in. Ignore it and click the "No thanks, just take me to the downloads!" link. After the page loads, scroll down until you locate a mirror in your country and start to download.

After your download completes, open the downloaded file to start the installation process. In the initial MySQL Tools welcome window, shown in Figure 1-20, click Next.

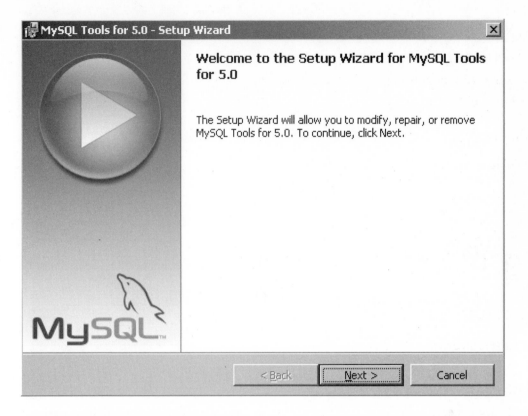

*Figure 1-20.* MySQL Tools welcome window

Accept the terms and conditions presented by MySQL on the next window by clicking "I accept the terms in the license agreement" button and then click Next to continue. The MySQL Tools Destination Folder window displays (see Figure 1-21). Click Change. In the Folder name field, type in the MYSQL_HOME/tools path, click OK, and then click Next.

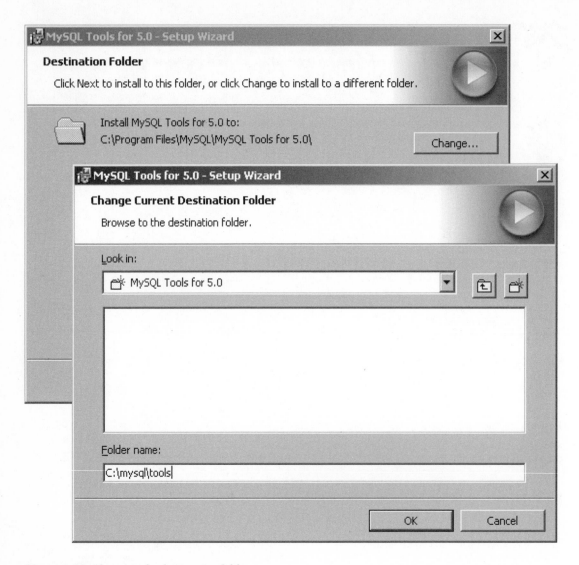

**Figure 1-21.** *Choosing the destination folder*

The MySQL Tools Setup Type window displays. Click Complete and then click Next to reach the Ready to Install the Program window. Click Install and let the setup do the rest. If you encounter any additional windows after this point, simply click Next until you reach the MySQL Tools Wizard Complete window. Click Finish, and you're done.

## Post-MySQL Installation

All should have gone well, but let's make sure. You'll create a database and add a table into the new database in the MySQL instance. Windows users: click the Start Windows button, typically located in the bottom-left of the screen, and open the MySQL folder. In the folder you'll find a few other applications, but you're currently interested only in the MySQL Query Browser, so click it and wait for it to load. You should see a window that prompts you for a few pieces of information (see Figure 1-22).

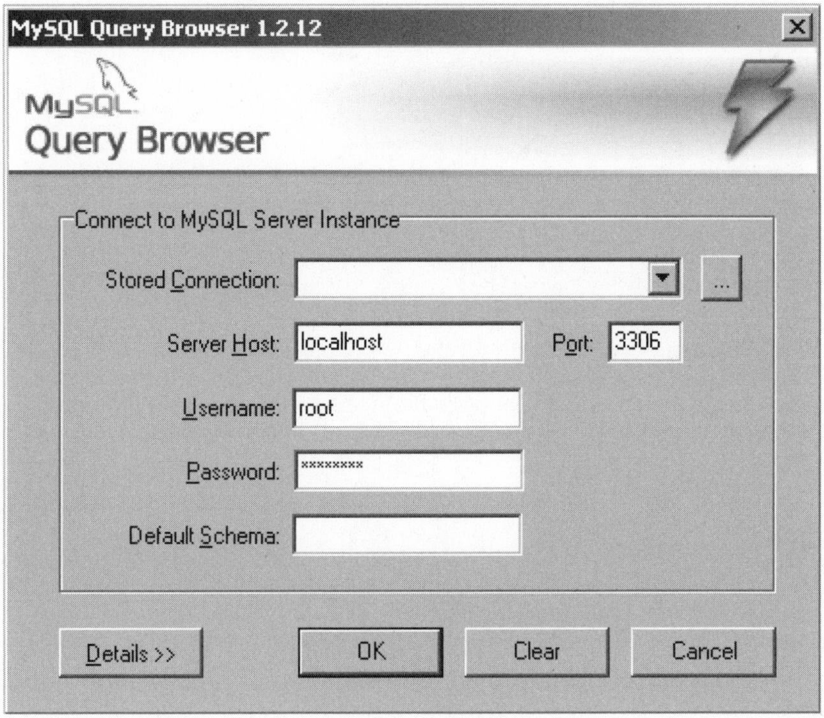

*Figure 1-22. MySQL Tools connection information window*

Type in the information you used during the MySQL server installation and then click OK. If you've been following along, you should enter **localhost** in the Server Host field, **root** in the Username field, and the password you used during the installation of MySQL.

You should now see the MySQL GUI window shown in Figure 1-23. By default, it contains a list of all your databases on the right side of the window, a place to write your SQL queries, and an Execute button with a lightning bolt on it. You will use these tools to write and execute your SQL statements.

21

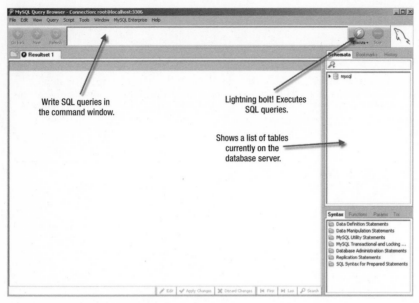

**Figure 1-23.** *MySQL tools GUI*

Mac users: open the MAMP manager once more and click the "Open start page" button on the right side of the manager. This will open up a web browser with a link to phpMyAdmin, a web-based MySQL manager, on the top navigation menu. Click the phpMyAdmin link and wait for the application to load. After phpMyAdmin has loaded, click the SQL icon on the left menu bar and continue to the next section to create your first database.

## Creating a Test Database

Create a test database by typing the following SQL command into the command window on the GUI tool for Windows users or the phpMyAdmin SQL window for Mac users:

CREATE DATABASE zend_test;

Click OK or the lightning bolt icon to run the SQL. If all went well, right-click the list of databases on the right side and click Refresh on the GUI tool, or look at the list of databases currently present in the left side of the phpMyAdmin window. You will see your zend_test database appear.

Now, select zend_test as the database you want to use (or click the database if you're using phpMyAdmin):

USE zend_test;

The database name should now be bold, indicating that you're working with the zend_test database (or the phpMyAdmin window should load a new window containing only zend_test options):
Create a table called Accounts, as follows:

CREATE TABLE Accounts (id int(11));

If all these commands ran without errors, MySQL is installed and waiting for calls from your application.

# PHP

One of the critical pieces of your application is PHP 5.2.4 or later. You must have PHP 5.2.4 at minimum installed because it contains the object-oriented features that Zend Framework requires. Without PHP 5.2.4, Zend Framework can't run. So let's go download it.

---

■ **Note** Mac users: MAMP installed the required PHP version. Continue to the "Installing Zend Framework" section.

---

## Installing PHP

The PHP installer can be downloaded at http://www.php.net. Again you have the option to either download a Linux installer or a Windows executable. In this case, if you are using a Windows environment, download the .zip file, not the Windows EXE installer. To find the .zip file, click the link for Current PHP 5 Stable on the right of the page under the Stable Releases header and look for the .zip package under the Windows Binaries heading. After you click that link, you'll see a list of mirrors from which you can download. Click the link for a mirror in your country to begin the download. The .zip file contains added extensions and libraries that you will need.

As soon as the PHP installer finishes downloading, extract the files to a directory of your choosing. I'm installing the files in the C:\PHP5\ directory, and I recommend you do the same.

---

■ **Note** For ease of use, this directory path will be referred to as PHP_HOME throughout the book.

---

## Getting PHP and Apache to Talk

When all the files are extracted, you need to modify the httpd.conf file that was installed by Apache. Go to the APACHE_HOME/conf directory and open the file.

This file allows Apache to be manually configured. Because Apache by default does not know how to interpret PHP files, you need to tell Apache what translator it needs to use when it is asked for a .php file by users. If you miss the step this far in the process of installing the environment, any time you try to load a .php file on any browser, the browser either prompts you to download the file or simply displays the PHP code on the page. So let's tell Apache what translator to use. In this case, the translator is the PHP engine you finished installing. Toward the end of the file, type in the following text:

```
AddType application/x-httpd-php .php
PHPIniDir "C:/PHP5/"
LoadModule php5_module "PHP_HOME/php5apache2_2.dll"
```

---

■ **Note** By issuing the commands apachectl start, apachectl stop, or apachectl restart in both the Windows shell (Run ➤ cmd) and the Linux shell, you can start, stop, or restart Apache. You can also click the Apache Monitor icon in the system tray and select Apache2 ➤ Stop or Apache2 ➤ Restart.

---

Save the file and restart Apache by using the Apache Service Monitor. Bring up the Apache Service Monitor window and click Restart on the right side. You see a success message if everything went well.

Let's test Apache and PHP now. Open a text file and type the following PHP code into it:

```
<?php
phpinfo();
?>
```

Save the file as phpinfo.php and place it into the directory that Apache looks into by default to retrieve any content that is called from the browser: APACHE_HOME/htdocs/. To view the page in a browser, type http://localhost/phpinfo.php, which is translated from the URL to the physical location APACHE_HOME\htdocs\phpinfo.php.

If all went well, you should now see your PHP script translated into a web page that looks like Figure 1-24.

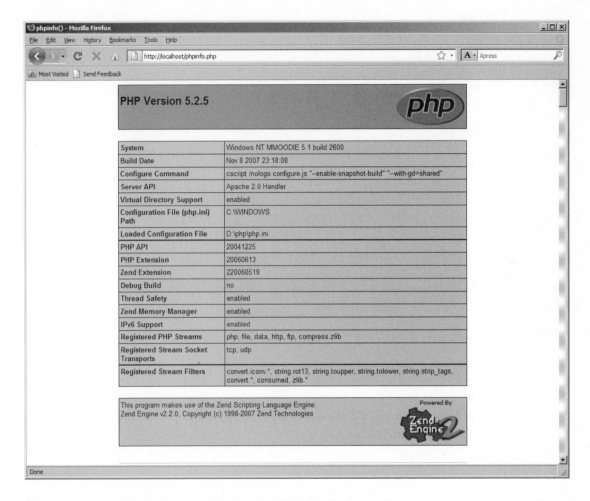

*Figure 1-24.* The phpinfo.php page, showing that PHP installed correctly

# Installing Zend Framework

Similar to a security guard pushing a rowdy, elbow-throwing crowd of 1,000 fans through a single entrance, you also need to funnel every user through a single figurative door when they request any document on the http://localhost web site. The door is the .htaccess file, which enables you to redirect every user to the index.php file used by Zend Framework, which you later learn is responsible for directing users to specific functionality in the application. Without this redirection, the application does not work.

Out of the box, the Apache web server has .htaccess support turned off, so you need to turn it on. Open up your httpd.conf file and look for the following line:

#LoadModule rewrite_module modules/mod_rewrite.so

Replace this line with the following; find all occurrences of AllowOverride None and replace them with AllowOverride All:

LoadModule rewrite_module modules/mod_rewrite.so

Stop the Apache web server and restart it by using the Apache Service Monitor. After it restarts, check that everything looks as it should and then continue.

By now, you should have all the required items installed: PHP, MySQL, and Apache. It's time to install what you came here for. Download the latest full Zend Framework installer, located at http://framework.zend.com (see Figure 1-25). Windows users should download the .zip file; Mac and Linux users should download the .tar.gz file.

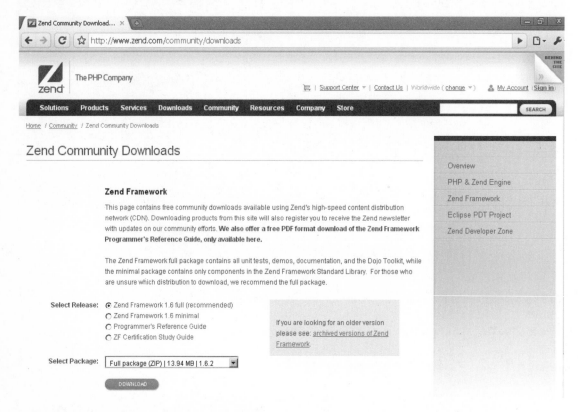

**Figure 1-25.** *Zend Framework Downloads page*

After the file download is complete, unzip the file to a location you can remember later, usually to the desktop. Create a project folder called APACHE_HOME/htdocs/helloworld and place the library directory from within the download here. You should now have the APACHE_HOME/htdocs/helloworld/library/Zend path, along with all the required files inside the Zend folder. You're finally done.

■ **Tip** I tend to host multiple web sites on a single web server. If you're like me and want to share the Zend Framework files across all projects, you should place the library/Zend folder in the path APACHE_HOME/htdocs.

# Your First Application

Your first application will be simple, but it will show you why Zend Framework is not only beneficial but also helpful. You will create the oh-so famous "Hello World" application. This simple application will display the message on the screen: "Hello, I was built using Zend Framework" and also introduce you to Zend_Tool.

## Zend_Tool

I bet you weren't expecting to learn an important component in Zend Framework so soon; it's only the first chapter. Get ready because this component allows you to enjoy coding and also removes the repetitive nature of setting up the foundation of a project.

The Zend_Tool component of the framework helps you apply rapid application development (RAD) when creating a project. What does this mean exactly? For Zend Framework developers, this tool can accelerate the time in which you deliver a product and results for your clients.

As a RAD command-line tool, Zend_Tool allows you to focus on coding instead of creating project structures, required files, or the small nuances that may slow your progress from the start. Zend_Tool removes these roadblocks by creating bug-free project foundations in a fraction of the time it would normally take to create these items. It also provides additional project information with quick and easy commands (shown in Table 1.1).

In a nutshell, Zend_Tool creates the following:

- Project directory structure

- Controllers

- Actions

- Views

- Bootstrap file

- Project details

Let's install Zend_Tool and create our first Zend Framework project.

**Table 1-1.** *Zend_Tool Available Commands*

| Type | Parameters | Example Usage |
| --- | --- | --- |
| Controller | create [name, indexActionIncluded=true] | zf create controller Account |
| Action | create [name, controllerName=index, viewIncluded=true] | zf create action list Account |
| Profile | show | zf show profile |
| View | create [controllerName,actionName] | zf create view Account list |
| Test | create [libraryClassname] | zf create test my_foo_baz<br>zf disable test<br>zf enable test |
| Project | create [path=null, profile='default'] | zf create project /path/to/project |

The zf command is discussed in the next section.

## Installing Zend_Tool

Zend_Tool comes bundled with the latest release of Zend Framework and can be found inside the bin directory of your download.

If you still have the unzipped folder, head toward the bin directory. Inside you will find three files:

- zf.bat

- zf.php

- zf.sh

These three files power Zend_Tool. Windows users need the zf.bat and zf.php files; Linux users need the zf.sh and zf.php files. I suggest placing these files inside the PHP_HOME directory, but they can live anywhere on your system where you have permission to execute. I placed mine inside the PHP_HOME directory for ease of use.

Once you copy the files, you need to inform Zend_Tool where your copy of the Zend Framework files is located. The Zend_Tool requires the Zend_Tool_Framework component of the framework to properly work, so this step is critical.

There are different paths you can take from here. One path is to copy the Zend library into the PHP_INCLUDE directory. Another path is to set an environment variable that Zend_Tool understands, ZEND_TOOL_INCLUDE_PATH, pointing to your copy of Zend Framework located at APACHE_HOME/htdocs/helloworld/library. And yet another method specifically for Linux users is to create a symbolic link inside the PHP_INCLUDE directory to the location where the Zend Framework library is currently located. I suggest adding an environment variable for Windows users and creating asymbolic link for Linux users; this allows you to maintain only a single copy of Zend Framework. Once this is done, you're ready to test the installation.

## Testing the Zend_Tool Installation

Open a terminal window. Once the terminal appears, you can test the installation by pulling up the version number of Zend Framework. Type in the following command:

zf show version

You should see the following if everything was installed correctly:

Zend Framework Version: 1.8.0

If this appears, you installed Zend_Tool successfully and are ready to create your project.

## Creating Your Project

You'll build your Hello World application now. Fire up your terminal once more and type in the following to create the directory structure as well as all the required PHP files the project needs (make sure that the PHP executable is in your path as well):

zf create project APACHE_HOME/htdocs/helloworld

The preceding command creates the directory structure shown in Figure 1-26 in a matter of seconds instead of minutes (yes, I timed it) inside the path specified in the third parameter: APACHE_HOME/htdocs/helloworld.

**Figure 1-26.** *Zend Framework project structure*

Now open the application/views/scripts/index/ directory and update the index.phtml file with the XHTML shown in Listing 1-1; if content is already present in the file, simply replace it.

*Listing 1-1. index.phtml XHTML*

```
<!DOCTYPE html PUBLIC "-//W3C//DTD XHTML 1.0 Transitional//EN"
"http://www.w3.org/TR/xhtml1/DTD/xhtml1-transitional.dtd">

<html xmlns="http://www.w3.org/1999/xhtml">
<head><title>Hello World</title></head>
<body>

Hello, I was built using Zend Framework!

</body>
</html>
```

Save the file. Before you open the URL, you have to point Apache to the APACHE_HOME/htdocs/helloworld/public location and also verify that the DirectoryIndex is set to index.php. To do so, open the APACHE_HOME/conf/httpd.conf file and set the DocumentRoot location to this:

```
DocumentRoot "APACHE_HOME/htdocs/helloworld/public"
```

Set the DirectoryIndex to this:

```
DirectoryIndex index.php
```

These changes allow all incoming requests to the URL http://localhost to load content from the specified location set for DocumentRoot. The change will also inform Apache to look for a file called index.php when the user requests a directory location such as http://localhost instead of the default index.html.

Restart Apache and load the URL http://localhost/ now. You will see a web page containing these words: "Hello, I was built using Zend Framework!" You just created your first Zend Framework application.

# Looking Under the Hood

Before wrapping up this chapter, let's take a look at the directory structure as well as the PHP files created by Zend_Tool. Beginning with the .htaccess file located inside the application/public directory, you should see the Apache rewrite rules shown in Listing 1-2.

*Listing 1-2. .htaccess Rewrite Rules*

```
SetEnv APPLICATION_ENV development

RewriteEngine On
RewriteCond %{REQUEST_FILENAME} -s [OR]
RewriteCond %{REQUEST_FILENAME} -l [OR]
RewriteCond %{REQUEST_FILENAME} -d
```

```
RewriteRule ^.*$ - [NC,L]
RewriteRule ^.*$ index.php [NC,L]
```

Apache initially reads this file located in the DocumentRoot directory for all incoming requests made to any location in the domain. The rewrite rules state the following:

*If any of the requested files are saved within the public directory, Apache should render the resource. On the other hand, if the file is not in the public directory, Apache should redirect the user to the script location identified after the $ in the last RewriteRule line.*

In the example, you redirect the user to the index.php file located inside the public folder. Let's take a look at that file now.

---

■ **Note** If you are on a heavily visited site or are concerned with performance, please be aware that using an .htaccess file lowers performance. For additional information, please see the following Apache web page for information and solutions: http://httpd.apache.org/docs/2.0/howto/htaccess.html.

---

Open the index.php file; you should see the code shown in Listing 1-3.

***Listing 1-3.** index.php*

```php
<?php
// Define path to application directory
defined('APPLICATION_PATH')
  || define('APPLICATION_PATH', realpath(dirname(__FILE__) . '/../application'));

// Define application environment
defined('APPLICATION_ENV')
  || define('APPLICATION_ENV', (getenv('APPLICATION_ENV') ?
    getenv('APPLICATION_ENV') : 'production'));

// Ensure library/ is on include_path
set_include_path(implode(PATH_SEPARATOR, array(
  realpath(APPLICATION_PATH . '/../library'),
  get_include_path(),
)));

/** Zend_Application */
require_once 'Zend/Application.php';

// Create application, bootstrap, and run
```

```
$application = new Zend_Application(
    APPLICATION_ENV,
    APPLICATION_PATH . '/configs/application.ini'
);
$application->bootstrap()
        ->run();
```

The index.php file sets the include paths for both the application directory and the Zend library folder, sets the environment you're currently developing for, loads the configuration settings, and runs the bootstrap file located within the application directory.

As you might have guessed, you're following the path that a typical request goes through. The next file to reference is the Bootstrap.php file located within the application directory. Open the file; you should see the code shown in Listing 1-4.

*Listing 1-4. Out-of-the-Box Bootstrap.php file*

```
<?php

class Bootstrap extends Zend_Application_Bootstrap_Bootstrap
{

}
```

The Bootstrap.php file is the main file in which the modules and components the application will use are initialized. You will look at this file in greater detail throughout the book.

Finally, let's take a look at the important directories within the application. At the root of the directory structure are the library, application, public, and test folders; and the .zfproject.xml file.

The library folder contains Zend Framework files. I suggest placing other third-party extensions and components in this location as well.

The application directory contains a number of subdirectories such as controllers, views, configs, and models:

- The controllers directory contains all controllers for the application.

- The views directory contains all the views for the application.

- The models directory contains all the models for the application.

- The configs directory contains the config files for the application.

Because there are many more folders, I created the table shown in Table 1-2 to help you determine what each folder contains.

**Table 1-2.** *Zend Framework Folders and Files*

| Directory/File | Used For |
| --- | --- |
| application | Contains the core application code. You can find all the controllers, models, and views of any application here. |
| library | Contains Zend Framework library files. I recommend placing all third-party source code here. |
| test | Contains unit test cases for the controllers. PHP unit is used. |
| public | Contains the .htaccess and index.php files. I recommend placing all application CSS, JavaScript, images, and any static content here. |
| .zfproject.xml | File created by Zend_Tool to identify project. |
| application/controller | All controllers for the application should be placed here. |
| application/views | All helpers and views for the application should be placed here. |
| application/models | All models for the application should be placed here. |
| application/configs | All config files for the application should be placed here. |
| Bootstrap.php | Bootstrap.php file used to initialize components for the application. |

# Summary

In this chapter, you set up a development environment with PHP, MySQL, Apache, and Zend Framework. You also learned about the basic directory structure that every Zend Framework–enabled application must follow and took a look at the required PHP files every Zend Framework application is required to have. Most importantly, you learned about your first component in Zend Framework, Zend_Tool, by installing and creating your first application.

Now that you have your feet wet, the next chapter looks into the application that you'll create as you progress through the book before diving into the Zend_Controller component.

# CHAPTER 2

■ ■ ■

# The Application

When I picked up my first PHP book, it contained little that would help the reader develop something after reading 50 pages of code. As you might expect, I had a very bad taste in my mouth after reading all those pages and realizing that I really couldn't show something exciting for all the trouble I went through. I wanted something that could get me going in the first section of the chapter. I'm sure you're as eager as I am to get something up and running fast and eventually being able to demonstrate the power of Zend Framework. Before you jump into the application, though, the foundation for the overall architecture and flow of the application you'll build throughout this book needs to be in place.

I'll spend these few pages outlining what you'll eventually be able to show off to your manager, spouse, and even your pet dog: an application that is worthy of your time and Zend Framework. The application is not too big to manage, and it won't be too complicated to create and maintain; it won't be another online store, a to-do list, or a popular social networking application. What you'll be working on is a small online music mash-up site called LoudBite.com.

This section covers the outline, flow, and architecture of the application so you'll understand what you're building as you go through each chapter of the book. I also describe the pieces of Zend Framework so you can jump to any chapter and figure out whether that chapter is what you need.

## Music Mash-Up Application

It's been a few years since the first MP3 hit the street. Now people have amassed an unmanageable collection of hits, flops, and late night sing-alongs. With so many artists and more genres available to the eclectic ear, there is no way to keep track of which artist might be of interest, when your favorite artist(s) will be in town, and what the latest release is from the artist you listened to in high school. We want a site that will manage and provide users with artist information and new concert dates, and also keep them informed about current music interests.

The music mash-up will be a web application powered mostly by external content and requiring little submitted content to get users up and running when they initially start using the web site. Like most Web 2.0 sites, this site relies heavily on using external content and mashes all the pieces into a meaningful page that communicates new and exciting artist information to users.

The site is simple, but it will enable you to learn a few things along the way concerning not only Zend Framework but also RSS and representational state transfer (REST), a popular web service standard. After you're done with this book, you will have not only a nice site worthy of your portfolio but also a few skills to boot: parsing XML, reading RSS feeds, working with external web services, building a mash-up site, and (most importantly) working with and understanding Zend Framework and its extensive library.

# Mashing Up the Pieces

The site will be composed of three sections, and each section pushes you to learn more details about Zend Framework and exposes you to the many libraries it contains. Let's go through the sections and outline how they will help you learn a thing or two about the framework:

- Accounts module

- Artists module

- Web Services module

## Accounts Module

To start, you'll create the Accounts module, which allows users to sign up for new accounts. You'll also create update forms so users can update their personal profile information, create login and logout pages, and create a personal profile page that other users of the system can view that contains a list of artists the user enjoys and also a small avatar of the user.

The Accounts module allows you to open the door into the extensive library collection in Zend Framework. The following Zend Framework topics will be discussed with the Accounts module:

- Creating site components using Zend_Controller

- Adding functionality to the application using Zend_Controller_Action

- Creating forms using Zend_Form

- Validating user-submitted content using Zend_Validate

- Filtering user-submitted content using Zend_Filter

- Constructing and sending e-mail using Zend_Mail

- Applying URL mapping using Zend_Controller_Route

- Saving user-submitted information to a database using Zend_Db

## Artists Module

The second module is the Artists module. While working on this module, you will be dealing with the content the user will supply to the web site. You will create forms for the user to add new artists into both their artist list and the system. The user will also have the ability to distinguish an artist as a favorite artist among the artists on their list, a page to remove the artists from their profile; and an artist profile page in which the user can receive information regarding the artist based on information consumed by web services created in the Web Services module. This is a very simple section of the site but with a slight twist: Zend Framework.

The Artists module section contains the following Zend Framework topics:

- Creating forms using Zend_Form

- Filtering user-submitted content using Zend_Filter

- Validating user-submitted content using Zend_Validate

- Introduction to Zend_Http

## Web Services Module

This part of the web site powers pretty much everything—it populates the most visited pages on the site and will be the focal point for every user. You start by creating the functionality for the artists profile page using the collection of Zend_Services_* components. The functionality created in this section will include searching and retrieving CDs and movies from Amazon.com, pulling content from YouTube for the artist, receiving ticket information and news related to the artist, searching for related blogs in del.icio.us, locating pictures from Flickr, and creating RSS feeds for a user's specific artist. The following topics will be discussed:

- Overview of web services

- Overview of RSS feeds

- Creating and consuming RSS feeds using Zend_Feed

- Communicating with Amazon.com using Zend_Service_Amazon

- Communicating with YouTube using Zend_Gdata_YouTube

- Overview of all available services

    By the end of the book, you will be fully versed in the major components surrounding today's web industry: form creation and validation, database content manipulation, and web service creation and consumption.

# Designing the System

I'll go through each module, section by section, to point out the requirements for each section and the overall flow of the user's experience to get you ready to create the application. Again there are three main sections: Accounts, Artists, and Web Services. I'll also use a good number of activity flow diagrams to illustrate how each system is intended to work, as well as a system diagram to give you an overall look of the application before I dive into the details.

## An Overall Look

Before I move into the details of the application, let's take a step back and get an overall picture of how each section interacts with one another and how the database and web services are incorporated into the application (see Figure 2-1).

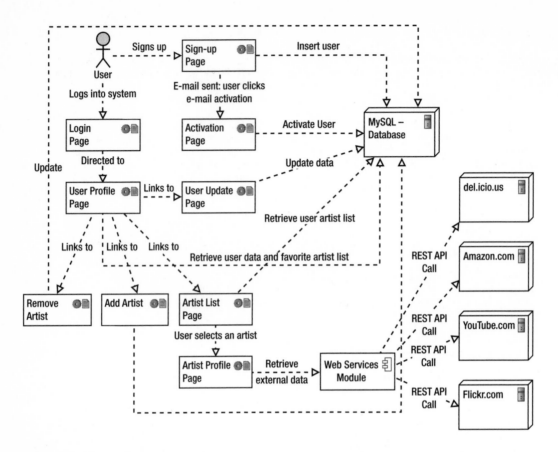

**Figure 2-1.** *System diagram*

The starting point is the user icon, located in the top-left corner. The user has two options at this point: either sign up or log in to an account that was previously created. In the sign-up process, the user activates the existing account; in the login process, the user is directed to a profile page, in which the user's data is fetched, along with a favorite artists list to display on the user profile page.

Lists of links are also available to the user from this page: links to remove artists, add artists, and view all artists on the list. To view all the artists on the list, the user can click the artist's name and visit the artist profile page, which pulls data from the Web Services module. The Web Services module then consumes data from four external sources to display on the artist profile page.

## Designing the Accounts Module

Let's first look at the Accounts module because this is where a user starts when interacting with the application.

## Signing Up

The sign-up page allows the user to sign up for an account in a very straightforward way. The page contains three form input fields and two check boxes to allow the user to receive e-mail newsletters about specific artists:

- E-mail field (required)

- Password field (required)

- Username field (required)

- Receive weekly artist newsletter check box

- Receive weekly artist newsletter as HTML check box

Take a look at Figure 2-2; I'll use it to explain what's going on with the sign-up form.

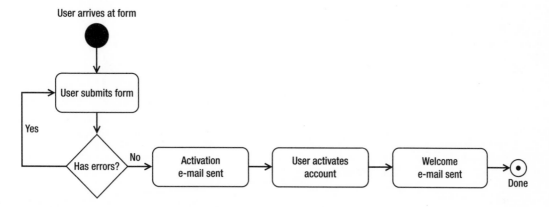

***Figure 2-2.*** *Accounts module: signup flow*

Arriving at the form, the user clicks the submit button. The application then checks whether the username and e-mail address are already in the system. If either test fails, the user is shown an error and must try to sign up again.

Each input field also validates the type of input that is entered. The e-mail address has to be valid in the e-mail field, and the entered text must be between 4 and 20 characters long in both the password and username fields. Once the user successfully signs up, two e-mail messages are sent. The first e-mail is sent to the user to activate the account. After the user activates the account, the user receives a welcome e-mail message.

## Logging In and Out

Login and logout functionality is standard across many sites, so it's no surprise that this aspect of the application is covered here. The login and logout functionality of Zend Framework does not have anything special to it; it just does what it's intended to do: log users in and out of the system.

In terms of the login process, there are a few things we want to do when the user logs into the system; for instance, we want to fetch and store any data that will be used throughout the site. Let's go through that process to get a clear understanding (see Figure 2-3).

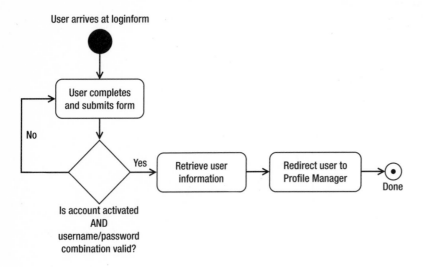

**Figure 2-3.** Accounts module login

When the user logs into the system, the system checks whether the user has activated the account. If so, the system will see whether the username and password combination is correct. If there are no errors, the process of fetching a few details from our database begins. The following user information is retrieved from the database:

- User ID

- Username

These two items are requested upon a successful login and stored within the user's session. The application can then fetch user preferences throughout the site based on the user ID or username stored in the session instead of requesting the username or user ID on every page to personalize the site. After the information is received, the user is redirected to a profile page.

The logout process is much easier, so I didn't create a user activity diagram for it. The logout functionality will simply allow the user to click on a logout link. Once the logout page is loaded, all session information will be cleared. That's it.

## User Profile Page

After successfully logging in, the user is redirected to the user profile page, which is where a user can access additional links to update the profile and artist information, and is also where users have direct access to other users' information. It contains the username and avatar, a list of favorite artists, and an additional link to the complete list that links to the artists' profile page. This page plays a critical part in the application because it is where the user controls preferences for the application.

Let's take a look at the overall layout of this page because there are more links here to other sections of the site than in other pages (see Figure 2-4).

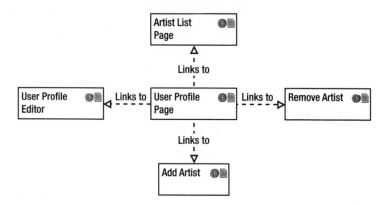

**Figure 2-4.** User profile page

The user profile page acts as the springboard for the rest of the site. It contains links to the edit page and the artist edit page, and contains a set of relevant modules.

## User Update Page

The user update page is where users can modify everything they have entered into the system. Let's take a look at Figure 2-5 and go through the process of updating the user information.

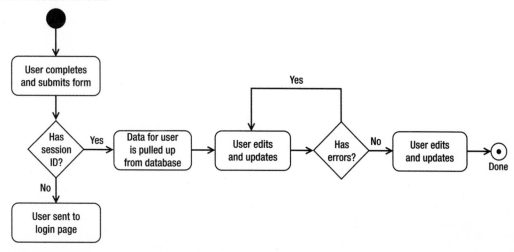

**Figure 2-5.** Activity diagram: user update page

When the user arrives at the user update page, the information presented is retrieved by using the userId stored in the user's session. If the user does not contain the required session information, the user is sent to the login page; otherwise, the userId from the session is used to retrieve the data in the database. The data on the form is presented, and the user is allowed to edit it. The user will have the option to update the e-mail address, password, and username.

When the form is submitted, the same error checks applied on the sign-up form are applied here as well to determine whether the form has any errors. If errors are found, the user can make corrections; otherwise, the data is saved in the database, and a success message is displayed.

## Designing the Artists Module

The Artists module contains the functionality for the user to add artists to (and remove artists from) the list, designate which artists should be placed into a favorite artists list, and add new artists into the system. It also contains an artist profile page that has information gathered by the Web Services module.

### Add Artist to User's List

The add artist section enables a user to add an artist to the overall list from existing artists in the system, designate an artist as a member of a favorite artists list, and save the artist into the system if it does not currently exist. Figure 2-6 shows how to add an artist, so I'll refer to it while describing this process.

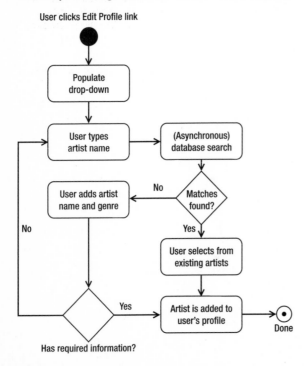

**Figure 2-6.** Activity flow diagram: add artist

The add artist link takes the user to the form with the following input fields:

- Artist name (required)

- Genre (required)

- Add to favorite artists (optional)

The Genre field is a pre-populated drop-down menu containing a list of genres in the database, and the Add To Favorite Artists check box allows the user to mark the artist as a favorite artist among all others in the list.

When the user begins to type the artist name, an asynchronous search for artists matching the text currently in the artist name field is performed. If there are any matching results, the user sees a drop-down menu to select the artist. If the artist is not yet in the system, the user fills in the name of the artist and selects the genre. Before submitting the form, the user has the option to add the artist to the favorite artists list by selecting the Add To Favorite Artists check box. This will save the information into the database and link the user to the artist. After the user has completed the process of adding an artist, the user is taken to a thank you page.

## Removing an Artist from the List

I remember when "Ice Ice Baby" by Vanilla Ice was the *it* song of the century, but nobody is currently bopping to it. So we will allow users to also remove artists from their list because users' tastes constantly change. You'll create a page containing a list of all artists the user has added to the list, with the option to remove the artist from the list and not completely from the system (see Figure 2-7). If the user decides to remove an artist from the list, it is also removed from the favorite artists list.

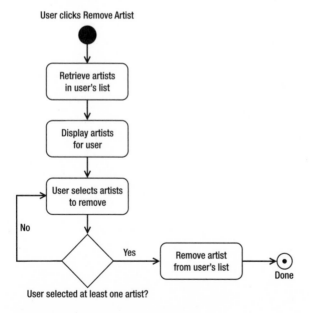

*Figure 2-7.* Activity diagram: artist removal

After clicking the remove artist link, the user is taken to the remove artist page. The database is queried to fetch all the user's artists, the artists are presented on the page, and the user can click the check boxes on the side of the artists' names to remove one or more artists at a time. When the user finishes selecting the artists to remove, the user clicks the Remove Artist button. If there are no artists selected to remove, an error displays and prompts the user to try again. If the user has selected any artists, they are removed from the list, and a thank you page displays.

## Update Artist List

Users also need a page to add an artist currently in their list to their favorite artists list. What's the difference? The difference between an artist on the list and an artist on a user's favorite artists list allows you to determine which artist the user likes better. It's like saying, "I listen to U2 and I think U2 is a good artist to listen to, but I would pay hard cash to see Paul Oakenfold live, buy all his CDs, and maybe buy other things with his name on it." In the application, the artist on the favorite artists list is shown on the user profile page, and the user will receive e-mail about these artists on a weekly basis (depending on the user's settings).

Figure 2-8 shows the complete activity diagram of a user updating an artist list. It starts with the user clicking the update artists list link. The application then retrieves all the artists in the user's artist list and displays each artist on the page, along with an Add To Favorite Artists check box to the right of the artist name. The user then has the option to select one or many artists to add to the favorite artists list. After the user submits the form, you check to see whether the user selected any artists; if the user selected at least one artist, the artist's status is updated, and a thank you page displays. Otherwise, the user can either select an artist or cancel the process by leaving the page.

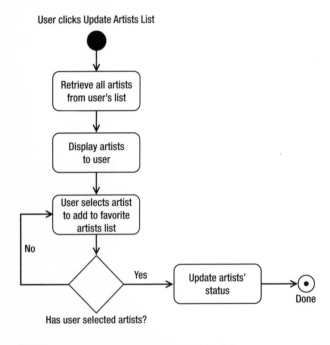

*Figure 2-8.* Activity diagram: update artist list

# Artist Profile Page

The artist profile page, which is the brains of it all, contains information for each artist in the form of news, general information, YouTube videos, Flickr images, concert schedules, and items the user can purchase from Amazon.

When users arrive at their own profile pages or at other users' pages, they can access the artist profile pages by clicking one of the artists in the artists list. When the artist profile page loads, a number of web services are called. Let's review each web service.

First is the Flickr web service, which retrieves any images containing the name of the artist. When the user arrives at the artist's profile page, the artist name is passed into the Zend_Service_Flickr, which then uses REST to fetch any images with the name of the artist. If the service locates any images with the artist name as a tag, the images are retrieved, and the images display on the page; otherwise, an apology message displays. The activity diagram can be seen in Figure 2-9.

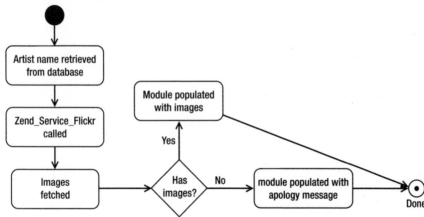

***Figure 2-9.*** Activity diagram: Flickr web service integration

The next web service implemented on the artist profile page is the YouTube service, which finds and displays relevant videos containing the artist's name as a tag. Referring to Figure 2-10, the artist name for the profile page is retrieved, it is passed into the Zend_Gdata_YouTube service, and Zend Framework uses REST to fetch any videos relevant to the artist. Like the web service call to Zend_Service_Flickr, an apology message displays instead of the videos if there are no results.

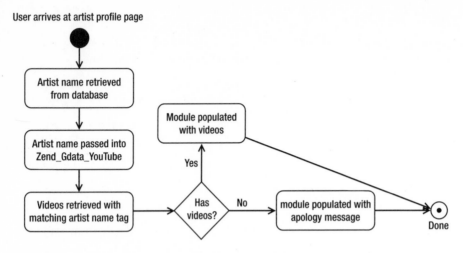

User arrives at artist profile page

Artist name retrieved from database

Artist name passed into Zend_Gdata_YouTube

Videos retrieved with matching artist name tag

Module populated with videos

Has videos?

Yes

No

module populated with apology message

Done

**Figure 2-10.** Activity diagram: YouTube web service integration

You can also integrate the del.icio.us web service to find any blogs that deal with the artist. Like the previous two web services, you use a tag-based search to locate matching entries containing the artist name as a tag. I won't show an activity diagram for this web service because there is no change except for the service name.

Do you remember when your artist used to be a simple garage artist trying to push those $.25 stickers, $1 demo tapes, and $5 t-shirts? We all have to make money somehow, so no artist profile page is complete without a section to buy CDs, books, and other artist-related merchandise. So we'll integrate a little bit of the entrepreneurial spirit into this section by integrating the Amazon application programming interface (API) into the application by using the Zend_Service_Amazon library to search and display merchandise related to the artist. Again, just like the Flickr and the YouTube activity diagrams, there is only a small change to the diagram: replacing Zend_Service_Flickr with Zend_Service_Amazon.

# Designing the Database

You might have already made up your mind about how the system will track and save user information, and started on your database design for this application. To make this process as easy as possible, I'll discuss the database that I created and used for this sample application. Although the database can be greatly improved upon, I wanted to keep it small and simple.

I'll stick with MySQL for this application, so most of the code will be written for that relational database management system (RDBMS), but it can just as easily work for other databases such as PostgreSQL. There are three tables in the system: the accounts table, artists table, and accounts_artists_table.

## Accounts Table

The accounts table contains all user information supplied during the sign-up process. The user data stored in this table can be updated and contains preference information that the user sets. The columns in the table are as follows (see Figure 2-11):

- id: User ID and table primary key

- username: User's username

- email: User's e-mail address

- password: User's password

- status: Either pending or active

- email_newsletter_status: Records whether the user has decided to opt in or opt out of receiving monthly newsletters concerning updates and enhancements to the site

- email_type: Either html or text, which tells you if the user wants to receive an e-mail in text or HTML format

- email_favorite_artists_status: A flag is set to true if the user wants to receive weekly information about favorite artists

- created_date: Timestamp for when the entry was created

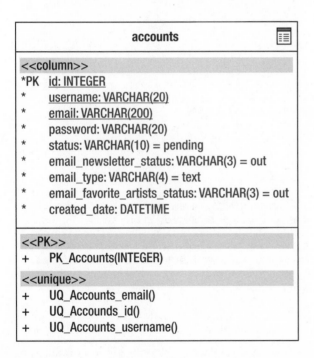

***Figure 2-11.*** accounts table

## Artists Table

The artists table stores the information of all artists in the system. It contains only four columns (see Figure 2-12):

- id: Artist ID and table primary key

- artist_name: Artist's name

- genre: Associated genre for the artist

- created_date: Timestamp for when the entry was created

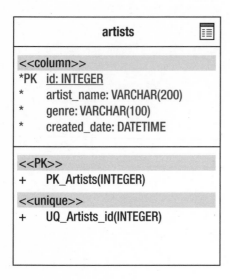

*Figure 2-12.* Artists table

There are also a few restrictions on the table. For starters, the artist_name and genre columns can't be empty, and there can be only one combination of artist name to artist genre. This will limit the possibility that an artist and genre combination is entered twice. There are a few flaws in this example, but I'm trying to keep it simple. For example, a user can enter a local artist in Los Angeles called "The Puffy Puffs Puffs" in the rock genre, and another user can enter the same artist name and the same genre for a completely different artist in Ohio. Given the restrictions, the artist in Ohio will not be saved, and the user will receive information from the artist in Los Angeles.

## Accounts_Artists Table

The final table required for the application is the accounts_artists table. This table allows users to add more than one artist to their account without repeating data in the database. It also enables each artist to have many fans. In other words, this table facilitates a many-to-many relationship between users and artists.

Take a look at Figure 2-13. The table is simple; only six columns (see Figure 2-13):

- id: Table primary key

- account_id: ID of the account

- artist_id: ID of the artist

- created_date: Timestamp for when the entry was created

- rating: Rating of this artist

- is_fav: Flag that indicates whether this artist is on the user's favorite list

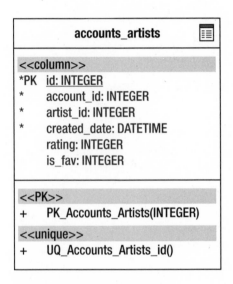

*Figure 2-13.* Accounts_artists table

Finally let's take a look at the complete entity relationship diagram (ERD), which shows how all the tables fit into the large picture of the application (see Figure 2-14).

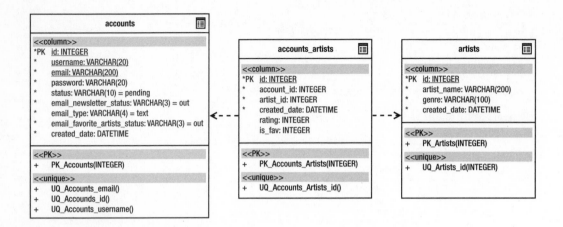

***Figure 2-14.*** Complete application ERD

# Creating Tables in MySQL

What book discusses the database ERD and doesn't allow you to save a bit of time to fully integrate the ERD into a database? Following is the Data Definition Language (DDL) for each table using MySQL commands:

```
# Database creation
CREATE DATABASE loudbite;

# Change into the database to run commands
USE loudbite;

# accounts Table Creation
CREATE TABLE accounts (
  id int(11) AUTO_INCREMENT PRIMARY KEY,
  username varchar(20) NOT NULL UNIQUE,
  email varchar(200) NOT NULL UNIQUE,
  password varchar(20) NOT NULL,
  status varchar(10) DEFAULT 'pending',
  email_newsletter_status varchar(3) DEFAULT 'out',
  email_type varchar(4) DEFAULT 'text',
  email_favorite_artists_status varchar(3) DEFAULT 'out',
  created_date DATETIME
);

# artists Table Creation
CREATE TABLE artists (
id int(11) AUTO_INCREMENT PRIMARY KEY,
artist_name varchar(200) NOT NULL,
```

```
genre varchar(100) NOT NULL,
created_date DATETIME
);

# accounts_artists Table Creation
CREATE TABLE accounts_artists (
id int(11) AUTO_INCREMENT PRIMARY KEY,
account_id int(11) NOT NULL,
artist_id int(11) NOT NULL,
created_date DATETIME,
rating int(1),
is_fav int(1)
);
```

Copy the previous SQL into your MySQL command prompt, run the commands, and you should have three new tables ready for use.

# Summary

At the end of each chapter, I'll give you a brief summary—a refresher—to remind you about what you did. You can use this summary to jump from chapter to chapter to determine whether the chapter created something worth implementing.

This chapter discussed the following:

• The application you will build using Zend Framework

• Background information regarding the mash-up

• The system's design using activity diagrams and an ERD

• How to set up the application database and tables

# CHAPTER 3

# Writing Controllers Using Zend_Controller

"Ugh, is this over yet? I should be watching 'ALF' reruns!" My disdain for the concert was apparent. As a developer who spends his time reading code, watches a bit of TIVO-recorded shows, and is just not a classical music type of guy, watching a concert was just not me. However, as the concert continued, I watched in amazement as the composer raised his hands up and down, swayed side to side, and brought order to the sounds that these complicated instruments made to create music.

Like the orchestra, Zend Framework contains its own classical music wizard: the Zend_Controller, which is ready to bring order to all the steps and components the Framework is required to call to make an application run properly. The Zend_Controller brings order and is the figurative glue that binds together all the steps and libraries to make your application worth the trouble to build.

This chapter begins by taking a look at the model-view-controller (MVC) pattern. You want to set the foundation for Zend Framework and know why it promotes the use of the MVC pattern. You'll look at what the MVC pattern is; why it was introduced into the web industry; and how it has become a leader in creating fast, loosely coupled applications. You will then work with the Zend_Controller component, learn what controllers are, implement best practices when creating controllers, and add functionality to them by extending the Zend_Controller_Action class. You'll also see how Zend Framework processes a URL so it maps to a controller action pair and learn how to manipulate this mapping feature using the Zend_Controller_Router_Route class.

With an understanding of how a controller is created and accessed, you'll learn how to use the Zend_Controller_Request_Http class to retrieve HTTP data, such as data from a form submission, and how Zend Framework handles errors using Zend_Exception.

## Model-View-Controller Pattern

The MVC pattern is a computer science pattern widely used in today's web industry, but that was not always the case. The MVC pattern, introduced in 1979 by Trygve Reenskaug, had a following in the software engineering field, specifically in the SmallTalk communities at the time. Software engineers adopted the pattern because it offered an efficient method of creating loosely coupled applications and maintaining software applications. With the MVC pattern's success in software engineering, the web industry took the figurative plunge into the MVC world.

### Why Use MVC?

The MVC pattern made a lot of positive noise in the software engineering field. Why, after so many years, should you continue to use and build software under this pattern? Because the MVC pattern is the logical step when creating web applications, as you'll see.

As a web developer for 10 years, I've seen the process of developing and launching a web application change. In the past, a web developer had to be versed in both the front end and back end.

Now, however, there is a systematic way to build web applications. In most cases, the back-end developer is not the front-end developer or the person with all the knowledge concerning the business rules/logic the product is required to use. In most cases, these positions are held by different individuals in the company, and the layout and the back-end code usually must be simultaneously developed to keep up with deadlines and milestones the team has set.

The two positions, front-end developer and back-end developer, are easily represented in the MVC pattern. While the front-end developer works on the view, where the display markup resides, the back-end developer can focus on creating the controller and the models that contain the logic that powers the application. This separation of power decreases the overall time it takes to create the application.

The MVC pattern also solves the issue of how to reuse major features. By separating features into distinct and loosely coupled modules, you can easily plug these features into other applications without having to copy the bulk of the application that initially implemented it. Before MVC, this was a time-consuming task. If you required only the design of a login form, you had to take the time to remove all the additional code that might have retrieved any incoming data and checked whether the submitted login information was valid. If you wanted to use only the authentication features, you had to remove the design markup.

Using the MVC pattern the functionality built for one application can be easily reused. The login and authentication feature has three components: the view, a controller, and a model. If you want to reuse the look and authentication logic, you can easily copy just the model and the view files, and disregard the controller file.

## What Is the MVC Pattern?

The MVC pattern breaks a project into three manageable modules to satisfy the separate functions in a development process and achieve the loosely coupled design mentioned previously.

Figure 3-1 demonstrates each distinct piece in the MVC pattern: a controller, a view, and a model. Without all three of these components, the MVC pattern could not help the web developer, and your application would not be considered a MVC application. I'll briefly go over the separate components before you dive into the code. (Of course, I'll discuss each piece in more depth when you work on some of the code.)

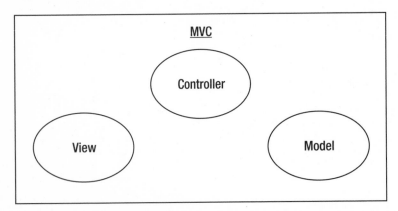

**Figure 3-1.** MVC pattern components

The *controller* contains code to handle all the allowed user events and coordinates the view and models—culminating with a response to the user. In Zend Framework, each user event is represented by a request, each request is handed to an *action* that knows how to deal with it, and each controller can have an infinite number of actions. If you constructed a controller that allowed the user to retrieve all accounts in the system, retrieve a specific account, and add a new account, code to handle these events would be contained in corresponding actions inside a controller that handles account functionality..

A *model* contains domain-specific instructions. Because the controller directs the functionality of specific sections/pages in your application, you need a place to keep all the business logic. The model is the place where you'll find how to retrieve different types of data—such as information stored in a database, the contents of XML files, or the results of a web service call—or simply return specific values for specific inputs. In the account example, when using an action to log into a system, you can implement a model containing all the logic to authenticate a user that the controller would instantiate and use.

The *view* is the user interface of the controller. It is the public face of the user event's response. Because you're building web applications, the view would contain HTML, cascading style sheets (CSS), JavaScript, forms, and the cool images you have learned to love.

## MVC Life Cycle

You now know what components the MVC pattern contains, so take a look at the life cycle of a user's request in a MVC application (see Figure 3-2).

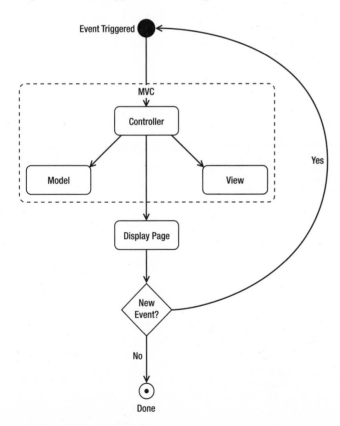

*Figure 3-2.* MVC life cycle

The figure can be a bit confusing, so I'll break it up into manageable pieces. Start at the top of the figure: the black dot. The user arrives at a web page, which is the initial step of the MVC pattern: the user triggering an event. Events always occur from the request for a specific URL by a user or another application such as a web service.

Move down into the MVC pattern and enter the controller. The user's event is translated into a request for a controller. This is where each piece of the MVC pattern begins to talk to the others. The controller determines whether it needs to load the model to format, transform, or process any information that the user has submitted or if the user simply wants to view a page. The model then returns any data it processed back to the controller. The controller finally specifies a design to render to the user by retrieving a view.

After the user is presented with the view (the XHTML side of the application), the user's request drops out of the MVC session and waits for the next request. If the user requests another page, the entire process restarts until the user stops or leaves the application.

Now that you know what MVC is and how each piece of the MVC pattern is used, you get to play around with some of the MVC functionality within Zend Framework.

# Zend Controllers

In this section, you'll start working on a small application to become acquainted with both Zend Framework and the role of the controller in Zend Framework. The controller contains different actions that allow the user to trigger different events for a specific feature. Figure 3-3 outlines the path the user's request takes after triggering an action to process form information (this demonstrates what the controller does and why you need it in greater detail).

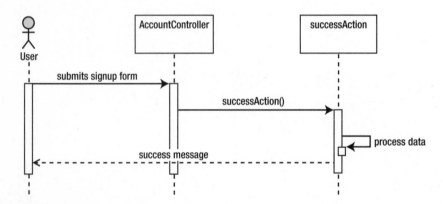

**Figure 3-3.** MVC controller

In Figure 3-3, start at the point where the user is ready to submit the sign-up form and send the information to the application by clicking the submit button. As soon as the submit button event is triggered, the AccountController, one of the controllers in the application, is called. Because the goal is to save the information, the controller calls successAction(), which will process the data submitted by the user and call external code, the model, to save the information. As soon as successAction() finishes, a message is sent to the user in the form of a thank you page.

To get started, create a loudbite directory in the Apache htdocs folder using Zend_Tool and set its public directory as your document root, as described in Chapter 1. (Make sure that the Zend library is available from this directory, too.) Open a command-line window and head toward the loudbite project directory. Once in the directory, create the new controller, AccountController, by typing the following command:

zf create controller account

It's important to remember that you must be in the project's directory for the preceding command to successfully create the controller because Zend_Tool requires the .zfproject.xml file. The .zfproject.xml file is an XML representation of your application's directory settings, list of controllers and their actions, and test information.

Once the command is executed, the new file, AccountController.php, is created and saved in your <APACHE HOME>/htdocs/loudbite/application/controllers directory. This directory is where you will keep all the controllers for the application going forward and is the default location where Zend Framework searches for your application's controllers.

Open the file and take a look at what the Zend_Tool created for you. The autogenerated code is shown in Listing 3-1.

**Listing 3-1.** *AccountController.php*

```php
<?php

class AccountController extends Zend_Controller_Action
{

    public function init()
    {
        /* Initialize action controller here */
    }

    public function indexAction()
    {
        // action body
    }


}
```

---

■ **Note** All the code examples omit the closing php tag ?>. Zend recommends the omission of the closing PHP tag ?> to reduce the possibility of additional whitespace in the response.

---

The new controller contains two methods: init() and indexAction(). By default, these two methods are created automatically when you use Zend_Tool. The init() method is executed before any action is called within the controller. For example, if the user requests the index action http://localhost/account/, the init() method will initially process followed by the index action. The second default method that is created is the indexAction(). This action allows you to add functionality to any request made to the URL http://localhost/account/. Let's now expand the controller by adding additional actions using Zend_Tool.

The first action added to the AccountController.php file is successAction(), which contains code to allow the user to save any data entered into the sign-up form. The second action, newAction(), renders the sign-up form for the user. And the third action, activateAction(), allows the user to activate the account. All these actions belong in the AccountController.php file because they are related to an account, but they can easily be placed into either the UserAccountsController or MyCoolController file. It doesn't matter what you name the controller, but I recommend that you name the controllers so it's easy for you to understand which features it controls at a later time.

Open the command-line window once more and type in the following Zend_Tool commands:

```
zf create action success account
zf create action new account
zf create action activate account
```

The commands not only create the three actions inside the AcountController.php file but also create the views for these actions (which you'll add to much later in this chapter). The final controller file will look similar to Listing 3-2.

**Listing 3-2.** *AccountController.php*

```php
<?php
/**
 * Account Controller
 *
 */
class AccountController extends Zend_Controller_Action
{

    public function init()
    {
        /* Initialize action controller here */
    }

    public function indexAction()
    {
        // action body
    }

    /**
     * Process the account form.
     *
     */
    public function successAction()
    {
        // action body
    }

    /**
     * Display the form for signing up.
     *
```

```
*/
    public function newAction()
    {
        // action body
    }

    /**
     * Activate Account.  Used once the user
     * receives a welcome email and decides to authenticate
     * their account.
     *
     */
    public function activateAction()
    {
        // action body
    }
}
```

To load some of the actions within the controller, open your favorite web browser and type http://localhost/account/new. Here, account corresponds to the name of the controller, and new is the name of the action you want to perform.

The next step is to learn the guidelines when creating a controller because you can't just create a controller with any name or write actions any way you want. Keep in mind, though, that you just created a running application in a matter of minutes that is easily manageable in a large team and is easily scalable.

# Controller Guidelines

The basic layout of a Zend controller is simple, so you'll learn the rules each controller must follow by creating another controller in the application manually. You'll create the ArtistController, and I'll point out each rule as you go.

The ArtistController will handle all the functionality that deals with musical artists. For now, the controller has only two actions that will allow users to view all the artists they have saved into the system and add new artists to their lists.

## Naming the Controller

The first rule of controller creation is as follows: each controller must start off with a word containing a capitalized first letter followed by the word *Controller*. If you require your controller to have multiple words such as *Member Artists*, the controller's file name needs to be in camel case, containing no spaces: MemberArtistsController.

To access a controller that implements camel-cased names using the URL, you must separate the words in the controller name with . or - (for example, http://localhost/member-artist/). Camel-cased contoller files also affect the location where you store your views (this is covered in Chapter 4).

The new controller will handle actions related to artists in the system, you'll call this new controller ArtistController. Let's create the controller that follows these initial naming conventions and save the file inside the application/controllers directory. Name the file ArtistController.php and enter the code shown in Listing 3-3.

*Listing 3-3.* *ArtistController.php*

```php
<?php
/**
 * Artist Controller.
 *
 */
class ArtistController
{

}
```

The code shown in Listing 3-3 is a class named ArtistController, which contains no methods or properties. If you try to run the preceding example, nothing will happen because you haven't completed this section and don't know the next few rules. So before you try to run the code, let's wrap up this section.

## Extending Zend_Controller_Action

The next rule that each controller must follow is: each controller in a Zend Framework application must extend the Zend_Controller_Action.php file.

This rule adds functionality to your controller. It allows Zend Framework to interpret your class methods as actions. Without this file, the controller would just be an object in your application. Listing 3-4 is the updated ArtistController.php file that includes the previous two rules.

*Listing 3-4.* *ArtistController.php*

```php
<?php
/**
 * Artist Controller.
 *
 */
class ArtistController extends Zend_Controller_Action
{

}
```

The keen developer might wonder how Zend Framework knows which file ArtistController needs to properly extend the Zend_Controller_Action class. To answer this, you need to look at another useful component, Zend_Loader, which is a wrapper for the include() PHP function. Similar to include(), it allows you to include specific files in the code; unlike include(), it automatically loads class files that follow a specific naming convention referenced anywhere in the application.

Let's take a look at the naming convention using Zend_Controller_Action. The Zend_Loader autoload feature translates the name of the class into the path Zend/Controller/Action.php, in which each folder is separated by _in the file name. Zend_Loader doesn't stop there: it doesn't just autoload Zend Framework–specific files; it also allows you to create your own classes and automatically load them if they conform to the naming convention.

In the context of your application, you registered the autoloader within the public/index.php file in Chapter 1 with the following code:

```
require_once "Zend/Loader.php";
Zend_Loader::registerAutoload();
```

Placing the autoloader within the index.php file enables the application to use the autoload feature throughout the code.

## Naming Actions

The next rule deals with actions: each action is represented as a function and must be a lowercased word followed by the word *Action*. If you require the action to have more than one word (for example, *list all artists*), the name of the action should be camel cased: listAllArtistsAction().

Now add a new action to the ArtistController, which will allow users to list all artists in the system. You could create a public method called listAction() or listAllArtistsAction() (both action names follow the naming convention).The final ArtistController, shown in Listing 3-5, abides by all the rules listed here.

***Listing 3-5.*** *ArtistController.php*

```php
<?php
/**
 * Artist Controller.
 *
 */
class ArtistController extends Zend_Controller_Action
{
    /**
     * List all the artists in the system.
     *
     */
    public function listAllArtistsAction()
    {
    }

}
```

Accessing the actions can be accomplished by loading the URL http://localhost/artist/list-all-artists. Try it for yourself.

There are also three types of acceptable method access types used in the controller:

- public

- private

- protected

All actions that are available for the user to request are public types. Any action that is used internally in the controller is set to either private or protected, depending on the level of security.

So far, you created two controllers, and for all intents and purposes you're almost done with your first proper Zend Framework application. But how do you route a specific URL to a specific action within a controller? This will be the next topic before you dive into controller error handling and views.

# Routing in Zend Framework

If you were adventurous and began to create new actions for the AccountController or the ArtistController, you might have encountered the problem of having very long action names that might not be ideal for the user to type into the browser. This section covers how a user's URL request maps to a specific controller-action pair and how to create user-friendly URLs.

## Transforming URLs to Controllers/Actions

The typical things users do while on a web site include filling out a form, clicking a link, or typing in the URL to a page in the application using the browser. All these clicks, submissions of forms, and typing in URLs are called *actions*. What all these actions have in common is that each translates into a URL request. Let's take a simple example. The following is a simple three-step process event by a user:

1. The first request by a user is to view the web site's index page. In the example, the user requests the URL http://localhost.

2. As soon as the user's request is satisfied, the user clicks the link to sign up for an account. The action taken results in the request for the URL http://localhost/account/new.

3. As soon as the request is satisfied (the page loads), the user is presented with the form to sign up for an account. The user promptly fills in the required form fields and fires off the last event by clicking the submit form button. This last action taken by the user turns into the URL http://localhost/account/success if there were no errors while submitting.

Each URL requested by the user in the preceding example is translated by Zend Framework into an action. Time to dissect the URL.

## Dissecting the URL

The action initiated by a user's URL request translates into a controller-action pair. If you dissect a typical URL within the context of Zend Framework, you can take a look at a URL and break it up into smaller manageable sections.

In Figure 3-4, the URL is broken into three pieces. The initial piece is the domain for the application. If the web site is hosted under the domain name loudbite.com, the address would be http://www.loudbite.com.

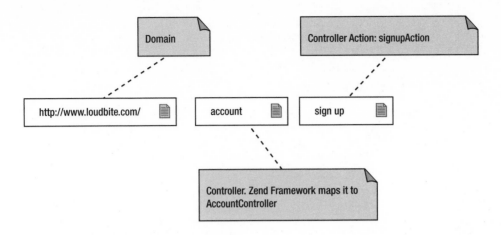

**Figure 3-4.** Mapping URL to controller action

The second component in the URL figure is the account portion, which is the controller of the application. In this example, the account section in the URL is mapped to the AccountController.php file. If you want to create a controller to control all actions for members in the site, you might create a MemberController; this controller would then handle requests where the URL is http://www.loudbite.com/member/. In the case of the ArtistController, the URL to load the controller is http://www.loudbite.com/artist/.

The third and final section in the URL is the action you want to take within the controller. In Figure 3-4, the action is the successAction() method within the AccountController.

Taking this example and using it on another URL pattern, http://www.loudbite.com/member/viewall, the URL will route the user to the MemberController and then route the user to the MemberController viewallAction() method. That wasn't so hard, was it? Now go ahead and start creating a few actions on your own with Zend Tool before you jump into the advanced routing setup.

## Creating Custom URLs

The last few examples used very simple action names, from listAllArtistsAction() for the ArtistController to successAction() in the AccountController. The URLs that map to these actions are simple enough: http://localhost/artist/list-all-artists and http://localhost/account/success, respectively. But if you're like me, you want to create actions with names that make sense to you for coding and debugging purposes, but they might not be intuitive to users.

In the application you want to give the user the ability to visit an artist page containing products the user might be interested in. This page will have a section in which the application retrieves all available music from Amazon using a web service and displays a list of books, CDs, and plush toys that the user might be interested in purchasing. I won't cover web services just yet, but let's add a new action to the ArtistController to begin the process of creating a user-friendly URL.

Open up the ArtistController.php file and introduce a new action into the controller called artistaffiliatecontentAction(); it should look like the code displayed in Listing 3-6.

**Listing 3-6.** *ArtistController.php: artistaffiliatecontentAction()*

```php
<?php
/**
 * Artist Controller.
 *
 */
class ArtistController extends Zend_Controller_Action
{

    /**
     * New Action
     */
    public function newAction()
    {
    }

    /**
     * List all the artists in the system.
     *
     */
    public function listAllArtistsAction()
    {
    }

    /**
     * Artist Items a user might be interested
     * in purchasing.
     *
     */
    public function artistaffiliatecontentAction()
    {
    }
}
```

If the user attempted to fetch this page, the URL would not be friendly because http://localhost/artist/artistaffiliatecontent is a bit too long. Try typing that three times! To turn this monstrosity of a URL into a user-friendly URL and change artistaffiliatecontent into something a user would not get tired of typing, such as http://localhost/artist/store, use the built-in controller-routing features Zend Framework has provided for you.

You want users to load the artistaffiliatecontentAction() method when they type the URL http://localhost/artist/store, so you need to tell Zend Framework to route all incoming requests for /artist/store to the ArtistController and the artistaffiliatecontentAction() method. To do this, you use Zend Framework's Zend_Controller_Router_Route class.

The Zend_Controller_Router_Route class requires two input parameters:

The first parameter requires a pattern you want Zend Framework to look for when a URL request is made.

The second parameter requires a hash containing the controller and action keys:

- The controller key accepts the name of your controller, minus the Controller portion. Using the ArtistController.php file, you would use the word artist as the value of the controller key value.

- The action key accepts the name of your action you want the user to reference but, like the controller key, it accepts the name of the action minus the Action portion of the name. Now open the index.php file located in the /public/ folder and modify it to look like Listing 3.7.

**Listing 3-7.** *index.php*

```php
<?php
// Define path to application directory
defined('APPLICATION_PATH')
    || define('APPLICATION_PATH', realpath(dirname(__FILE__) . '/../application'));

// Define application environment
defined('APPLICATION_ENV')
    || define('APPLICATION_ENV', (getenv('APPLICATION_ENV') ?
    getenv('APPLICATION_ENV') : 'production'));

// Ensure library/ is on include_path
set_include_path(implode(PATH_SEPARATOR, array(
    realpath(APPLICATION_PATH . '/../library'),
    get_include_path(),
)));

/** Zend_Application */
require_once 'Zend/Application.php';

// Create application, bootstrap, and run
$application = new Zend_Application(
    APPLICATION_ENV,
    APPLICATION_PATH . '/configs/application.ini'
);


/** Routing Info **/
$FrontController = Zend_Controller_Front::getInstance();
$Router = $FrontController->getRouter();

$Router->addRoute("artiststore",
        new Zend_Controller_Router_Route
        (
            "artist/store",
            array
            ("controller" => "artist",
             "action"     => "artistaffiliatecontent"
```

65

```
        )

    ));

$application->bootstrap()->run();
```

The updated index.php file contains new routing information by first fetching an instance of Zend_Controller_Front, then fetching its router, and finally adding a new route using addRoute().

The addRoute() method accepts two parameters: an identifier for the route and a Zend_Controller_Router_Route object. Save the file and load the URL http://localhost/artist/store, which then loads ArtistController::artistaffiliatecontentAction(). So how does it work?

When a URL is fetched within an application, the front controller looks at the URL and then looks at the declared routes to determine whether there are any URL patterns that apply to the user's request. If the URL matches one of the patterns specified by the routes, the request loads the controller-action pair specified in the Zend_Controller_Router_Route second parameter. On the other hand, if the URL pattern does not match any of the routes, the user is shown an error message.

With the changes saved, let's create a new view for the artist store. Create the artistaffiliatecontent.phtml file with the XHTML shown in Listing 3-8, and save the file in the application/views/scripts/artist/ directory. Bring up the URL in your browser: http://localhost/artist/store.

*Listing 3-8. artistaffiliatecontent.phtml*

```
<!DOCTYPE html PUBLIC "-//W3C//DTD XHTML 1.0 Transitional//EN"
"http://www.w3.org/TR/xhtml1/DTD/xhtml1-transitional.dtd">
<html xmlns="http://www.w3.org/1999/xhtml">
 <head>
  <title>LoudBite.com – Artist Products</title>
 </head>
 <body>
  Product #1 - Test
 </body>
</html>
```

You know how the controller handles the user's requests and how to mask the URLs to give them a more user-friendly pattern. Now let's see how to pass variables through the URL.

## Passing Parameters with Route

You might sometimes implement code that retrieves parameter information from a query string such as http://localhost/artists?name=metallica or http://localhost/user?username=armando. Using Zend_Controller_Router, you can allow users to use a much simpler URL such as http://localhost/artist/Metallica and have the application know that the last item in the URL path is the artist name or data you need.

To implement this feature, you need to declare the variable within the Zend_Controller_Router_Route object. To do so, initialize the name of the variable in the first parameter of the object using : followed by the name of the variable. The variable must contain only PHP-acceptable characters. To fetch the content within the controller-action, you can either use $_GET['name of variable'] or the Zend_Controller Request object.

**Listing 3-9.** *Setting variables in route*

```
Zend_Controller_Router_Route("artist/:artistname",
                array
                ("artistname" => "The Smiths",
                 "controller" => "artist",
                 "action"    => "profile"
                ))
```

The snippet of code shown in Listing 3-9 initializes a new variable, artistname, and sets its default value to The Smiths. Once this route is added, the user will able to load the URL http://localhost/artist/metallica or http://localhost/artist/the beatles. Let's now add this route into index.php, as shown in Listing 3-10.

**Listing 3-10.** *index.php*

```php
<?php

//Define path to application directory
defined('APPLICATION_PATH')
  || define('APPLICATION_PATH', realpath(dirname(__FILE__) . '/../application'));

// Define application environment
defined('APPLICATION_ENV')
  || define('APPLICATION_ENV', (getenv('APPLICATION_ENV') ?
    getenv('APPLICATION_ENV') : 'production'));

// Ensure library/ is on include_path
set_include_path(implode(PATH_SEPARATOR, array(
    realpath(APPLICATION_PATH . '/../library'),
    get_include_path(),
)));

/** Zend_Application */
require_once 'Zend/Application.php';

// Create application, bootstrap, and run
$application = new Zend_Application(
APPLICATION_ENV,
APPLICATION_PATH . '/configs/application.ini'
  );


/** Routing Info **/
$FrontController = Zend_Controller_Front::getInstance();
$Router = $FrontController->getRouter();

$Router->addRoute("artistprofile",
                new Zend_Controller_Router_Route(
```

```
                           "artist/:artistname",
                            array
                            ("artistname" => "The Smiths",
                             "controller" => "artist",
                             "action"     => "profile"
                            )));

$Router->addRoute("artiststore",
               new Zend_Controller_Router_Route(
                       "artist/store",
                        array
                        ("controller" => "artist",
                         "action"     => "artistaffiliatecontent"
                        )));
```

$application->bootstrap()->run();

Because the ArtistController.php file currently does not contain a profileAction method to support the new route, create the action, as shown in Listing 3-11.

***Listing 3-11.*** *ArtistController::profileAction method*

```
/**
 * Artist Profile
 *
 */
public function profileAction()
{
}
```

You'll now look at how to fetch these variables along with other user-defined data using the Request object.

# Request Object

Going back to the MVC life cycle, after the controller finishes processing with no errors, it initializes the user interface (UI) that the user will see, otherwise known as the *view*. Because the view is a critical component for the controller, the controller automatically creates three objects for immediate use:

- ViewRenderer

- Request

- Response

The Request object is covered in this section (you'll look at the ViewRenderer and the Response object in Chapter 4).

The Request object handles all incoming user data or any data sent from the user's browser to the application code. This data is always in the form of a POST submission, query submitted data, or raw header data.

Query data comes in the form of a URL such as http://localhost/account?u=armando, where u=armando is the data you want to process. POST data is form-submitted content. The request object allows you to fetch this data and manipulate it within the code. You'll expand on the sign-up form and add the artist form for this example.

Let's start with the AccountController. You already have the newAction() method, which deals with requests for the sign-up form, but you need an action to process any incoming form submissions. This requires an action in the AccountController.php file, so you'll be using the successAction() method, as shown in Listing 3-12. You want to learn how Zend Framework handles incoming data, so you'll fetch all incoming parameters.

**Listing 3-12.** *AccountController.php – updated successAction*

```
/**
 * Process the account form.
 *
 */
public function successAction()
{
    $email    = $this->_request->getParam('email');
    $username = $this->_request->getParam('username');
    $password = $this->_request->getParam('password');

    //Save the user into the system.

}
```

As you can tell from the preceding code, you added a few lines into the successAction() method. The new lines of code allows you to capture all incoming user data by using the request object's getParam() method. Here you capture three parameters from an XHTML form you will create in Chapter 4, containing three form input fields for the new.ptml page and store the data inside three variables: $email, $username, and $password. At the moment you won't be doing much with this data, but it's nice to have a foundation that allows you to successfully capture user data.

Expanding on the getParam() method, it accepts a parameter, which is the name of the parameter you want to capture. The form input field name values specified were email password and username. These unique identifiers are the parameters for the getParam() function. Easy, right? Yes, but there is a big security risk using this method, and the best way to understand why is to analyze how Zend Framework treats superglobal data.

## Superglobal Data in Zend Framework

You've used superglobal variables because they are part of PHP. COOKIE, SERVER, ENV, GET, and POST are the types of superglobal variables that Zend Framework uses and these are also the variables that the request object fetches.

Zend Framework uses a set way to capture these variables. Following is the order in which Zend Framework captures these variables:

1. GET

2. POST

3. COOKIE

4. SERVER

5. ENV

Because getParam() does not distinguish whether you want to fetch POST data or GET data, a malicious user can easily change any POST data by modifying the URL to pass in a GET value. To counteract this behavior, Zend Framework created a list of getters (see Table 3-1).

## Request Object's Getters

Suppose that you attempted the old tried-and-true method of creating a simple form for your users and you created that millionth form $_POST code on your PHP script. Let's use the secure Zend Framework getter now by updating AccountController successAction(), as shown in Listing 3-13.

*Listing 3-13. AccountController.php*

```php
<?php
/**
 * Account Controller
 *
 */
class AccountController extends Zend_Controller_Action
{

    public function init()
    {
        /* Initialize action controller here */
    }

    public function indexAction()
    {
        // action body
    }

    /**
     * Process the account form.
     *
     */
    public function successAction()
    {
```

```
    $email    = $this->_request->getPost("email");
    $username = $this->_request->getPost("username");
    $password = $this->_request->getPost("password");

    //Save the user into the system.

}


/**
 * Display the form for signing up.
 *
 */
public function newAction()
{

}

/**
 * Activate Account. Used once the user
 * receives a welcome email and decides to authenticate
 * their account.
 *
 */
public function activateAction()
{
}

}
```

In this example, successAction() takes the user's information that was previously entered in the form using the getPost() method, which retrieves only POST data.

The getPost() method allows you to fetch only data passed in using a POST request and nothing else. This is different from the getParam() method that allows users to use POST or query data. But sometimes you need to have query data such as account validation or a parameter that helps you fetch paginated data.

## Processing a GET Submission

POST data is nice, but what if you require the user to pass in a variable string through the URL? A good example is a user authenticating the account after signing up as a new user by clicking a link in an e-mail message (for example, http://localhost/account/activate?email=test@test.com or a user paginating through a list of images in your search result that uses the URL http://localhost/account/results?x=20 to determine which result index to start from). Apart from getParam(), how do you retrieve those values?

For this example, you'll update the activateAction() method in the AccountController.php file, as shown in Listing 3-14. The action will retrieve the e-mail address that needs to be activated from the requested URL clicked by the user. You'll fetch the data, but not fully activate the account just yet.

**Listing 3-14.** *AccountController.php: Using getQuery*

```php
<?php
/**
 * Account Controller
 *
 */

class AccountController extends Zend_Controller_Action
{

    public function init()
    {
        /* Initialize action controller here */
    }

    public function indexAction()
    {
        // action body
    }

    /**
     * Process the account form.
     *
     */
    public function successAction()
    {
        $email    = $this->_request->getPost("email");
        $username = $this->_request->getPost("username");
        $password = $this->_request->getPost("password");

        //Save the user into the system.

    }


    /**
     * Display the form for signing up.
     *
     */
    public function newAction()
    {

    }

    /**
     * Activate Account.  Used once the user
     * receives a welcome email and decides to authenticate
```

```
 * their account.
 *
 */
public function activateAction()
{
    //Fetch the email to update from the query param 'email'
    $emailToActivate = $this->_request->getQuery("email");

    //Check if the email exists
    //Activate the Account.

}

}
```

Compare the POST and GET examples; there isn't much difference. In both examples, you use the request object, but in this example you use the getQuery() method to retrieve all incoming query variables.

## Other Request Object Features

The request object doesn't stop there when it comes to fetching user data. It also allows you to fetch all raw POST and header information. Take a look at Table 3-1 for more information on the type of operations the request object can handle.

*Table 3-1.* Request Object Operations

| Function | What Does It Do? | What Does It Return? |
| --- | --- | --- |
| getParam(String key) | Retrieves an individual parameter to be accessible by the action. | Returns the value for the parameter key specified. |
| getParams() | Retrieves multiple parameters to be accessible by the action. | Returns an associative array of key/value pairs for multiple parameters of a request object. |
| getPost(String key) | Retrieves an individual parameter to be accessible by the action. | Returns the value for the parameter key specified. |
| getQuery(String key) | Retrieves an individual GET parameter to be accessible by the action. | Returns the value for the parameter key specified. |

## Zend Request Type Checkers

Besides allowing you to retrieve information sent to you by a user's request or a process, the request object can also determine the type of request that was made. This is great if you want to validate whether the request was a POST request or an Ajax request. Using request-type checkers reduces the chances of malicious users trying to manipulate POST variables with GET variables or send a POST to a process when your code expects an Ajax XmlHttpRequest call.

## Checking Whether the Request Is a POST

Zend Framework's request object comes equipped with the method isPost() that you can use to test for POST data, as shown in Listing 3-15.

*Listing 3-15. AccountController.php: Using isPost()*

```php
<?php
/**
 * Account Controller
 *
 */
class AccountController extends Zend_Controller_Action
{

    public function init()
    {
        /* Initialize action controller here */
    }

    public function indexAction()
    {
        // action body
    }

    /**
     * Process the account form.
     *
     */
    public function successAction()
    {
        //Check if the submitted data is POST type
        if($this->_request->isPost()){

            $email    = $this->_request->getPost("email");
            $username = $this->_request->getPost("username");
            $password = $this->_request->getPost("password");

            //Save the user into the system.

        }else{
          throw new Exception("Whoops.  Wrong way of submitting your information.");
        }
```

```
    }


    /**
     * Display the form for signing up.
     *
     */
    public function newAction()
    {

    }


    /**
     * Activate Account.  Used once the user
     * receives a welcome email and decides to authenticate
     * their account.
     *
     */
    public function activateAction()
    {
        //Fetch the email to update from the query param 'email'
        $emailToActivate = $this->_request->getQuery("email");

        //Check if the email exists
        //Activate the Account.

    }

}
```

Listing 3-15 expands the successAction() method to validate that the incoming request was a POST type. The important section in this example is the if statement. Here you use the default request object and its isPost() method. If the incoming request is not a POST type, the user sees an error message: "Whoops. Wrong way of submitting your information." The script then stops executing.

## Checking for a GET Request

Checking for a GET request type is straightforward and requires you to change only the if statement to read as follows:

```
    if($this->_request->isGet())
```

The new function that uses a GET request type looks like this:

```
//Action #1 - Sign up for an account form.
public function successAction(){

    //Check if the submitted data is GET type
```

```
    if($this->_request->isGet()){

        $email    = $this->_request->getQuery("email");
        $username = $this->_request->getQuery("username");
        $password = $this->_request->getQuery("password");

        //Save the user into the system.

    }else{
        throw new Exception("Whoops.  Wrong way of submitting your information.");
    }
}
```

## Checking for an Ajax Call Request

So you're tired of creating only one-dimensional POST and GET forms; you want to sink your teeth into a little asynchronous calling. You pop open that browser and start looking up for a nice Ajax framework. After you choose your framework, you might wonder how you can stitch the Ajax calls to Zend Framework. I won't cover the setup of an Ajax call because there are too many good Ajax frameworks out there: jQuery, Prototype, Scriptaculous, and Dojo. So I will cover only the back-end script that is called by the Ajax function.

Using the same successAction() function, you can expand it by allowing the script to accept only Ajax requests by checking for the XmlHttpRequest type (see Listing 3-16).

*Listing 3-16. AccountController.php: Checking for Ajax Calls*

```
//Action #1 - Sign up for an account form.
public function successAction()
{
    //Check if the submitted data is an Ajax call

    if($this->_request->isXmlHttpRequest()){

        $email    = $this->_request->getQuery("email");
        $username = $this->_request->getQuery("username");
        $password = $this->_request->getQuery("password");

        //Save the user into the system.

    }else{
        throw new Exception("Whoops.  Wrong way of submitting your information.");
    }
}
```

The preceding code changed the GET and POST versions only slightly. The bold line shows the new Request object method isXmlHttpRequest(). This method enables the script to check whether the incoming request was an Ajax call. The method returns true if it was an Ajax call and false if not. Depending on your Ajax framework, you can also change the way the data is sent to the script, either by a POST or a GET submission. In that case, you can check the incoming data using the isPost() or isGet() method instead of the more general isParam() method, which is an additional method of checking for submitted data. The isParam() function checks whether there was any data in any submitted variable.

## Request Type Checkers

Table 3-2 contains a complete list of checkers the request object allows you to use.

*Table 3-2.* Request Object Checkers

| Function | What Does It Do? | What Does It Return? |
| --- | --- | --- |
| isPost() | Checks whether the incoming request type is a POST request. | Returns true if it is a POST type; otherwise, returns false. |
| isGet() | Checks whether the incoming request type is a GET request. | Returns true if it's a GET request type; otherwise, returns false. |
| isPut() | Checks whether the incoming header request is a PUT request. | Returns true if it's a PUT header request; otherwise, returns false. |
| isDelete() | Checks whether the incoming header request is a DELETE request. | Returns true if is a DELETE header request; otherwise, returns false. |
| isHead() | Checks whether the incoming request contains header information | Boolean. |
| isOptions() | Checks whether the incoming request is an OPTIONS request | Boolean. |
| isXmlHttpRequest() | Checks whether the incoming request type is a XmlHttpRequest, which is used in JQuery, Mochikit, Yahoo! UI Library, and any libraries with core Prototype foundations. | Returns true if it's an Ajax call; otherwise, returns false. |

Now that you've seen the basics of controllers and views, it's time to see how to deal with situations in which things don't go according to plan.

# Zend Controller Error Handling

So far, I have covered everything from the controller to the view in a world in which there are no deadlines, the coffee flows from trees, magical fairies grant you wishes, and the code always works. Then you realize you don't live in that world—the code has bugs or (worse) it breaks the application. In this section, you'll use all the assets you previously learned to set up the error handlers by creating user-friendly error messages and handling.

When I'm in a hurry, I tend to type in a URL extremely quickly. I have come up with more than 100 ways to type in **Google**, for instance, and more than 20 ways to type in my full name. When it comes to the incorrectly typed-in URL, I get sent to a page I wasn't expecting or to a broken page. As far as you're concerned, a broken or blank page is PHP's way of telling you that there was a fault in the script or the user requested a bad URL.

It's your job to give the user a seamless experience when visiting the web application, so a blank page won't do. Zend Framework has introduced the ability to handle the behavior of controlling what users see when they encounter an error in the application by allowing you to turn on (or off) error/exception handling within the application. This functionality is on by default.

Let's create a generic error handler. You want to avoid showing the user a blank page or a long PHP error detailing at what line the error occurred. The default exception handler contains three parts because, like all components in Zend Framework, it is also treated like a page request. So you'll need a controller, an action in the controller, and an HTML page to render all errors or any default message you want to display to the user.

Open the application/controllers directory and open the file called ErrorController.php, which Zend Framework uses as the default error controller. This file contains a single action that handles any errors the user might come across, as shown in Listing 3-17.

**Listing 3-17.** *Error Handler Controller: ErrorController.php*

```php
<?php
class ErrorController extends Zend_Controller_Action {
    public function errorAction(){}
}
```

After you have the controller, go to the views/scripts/error directory and save the markup shown in Listing 3-18 into error.phtml.

**Listing 3-18.** *Error Handler View: error.phtml*

```html
<html xmlns="http://www.w3.org/1999/xhtml">
  <head>
   <title>LoudBite.com</title>
  </head>
  <body>
   We're sorry, you have located a page that does not exist or contains an error.
  </body>
</html>
```

The controller contains only one default action that is called automatically by Zend Framework every time the user encounters an error. The HTML file contains the message that you want to display to users when they encounter an error. In this case, it is a simple message.

## Extending Error Handling

Zend Framework allows you to take full control of error handling and drill down into key messages created by the framework for debugging purposes. If you don't want to display an error message, but want to simply allow the script to crash, that can be done. If you want to trace any messages for better error handling, that also can be done.

You can set the name of the controller that handles errors using built-in functions such as setErrorHandlerModule(), setErrorHandlerController(), setErrorHandlerAction(), and setErrorHandler(). Let's take a look at a few examples of manipulating the error handler controller within the front controller.

# Setting a Different Error Handler

To set a different error handler, update the public/index.php file and add in a few more lines to allow the front controller to forward any errors to the new error handler (in this case, ApplicationError). You don't have to add the Controller suffix to the name because Zend Framework automatically does this for you. You also forward the user to indexAction within the ApplicationErrorController instead of errorAction. This is all done using the Zend_Controller_Plugin_ErrorHandler object's setErrorHandlerController() and setErrorHandlerAction() setters (see Listing 3-19).

**Listing 3-19.** *Updated FrontController in index.php: Using Setters*

```
$FrontController = Zend_Controller_Front::getInstance();

$plugin = new Zend_Controller_Plugin_ErrorHandler();
$plugin->setErrorHandlerController("ApplicationError");
$plugin->setErrorHandlerAction("index");

$FrontController->registerPlugin($plugin);
```

Another simple way to condense the preceding code into a single line is to use the setErrorHandler() function that accepts a key-value pair array (see Listing 3-20).

**Listing 3-20.** *Updated Front Controller*

```
$FrontController = Zend_Controller_Front::getInstance();

$plugin = new Zend_Controller_Plugin_ErrorHandler();
$plugin->setErrorHandler(array("controller" => 'ApplicationError',
"action" => 'index'));

$FrontController->registerPlugin($plugin);
```

# Using Error Variables in the View

Another exciting feature of Zend Framework error handling is the capability to display internal Zend Framework errors that occur while rendering a page or calling a controller-action pair. To do this, you need to modify the controller that handles the errors. If you follow the preceding code, it will be the ApplicationErrorController.php file.

In the indexAction() function, make the adjustments shown in Listing 3-21.

**Listing 3-21.** *Application Error Handler: indexAction()*

```
public function indexAction(){
    //Get the controller's errors.
    $errors = $this->_getParam('error_handler');
    $exception = $errors->exception;

    //Initialize view variables.
    $this->view->exception = $exception;
}
```

The new lines capture all the controller's internal error messages and place them into the $exception variable. By utilizing _getParam(), you can retrieve any errors encountered from the current request object by passing the error_handler parameter. This parameter contains more information than you might need, but the exception attribute is most important for now. After you have the exception attribute information stored in its own object, you can do a lot with it. For starters, you can display the internal Zend Framework error message using getMessage(), as you do in Listing 3-22, or you can display the steps that Zend Framework took to get to the current error using getTrace().

The following line is required if you want to display the error in the .phtml file by making the exception object available there:

$this->view->exception = $exception;

Take a look at the functions shown in Table 3-3; Zend Framework provides you with a lot of useful information. You can use these functions to display the information stored in the exception object.

**Table 3-3.** Zend_Exception Operations

| Method | Description | Return Type |
| --- | --- | --- |
| getMessage | Returns Zend Framework–created error message. | String |
| getTrace | Returns a complete flow of the way Zend Framework arrived at the error. | Array |
| getLine | Returns the line where the error was located. | String |
| getTraceAsString | Returns a formatted string of the trace. | String |
| getCode | Returns the code for the exception. | String |
| getFile | Returns the absolute file path that threw the error. | String |

Listing 3-22 shows how to use the getMessage() function to get details of the exception in the view. This file is index.phtml in views/scripts/application-error/.

**Listing 3-22.** *index.phtml:Using getMessage()*

```
<html>
 <head>
  <title>Untitled</title>
  <link rel="stylesheet" type="text/css" href="my.css">
 </head>
 <body>
  Whoops you encountered the below error.
  <?php echo $this->exception->getMessage();?>
 </body>
</html>
```

Because you have initialized the variable in the controller to use in the view, you can call up all functions available to you. If you want to display the trace, you can easily change the getMessage() call to getTrace() and print out the variable in your own way.

# The Model

After the user has entered into the action inside the controller, the second step the controller takes is to process any information stored in any necessary models. Unlike the controller, the model exists to help the developer decouple business logic from the application. Domain logic, or logic and rules that are specific to the application, will reside inside the model. In most cases, the model consists of scripts that connect to a database and processes any number of create, read, update, delete (CRUD) commands. Nothing besides business logic resides here to consider the script a model and loosely coupled with the other components of the MVC pattern.

Let's look at another example of what might be inside one of the models. If you created an application that required the user to fill out a form and submit, as shown in Figure 3-3, the application will initialize the submitted data inside the action, but will save the information to a database inside a model (refer to Figure 3-4).

Figure 3-5 expands on Figure 3-3, in which you took a look at how the user's event triggers the appropriate action in a controller. In Figure 3-5, after the user has successfully submitted the form information for signup, the example is expanded by introducing the model into the controller's action. In this example, the model will receive all the user's information sent in by the controller and save it into a database. If there are no errors, the model will return some type of value back to the controller to inform it that the data is processed. After that happens, the user is sent a message that all the data has been successfully processed.

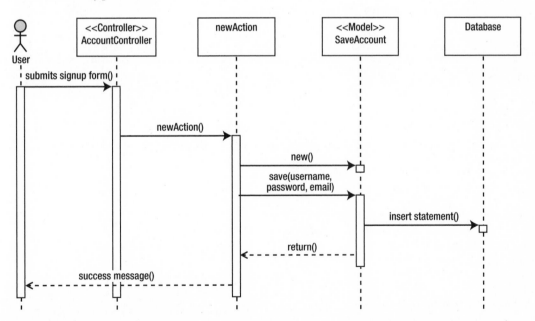

**Figure 3-5.** MVC controller and model

The model allows you to decouple the business logic from both the controller and the view. Decoupling the process from the controller by placing it inside the model will allow the developer to use the code in not only this particular application but also in a new application. Using PHP, you'll create a simple model for saving account information that is reusable and can be called from the controller (see Listing 3-23).

**Listing 3-23.** *SaveAccount.php*

```php
<?php
/**
 * Model - Save the data into the DB.
 * This code base can be used in other applications that need
 * data to be stored for new users.
 *
 **/
class SaveAccount {


    /**
     * Save Account
     *
     * @param String $username
     * @param String $password
     * @param String $email
     */
    public function saveAccount($username, $password, $email){

        //Clean up data
        $username = $this->_db->escape($username);
        $password = $this->_db->escape($password);
        $email    = $this->_db->escape($email);

        //Set up mysqli instance
        $dbconn = mysqli('localhost',
                '<Your Username>',
                '<Your Password>');
        $dbconn->select_db('loudbite');


        //Create the SQL statement and insert.
        $statement = "INSERT INTO Accounts (username, password, email)
                VALUES ('".$username."',
                    '".$password."',
                    '".$email."')";

        $dbconn->query($statement);

        //Close db connection
        $dbconn->close();
```

```
    }
}
```

The model you just created is a crude implementation that uses the mysqli to connect to a database, cleans the data passed into the function, and then saves the data into the database. To incorporate the model into the controller, let's update the AccountController successAction() (see Listing 3-24).

**Listing 3-24.** *Updates to the AccountController's successAction()*

```
//Action #1 - Sign up for an account form.
public function successAction(){

    //Check if the submitted data is POST type
    if($this->_request->isPost()){

        $email    = $this->_request->getParam("email");
        $username = $this->_request->getParam("username");
        $password = $this->_request->getParam("password");


        //Initiate the SaveAccount model.
        require_once "SaveAccount.php";
        $SaveAccount = new SaveAccount();
        $SaveAccount->saveAccount($username, $password, $email);

    }else{
        throw new Exception("Whoops. Wrong way of submitting your information.");
    }
}
```

The first few lines in successAction() retrieve any data the user has submitted as a POST. This example assumes that the form has three fields: a username, a password, and an e-mail address. After the data is fetched, you initialize the SaveAccount model and save the three fields by calling saveAccount().

# Summary

This chapter took Zend_Controller from its architectural foundation to the way the controller itself lives. This chapter is an essential step to understanding not only the MVC pattern but also MVC Zend Framework applications.

The following topics were discussed:

- Understanding the MVC pattern and its benefits

- Constructing a Zend_Controller using best practices

- Adding actions to a controller

- Routing URLs to their proper controller action pair

- Creating basic views

- Implementing request objects to fetch user-submitted data

- Implementing error handling

- Covering the role of the model in an MVC application

■ ■ ■

# CHAPTER 4

# Views, Forms, Filters, and Validators

Chapter 3 dissected the ins and outs of the Zend_Controller object and covered the separation that is recommended and allowed between the controllers and models using the model-view-controller (MVC) pattern. In this chapter, you'll now turn your attention to the front end, the public-facing side of the application. This is the side of the application that allows the user to interact with it. The goal of this chapter is to cover the concept of the *V* in the MVC pattern: the view. You'll see how it interacts with the controller, how you pass valuable information from the controller to the view, and how you can use PHP as a template language in your views.

The chapter also covers how forms are created, validated, and processed using Zend Form. You'll go through the majority of form elements supported by Zend Framework_such as text fields, password fields, select menus, radio buttons, and check boxes. You'll then apply each form field into the LoudBite application.

Once you're done with the Zend_Form and Zend_Form_Element objects, you'll move into filtering and validating data that users enter into the newly created Zend_Form forms with the Zend_Filter and Zend_Validate classes. You'll see how you can validate patterns in a string, determine whether an e-mail address is valid, check for string length, transform a string to lowercase, and much more. Finally, the chapter closes by discussing file uploading and applying CAPTCHA.

## Working with Views

Take a look at that coffee cup on your desk. My cup has a mermaid on it, surrounded by a green/white trim on a plastic clear container. Your coffee cup might be made out of paper with no logo or it might be a ceramic mug. All cups serve the same purpose, in this case to hold coffee, but have different designs and shapes that do not affect the liquid it holds. Views serve the same purpose for an application: they allow you to place different designs on the application without changing the way the application functions.

The view contains front-end code. The front end in the application is the XHTML, JavaScript, CSS, Flash, and anything else necessary for the user to interact with the application. The front-end code also includes PHP code used for rendering logic in your view, such as if-else statements to render a particular response and include() or require () functions that load navigational menus, headers, or external .php files. These are all technologies used in a view. The user, on the other hand, uses the view to complete and submit forms, read content on a web page, click a button to log in to the site, and interact with a Flash application.

To understand where the view comes into the MVC request picture, see Figure 4-1. The user makes a request to an MVC application. The request is then dispatched to a specific controller-action pair. The controller initializes all the data, processes any information, and ultimately specifies the view that renders the page for the user. Let's take a look at a simple example to see Figure 4-1 in action.

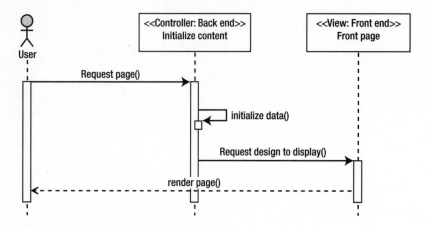

**Figure 4-1.** High-level view process

# A Simple Example View

You can implement the process outlined in Figure 4-1 by using Zend_View and Zend_Controller. Let's create a controller-action pair along with its view, paying particular attention to the setup of the view object within the controller.

In the previous chapter, you created a simple login form by creating the controller and the view. Now let's take a closer look at the steps you took by creating another piece of the application. You'll create the "add new artist" section, which will allow users to add new artists to their favorite artists list (see Listing 4-1).

**Listing 4-1.** ArtistController.php: New Additions

```
/**
* Add a new artist to the user's profile
*
*/
public function newAction()
{

    //Get all the genres
    $genres = array("Electronic",
            "Country",
            "Rock",
            "R & B",
            "Hip-Hop",
            "Heavy-Metal",
            "Alternative Rock",
```

```
        "Christian",
        "Jazz",
        "Pop");

    //Set the view variables
    $this->view->genres = $genres;


}
```

Let's focus on the newAction() method, which allows users to add artists to their favorite artists list. By default, the controller contains a Zend_View object for you to access using the $this class property. You store the genres in an array, $genres, and continue by storing the variable into the genres view property in the following line. Finally, the controller automatically loads the new.phtml view after the action method has finished. The new.phtml is rendered automatically based on the action name.

By default, the view object will look for the file under the views/scripts directory in a folder that corresponds to the name of the controller. In this case, the file will be found in the views/scripts/artist/ directory.

With the controller now in place, you can focus on the view itself. The View Helper contains a set of concrete placeholder methods. The methods allow you to set the doctype, set the page title, add metadata elements, add link elements, and insert inline scripts in your view with a single line of PHP code. A complete list is shown in Table 4-1.

***Table 4-1.*** *View Helper Placeholders*

| Method | Description |
| --- | --- |
| doctype(String) | Creates the <doctype> element for the markup. Acceptable values: XHTML11, XHTML1_STRICT, XHTML1_TRANSITIONAL, XHTML1_FRAMESET, XHTML_BASIC1, HTML4_STRICT, HTML4_LOOSE, HTML4_FRAMESET, HTML5 |
| headLink() | Creates the <link> element within your markup.<br>**Available methods:**<br>appendStylesheet($href, $media, $conditionalStyleSheet, $extras) setStylesheet(($href, $media, $conditionalStyleSheet, $extras)<br>**Example:**<br>$this->headLink()->appendStylesheet(); |
| headMeta() | Creates the <meta> element within your markup.<br>**Available methods:**<br>appendName($keyvalue, $content, $conditionalName)<br>setName($key, $content, $conditionalName)<br>setHttpEquiv($key, $content, $modifiers)<br>**Example:**<br>$this->headMeta()-.>setHttpEquiv(); |

*(Continued)*

| | |
|---|---|
| headScript() | Creates the <script> element within your markup. **Available methods:** appendFile($src, $type, $attributes) setFile($src, $type, $attributes) appendScript($script, $type, $attributes) setScript($script, $type, $attributes) |
| headStyle() | Creates the <style> element within your markup. **Available methods:** appendStyle($content, $attributes) setStyle($content, $attributes) **Example:** $this->headStyle()->setStyle(); |
| headTitle(String) | Creates the <title> element within your markup. |

Applying these placeholders to a view, you'll now create the view for the newAction() method.This view will contain the form the user will use to enter an artist. Let's add a few form fields that will allow users to enter an artist name, rating, and genre. They can also optionally check a box to add the artist to their favorite artists list.

Create the views/scripts/artist/new.phtml file and add the XHTML shown in Listing 4-2.

***Listing 4-2.*** *new.phtml*

```
<?php echo $this->doctype('XHTML1_STRICT'); ?>
<html xmlns="http://www.w3.org/1999/xhtml" xml:lang="en" lang="en">


<head>
<?php echo $this->headTitle('LoudBite.com - Add Artist'); ?>
</head>
<body>


<?php echo $this->render('includes/header.phtml') ?>

  <h2>Add Artist</h2>
  <form method="post" action="save-artist">
  <table width="500" border="0" cellpadding="5">
  <tr>
    <td>Artist Name:</td>
    <td><input type="text" name="artistName" /></td>
```

```
   </tr>
   <tr>
     <td>Genre:</td>
     <td>
       <select name="genre">
         <?php foreach ($this->genres as $genre){ ?>
         <option value="<?php echo $genre ?>"><?php echo $genre ?></option>
         <?php } ?>
       </select>
     </td>   </tr>
   <tr>
     <td>Add to Favorite List</td>
     <td>Yes <input type="radio" value="yes" name="isFav"/> |
     No <input type="radio" value="no" name="isFav" /></td>
   </tr>
   <tr>
     <td>Rate:</td>
     <td>1 <input type="radio" name="rating" value="1"/> |
     2 <input type="radio" name="rating" value="2"/> |
     3 <input type="radio" name="rating" value="3"/> |
     4 <input type="radio" name="rating" value="4"/> |
     5 <input type="radio" name="rating" value="5"/></td>
   </tr>
   <tr>
     <td colspan="2"><input type="submit" value="Add Artist" /></td>
   </tr>
   </table>
   </form>
   </body>
</html>
```

Listing 4-2 contains both XHTML markup as well as PHP code such as foreach to iterate over the genres (you'll learn more about looping later). You also used two of the View Helper placeholders, one to set the doctype and another to set the title of the page. The other interesting part of Listing 4-2 is the reference to an include/header.phtml file. This file contains a global navigation header that remains consistent throughout the application. The call to render() tells the view to render the specified resource.

Open the application/views/scripts/ directory and create a new folder called includes. Create a new file called header.phtml and type in the XHTML shown in Listing 4-3.

**Listing 4-3.** *Global Navigational Header*

```
<table width="100%" cellpadding="0" cellspacing="0">
<tr bgcolor="#eeeeee"><td><h1>LoudBite.com</h1></td></tr>
<tr><td>Sign Up | View All Artists | Add Artists | My Store</td></tr>
</table>
<br /><br />
```

Pull up the URL http://localhost/artist/new; you should see the form shown in Figure 4-2.

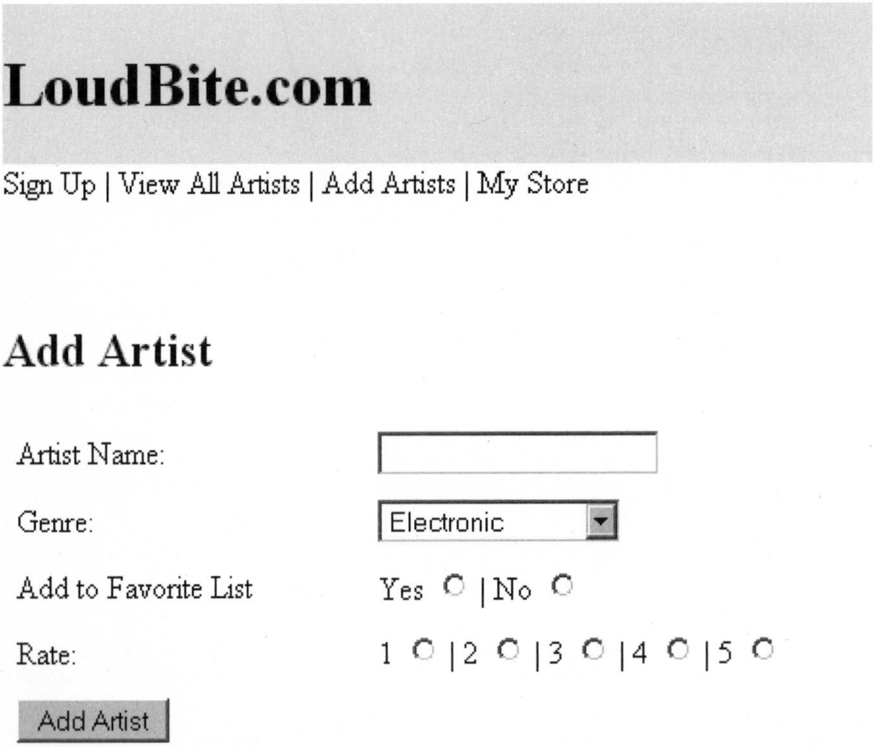

# LoudBite.com

Sign Up | View All Artists | Add Artists | My Store

## Add Artist

| | |
|---|---|
| Artist Name: | |
| Genre: | Electronic |
| Add to Favorite List | Yes ○ | No ○ |
| Rate: | 1 ○ | 2 ○ | 3 ○ | 4 ○ | 5 ○ |

Add Artist

**Figure 4-2.** *Adding a favorite artist*

You need a way to process the data the user submits using the add artist page. Create an additional action, saveArtistAction(), in the ArtistController.php file, as shown in Listing 4-4.

*Listing 4-4. ArtistController.php: New Additions*

```
/**
 * Save the Artist entered by the user.
 */
public function saveArtistAction(){

    //Initialize variables
    $artistName = $this->_request->getPost('artistName');
    $genre      = $this->_request->getPost('genre');
    $rating     = $this->_request->getPost('rating');
    $isFav      = $this->_request->getPost('isFav');

    //Validate
    //Save the input into the DB

}
```

The new action, saveArtistAction(), is invoked after the user has submitted the form rendered by newAction() in ArtistController. The action initializes four variables ($artistName, $genre, $rating, and $isFav) that have been submitted using a POST request. Using the controller's request object, you fetch the POST data using the getPost() method by passing in the name of the POST parameter to fetch. After you initialize the data, you can validate the data using Zend_Validate (covered later in this chapter) and save it to the database, among other operations. A comment is placed that acts as a placeholder for validation and persisting for now.

If you have already filled out the form and tried submitting it, you will receive a similar error message:

---

script 'artist/save-artist.phtml' not found in path

(C:\Apache\htdocs\loudbite\application\views\scripts\)

---

If you received such an error, don't panic; it's simply Zend Framework telling you that it did not find a view to render. By default, it looks for the file under the views/scripts/<NAME OF CONTROLLER> directory, even if you did not explicitly ask the action to render a view.

Let's go ahead and create the save-artist.phtml file, which is a thank you page for the action and save it in the directory views/scripts/artist. The file should contain the XHTML shown in Listing 4-5.

**Listing 4-5.** *save-artist.phtml*

```
<?php echo $this->doctype('XHTML1_STRICT'); ?>
<html xmlns="http://www.w3.org/1999/xhtml" xml:lang="en" lang="en">
<head>
<?php echo $this->headTitle('LoudBite.com - Add Artist'); ?>
</head>
<body>
<?php echo $this->render('includes/header.phtml') ?>
  <h3>Add Artist</h3>
<p>
  Thank you.  The artist has successfully saved.<br/>
  <a href='new'>Add another artist</a>
</p>
</body>
</html>
```

Reload the form and resubmit it. The error is gone, and you should now be able to submit the form without any problem.

You'll now create a view object and not use the autoinitialized Zend_View object created for you. To demonstrate the feature, you'll create the controller, action, and view for the account update page. The page displays all the information the user provided during the sign-up process and allows users to update the information. Add the updateAction() method to the AccountController.php file as shown in Listing 4-6.

**Listing 4-6.** *AccountController.php: New Additions*

```
/**
 * Update the user's data.
 */
public function updateAction()
{
  //Check if the user is logged in

  //Get the user's id

  //Get the user's information

  //Create the Zend_View object
  $view = new Zend_View();
```

//Assign variables if any

$view->setScriptPath("<ABSOLUTE PATH TO VIEW DIRECTORY>");

$view->render("update.phtml");


}

   Beginning with the placeholder comments, check whether the user is authenticated. If so, you retrieve the user ID from the session and the data stored in the database using the user ID. You then prepare the view.

   You instantiate the Zend_View object and set the path that Zend Framework will use when looking up views by calling setScriptPath(). The setScriptPath() method accepts a string parameter containing the path to the directory containing your views. The last line instructs the Zend_View object to render the specified script. In this case, it's the update.phtml view, shown in Listing 4-7.

***Listing 4-7.*** *update.phtml*

```
<?php echo $this->doctype('XHTML1_STRICT'); ?>
<html xmlns="http://www.w3.org/1999/xhtml" xml:lang="en" lang="en">
<head>
  <?php echo $this->headTitle('LoudBite.com – Update Info'); ?>
</head>
<body>

<?php echo $this->render('includes/header.phtml') ?>


  <h3>Update My Profile</h3>
  <form action="saveprofile" method="POST">
  <table width="500" border="0">
  <tr>
    <td>Username: </td>
    <td><input type="text" name="username"
       value="<?php echo $this->username?>" /></td>
  </tr>
  <tr>
    <td>Email: </td>
    <td><input type="text" name="email"
       value="<?php echo $this->email?>" /></td>
  </tr>
  <tr>
    <td>Password: </td>
```

```
    <td><input type="password" name="password"
      value="<?php echo $this->password?>" /></td>
  </tr>
  <tr>
    <td colspan="2">
      <input type="submit" value=" Update my account! " />
    </td>
  </tr>
  </table>
  </form>
</body>
</html>
```

Listing 4-7 demonstrates the form used for sign-up. The only difference is the value attribute in each input field. This new addition allows you to add the user's information as soon as the page is loaded.

Load the URL http://localhost/account/update in your browser, and you should see Figure 4-3.

**Figure 4-3.** *Updating the profile*

So if it's this easy to create and use the view, what is the big deal about using views? In other words, why devote an entire chapter to the Zend_View component?

# Why You Need Views

Understanding the implementation of views is beneficial to you as a developer because you can create maintainable and manageable applications. Without such a layer, you would have a hard time implementing new designs suitable for changing web trends.

To drive the point home, let's take the sign-up form you created in Chapter 3 and "de-MVC" it. Listing 4-8 first checks that the user has submitted the data via the form as a POST. If the user submitted the form, the $username, $email, and $password variables are initialized. These variables aren't used initially, but are used after the page has passed the validation. This part of the sequence belongs in the controller if you were using the MVC pattern.

*Listing 4-8. NonMVCSignupForm.php*

```php
<?php
if($_POST){

    //Initialize user input.
    $username = $_POST['username'];
    $email    = $_POST['email'];
    $password = $_POST['password'];
    $errors   = array();

    //Validate data
    if($username == ''){
      array_push($errors, "The username can not be empty");
    }

    if($email == ""){
      array_push($errors, "The email can not be empty");
    }

    if($password == ""){
      array_push($errors, "The password can not be empty");
    }

    //If no errors add otherwise show error.
    $conn = mysql_connect($app_server, $app_username, $app_password);
    mysql_select_db($app_db, $conn);

    $statement = "INSERT INTO Users (username, password, email)
        VALUES ('".$username."', '".$password."', '".$email."')";
```

```php
  if(mysql_query($statement)){
    $success = true;
  }else{
    $sucess = false;
  }
}
?>
<!DOCTYPE html PUBLIC "-//W3C//DTD XHTML 1.0 Strict//EN" "http://www.w3.org/TR/xhtml1/DTD/xhtml1-
strict.dtd">
<html xmlns="http://www.w3.org/1999/xhtml" xml:lang="en" lang="en">
  <head>
    <title>LoudBite.com</title>
  </head>
  <body>
    <?php
    if($errors){
      foreach($errors as $error){
        echo $error."<br/>";
      }
    }

    if($success === true){
      echo "Thank you!. You're now part of the site.";
    }else{
    ?>
    <form action="/account/signup" method="POST">
      Username: <input type="text" name="username" /><br/>
      Password: <input type="password" name="password" /><br/>
      Email: <input type="text" name="email" /><br/>
      <input type="submit" value=" Create my account! " /><br/>
    </form>
    <?php } ?>
  </body>
</html>
```

Moving down the code, if the user submitted the form, the input is validated. If the user passes validation, the data is saved. In this example, the entire MySQL flow from the connection to the query is created to demonstrate how messy it can get. You initialize a connection using mysql_connect(), pass in three variables (the server you want to connect to, the username, and the password), and then connect to the database using mysql_select_db(). Finally, you create the query statement and submit it using mysql_query(). The lines just described all belong in a model. If there were no errors with the call, set the success flag to true and render a thank you page.

Here's a problem, however: if you handed this code to a front-end developer, the developer would need to be proficient in PHP because the XHTML is interspersed with the PHP code. If the front-end developer does not know PHP, you'll find yourself spending valuable time helping during the design phase of the site. The most important argument for using views (similar to controllers and models) is that you can pick and choose the views already created. You can easily customize and reuse them in other applications without worrying about any supporting code that might change the functionality of the design.

You'll now migrate the code in Listing 4-8 to use the MVC pattern for comparison, placing the focus on only the views for now.

The spaghetti code that you initially had to work with was a long file containing PHP and XHTML. Now take a look at the new XHTML views shown in Listings 4-9 and 4-10. For ease of use, two views were created: one to handle the form itself and another to provide a thank you message after the user submits the form. Notice the amount of PHP code the front-end developer must deal with: you removed more than 90 percent of the PHP code. You can even go further and remove the error-message handling by replacing it with an include file so the designer does not have to see any PHP.

Notice how loosely coupled the views are to the underlining code. By having the loosely coupled view to the controller, you can easily take these views and reuse them as-is in another application in the future.

***Listing 4-9.*** *Sign-up Form View*

```
<html>
  <head><title>LoudBite.com</title></head>
  <body>
   <?php
   if($errors){
    foreach($errors as $error){
     echo $error."<br/>";
    }
   }
   ?>

   <form action="/account/signup" method="POST">
    Username: <input type="text" name="username" /><br/>
    Password: <input type="password" name="password" /><br/>
    Email: <input type="text" name="email" /><br/>
    <input type="submit" value=" Create my account! " /><br/>
   </form>
  </body>
</html>
```

**Listing 4-10.** *Thank You Page View*

```
<html>
  <head><title>LoudBite.com</title></head>
  <body>
    Thank you! You're now part of the site.
  </body>
</html>
```

# Manipulating the Directory Structure

By default, Zend Framework expects the standard directory structure shown in Figure 4-4.

**Figure 4-4.** *Default Zend Framework application directory structure*

This layout contains three main folders: controllers, models, and views. In the views folder you see a breakdown of two additional folders: scripts and helpers. At this stage, you're working in the scripts folder, so open it up. You'll see another level of folders created primarily for the application controllers (shown in Figure 4-5).

*Figure 4-5.* *Application-specific folders*

By default, you need to maintain the folders in this structure to have the application run smoothly and run under the default settings shown in previous examples. Sometimes breaking from such a structure is necessary when storing the views, however. For example, the architect of the application has decided to pursue an alternative directory structure that benefits the application you're creating. In any case, the Zend_View can easily adapt to this change.

Because examples are always good, let's take an instance where you create a controller to render a completely different view outside the default directory structure Zend Framework anticipates. You'll create the artist news page, which renders the details of all the user's artists and will later display RSS feeds for users and their favorite artists. Let's start by creating the view for this action, news.phtml, and save it outside the application (just for this example).

Listing 4-11 shows a simple HTML table to which you will later add a loop to display the many favorite artists a user might have. Place this file somewhere in your computer (in this example, it is placed in the <APACHE HOME> directory).

*Listing 4-11.* *news.phtml*

```
<?php echo $this->doctype('XHTML1_STRICT'); ?>
<html xmlns="http://www.w3.org/1999/xhtml" xml:lang="en" lang="en">
<head>
<?php echo $this->headTitle('LoudBite.com – News &amp; Info '); ?>

</head>
<body>

<?php echo $this->render('includes/header.phtml') ?>

  <h3>News and Info</h3>
  <table>
   <tr><td>Artist name goes here</td></tr>
   <tr><td>News items will go here</td></tr>
   <tr><td>Items of interest</td></tr>
   <tr><td>Pictures</td></tr>
```

```
    </table>
  </body>
</html>
```

Now let's take a look at the controller-action pair. In Listing 4-12, the placeholders check whether users are logged in and retrieve the session user ID if they are. You create a set of artists for testing. In this case, you'll use three artists: Thievery Corporation, The Eagles, and Elton John. You store these test artists in the $artists array and store the array in the view object property artists for use in the view. After you're ready to render the view, you change the base location in which you contain the views by using the function setScriptPath().

***Listing 4-12.** ArtistController.php: New Additions*

```
/**
* Display news for users artist.
*/
public function newsAction()
{

  //Check if the user is logged in

  //Get the user's Id

  //Get the artists. (Example uses static artists)
  $artists = array("Thievery Corporation",
          "The Eagles",
          "Elton John");

  //Set the view variables
  $this->view->artists = $artists;

  //Find the view in our new location
  $this->view->setScriptPath("<APACHE_HOME>");
  $this->render("news");

}
```

Because the view is not located within the standard path, views/scripts, the controller will issue an error. By using the setScriptPath() method, you force Zend_View to change the default directory it normally uses to locate the views to the one specified using the method. In this example, you set the script path to the APACHE_HOME directory. The only requirement is that each controller must have its own folder within this new base directory.

Now pull up the page in your browser to see it in action: http://localhost/artist/news, shown in Figure 4-6.

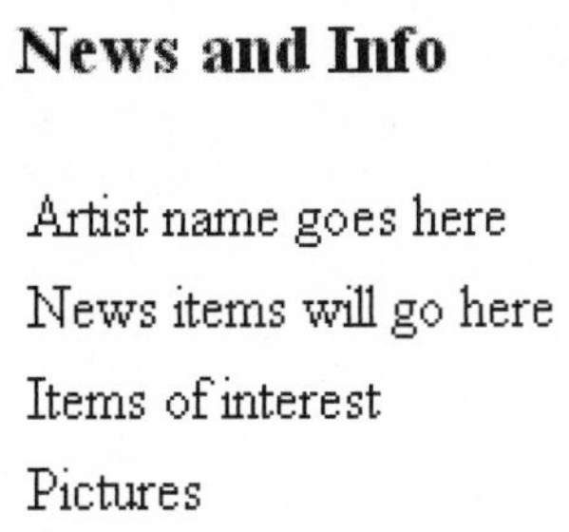

## News and Info

Artist name goes here

News items will go here

Items of interest

Pictures

*Figure 4-6. News page*

# Adding Logic and Control to Views

So far, you've learned how to initialize a view object, how to render that view in the application, and how to set view variables in the controller. Now I'll cover how to use variables created within your controller-action pair and PHP logic into any view. Lucky for you, if you have any level of PHP experience, you're already ahead of the game.

## Variable Handling

The Zend_View object has many ways to initialize variables within a controller for use in the view. I'll cover all the ways to do this, but you can choose the one that best fits your style of coding. The Zend_View object allows you to pass full arrays, single-valued strings, and objects containing property data into the view.

Let's take the code you're already familiar with—the ArtistController.php file—and add new functionality. The new functionality will allow the user to remove artists from the favorites list. The controller-action pair will display a list of all artists and will display a check box next to each name, allowing the user to remove the artist.

Listing 4-13 contains the new action in the ArtistController.php file. The initial method of initializing data from the controller for use in the view begins with the standard method you have used so far. The action contains the standard placeholders, followed by setting of the variable artist containing an array with three elements. The elements are names of artists you'll use to populate the view. Rounding out the example, you use the default ViewRenderer created by the controller and set the artists property before you allow the controller to render the remove.phtml view.

***Listing 4-13.*** *ArtistController.php: New Additions*

```
/**
* Remove favorite artist..
*/
public function removeAction()
{

    //Check if the user is logged in

    //Get the user's Id

    //Get the user's artists.
    $artists = array("Thievery Corporation",
            "The Eagles",
            "Elton John");

    //Set the view variables
    $this->view->totalArtist = count($artists);
    $this->view->artists = $artists;

}
```

You can access the artists property in the view like any other class variable (see Listing 4-14).

***Listing 4-14.*** *remove.phtml*

```
<?php echo $this->doctype('XHTML1_STRICT'); ?>
<html>
<head>
<?php echo $this->headTitle('LoudBite.com – Remove Artist'); ?>
</head>
<body>

<?php echo $this->render('includes/header.phtml') ?>

  <h3>Remove Artist </h3>

  <table>
  <tr>
```

```
<td>Artists - <i>Total Artists (<?php echo $this->totalArtist; ?>)</i></td>
</tr>
<tr><td><input type="checkbox" /><?php echo $this->artists[1]?></td></tr>
<tr><td><input type="submit" value="Remove"/></td></tr>
</table>

</body>
</html>
```

The XHTML call the $this->$artists index, 1. If you pull up the URL http://localhost/artist/remove, you'll see the page shown in Figure 4-7.

# LoudBite.com

Sign Up | View All Artists | Add Artists | My Store

## Remove Artist

Artists - *Total Artists (3)*

☐ The Eagles

Remove

***Figure 4-7.*** *Removing an artist*

The second method that allows you to assign variables for use in views is the Zend_View assign() method. This method allows you to explicitly specify the name of the variable you want to initialize, and the value the variable will contain. If the user specifies an array as the initial parameter, it must be a key-value array in which the key is the variable to initialize and the value is the value to assign it.

```
assign(<mixed value>, <optional value to assign it>)
```

Using the same remove artist example, you'll update the code to use the new method (see Listing 4-15).

**Listing 4-15.** *ArtistController.php*

```
/**
* Remove favorite artist.
*/
public function removeAction()
{

    //Check if the user is logged in
    //Get the user's Id


    //Get the user's artists.
    $artists = array("Thievery Corporation", "The Eagles", "Elton John");

    //Set the total number of artists in the array.
    //Demonstrates the use of a key-value array assignment.
    $totalNumberOfArtists = array("totalArtist" => count($artists));

    //Set the view variables
    $this->view->assign("artists", $artists);
    $this->view->assign($totalNumberOfArtists);


}
```

Listing 4-15 demonstrates both assign() approaches. You set the $artists view variable using the values stored in the array by using the assign()'s second parameter. You also set the $totalNumberOfArtists view variable by passing in a key-value array as the initial parameter in the assign() method. Accessing these variables doesn't change in the view, so using $this->totalArtist works the same way. Reload the http://localhost/artist/remove page; you'll see an additional piece of the page: the count.

The final approach to assigning values to use in the view uses the StdClass base class, which is a built-in feature in PHP 5.0. By constructing a class of type StdClass and assigning the class property values, you can easily pass the class into the assign() view operation, as shown in Listing 4-16.

**Listing 4-16.** *ArtistController.php: Updated removeAction*

```
/**
* Remove favorite artist.
*/
public function removeAction()
{
```

```
//Check if the user is logged in
//Get the user's Id


//Get the user's artists.
$artists = array("Thievery Corporation", "The Eagles", "Elton John");

//Set the total number of artists in the array.
//Demonstrates the use of a key-value array assignment.
$totalNumberOfArtists = array("totalArtist" => count($artists));

//Create the class
$artistObj = new StdClass();
$artistObj->artists = $artists;

//Set the total number of artists in the array.
//Demonstrates the use of a key-value array assignment.
$totalNumberOfArtists = array("totalArtist" => count($artists));

//Set the view variables
$this->view->assign((array)$artistObj);
$this->view->assign($totalNumberOfArtists);



}
```

As in the previous two examples, you assign the $artists variable to the $artistObj object to use in the view by using the assign() method. In this example, you initialize the variable information and store the information into a StdClass class property: artists. Using the assign() method, pass in the $artistsObj and typecast the variable as an array.

Try all three methods and see which one you like best. In all three instances, the information is rendered the same way as remove.phtml, so the only thing you have to change is the way you initialize the variables.

Because PHP can be used as a template language, you can use it here as well. Using PHP as a template language will give you the ability to not only display the variables on the page but also use if-then statements and for loops.

## Looping in the View

As discussed at the start of the chapter, a view also supports the standard PHP looping capabilities such as for, foreach, and while; they are used no differently from a regular PHP file.

Using the array of artists created in the controller, let's display each value in the array so users can remove the artists they no longer want to have on their favorites list (see Listing 4-17).

***Listing 4-17.*** *remove.phtml*

```
<?php echo $this->doctype('XHTML1_STRICT'); ?>
<html xmlns="http://www.w3.org/1999/xhtml" xml:lang="en" lang="en">
<head>
   <?php echo $this->headTitle('LoudBite.com – Remove Artist'); ?>
</head>
<body>

   <?php echo $this->render('includes/header.phtml') ?>

<h3>Remove Artist </h3>

   <table>
   <tr>
    <td>Artists - <i>Total Artists (<?php echo $this->totalArtist; ?>)</i></td>
   </tr>

   <?php foreach($this->artists as $artist){ ?>
   <tr><td><input type="checkbox" value="<?php echo $artist?>"
          name="remove[]" /><?php echo $artist?></td>
   </tr>
   <?php } ?>

   <tr><td><input type="submit" value="Remove"/></td></tr>
   </table>

</body>
</html>
```

The updated remove.phtml file now contains a foreach loop so it can loop through the $artists array much as you would use a foreach loop in a standard PHP script. Open up the URL http://localhost/artist/remove and take a look at the form again; it should look like Figure 4-8.

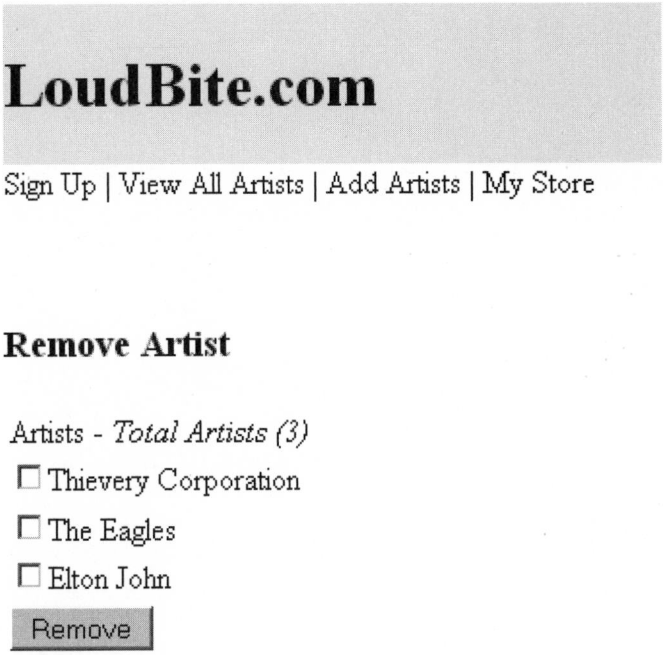

# LoudBite.com

Sign Up | View All Artists | Add Artists | My Store

**Remove Artist**

Artists - *Total Artists (3)*

☐ Thievery Corporation

☐ The Eagles

☐ Elton John

[ Remove ]

***Figure 4-8.*** *Removing artists*

## If-Else Statements

The previous example took the $artists view variable and looped through each index in the array to display the artist name next to a check box. Let's take the view one step further and add an if-else statement. If the user has rated the artist as a 5 (among the user's most-liked artists), add an asterisk next to the artist's name.

You'll make a few changes to the array first. Instead of a simple array, let's create a key-value array that contains the name of the artist and the rating. Modify the removeAction() method in ArtistController, as shown in Listing 4-18.

***Listing 4-18.*** *ArtistController.php*

```
/**
* Remove favorite artist..
*/
public function removeAction()
{

  //Check if the user is logged in
```

```php
//Get the user's Id

//Get the user's artist with rating.
$artists = array(
                array( "name" => "Thievery Corporation", "rating" => 5),
                array("name" => "The Eagles", "rating" => 5),
                array("name" => "Elton John", "rating" => 4)
        );

//Create the class
$artistObj = new StdClass();
$artistObj->artists = $artists;

//Set the view variables
$this->view->assign((array)$artistObj);

//Set the total number of artists in the array.
//Demonstrates the use of a key-value array assignment.
$totalNumberOfArtists = array("totalArtist" => count($artists));

//Set the view variables
$this->view->assign((array)$artistObj);
$this->view->assign($totalNumberOfArtists);

}
```

The updates made to the removeAction() method contain a multidimensional array containing key-value pairs: the name and rating as the key, and the artist name and artist rating as the values. With an if-else statement, you can use the data to display an asterisk next to the artist name if the rating is 5, as shown in Listing 4-19.

### Listing 4-19. *remove.phtml*

```php
<?php echo $this->doctype('XHTML1_STRICT'); ?>
<html xmlns="http://www.w3.org/1999/xhtml" xml:lang="en" lang="en">
<head>
  <?php echo $this->headTitle('LoudBite.com – Remove Artist'); ?>
</head>
<body>

  <?php echo $this->render('includes/header.phtml') ?>
```

```
<h3>Remove Artist </h3>

<table>
<tr>
  <td>Artists - <i>Total Artists (<?php echo $this->totalArtist; ?>)</i></td>
</tr>

<?php foreach($this->artists as $artist){ ?>
<tr><td><input type="checkbox" value="<?php echo $artist['name']?>"
        name="remove" /><?php echo $artist['name']?>
        <?php if($artist['rating'] == 5){ ?> * <?php } ?></td></tr>
        <?php } ?>
<tr><td><input type="submit" value="Remove"/></td></tr>
</table>

</body>
</html>
```

The view shown in Listing 4-19 expands on the example created initially to loop through the array elements and each artist, so users can remove artists they no longer want to have on their list. This example introduced the if-else statements; like the foreach loop, you use PHP in much the same way as you would in any other situation. A .phtml file should now be seen as a PHP file.

Figure 4-9 shows the results of this code.

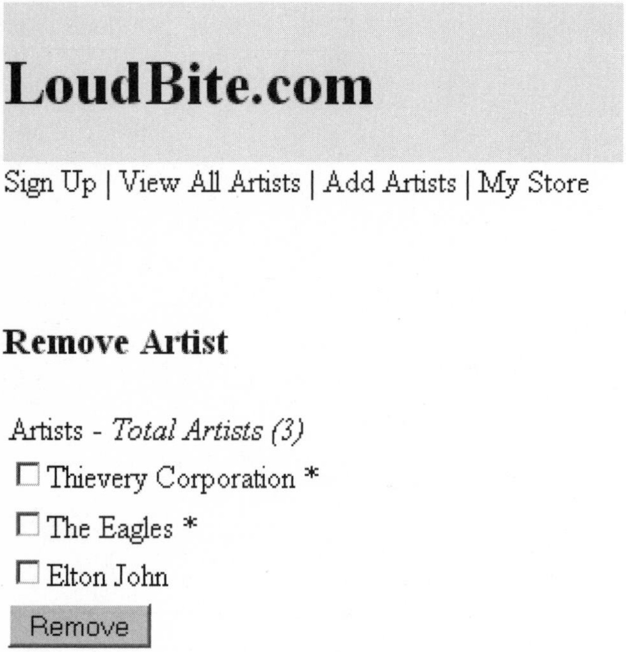

# LoudBite.com

Sign Up | View All Artists | Add Artists | My Store

## Remove Artist

Artists - *Total Artists (3)*

☐ Thievery Corporation *

☐ The Eagles *

☐ Elton John

[ Remove ]

**Figure 4-9.** *Removing artists with ratings*

# Escaping User Input

Some users are not interested in using the application for its intended purpose; they want to steal user information using the many methods available to them. To limit these possibilities, you can build your own escape() method to clean incoming user data. You will typically use the strip_tags() function, the htmlentities() function, or a combination of these functions—along with your own filtering.

Clean input must be a high priority when working with any application in which the user enters data for you to save or manipulate in the back end. Zend Framework added a Zend_View method, escape(), which allows you to not only clean user input but also overwrite default filtering and create your own escape() method.

The escape() method by default acts as a wrapper to the internal PHP function htmlspecialchars(). The htmlspecialchars() PHP function replaces <, >, &, ", and ' with their respective HTML encoded equivalents: &amp, &lt, &gt, &quot, and &#039. For example, consider the following string:

<tag>PHP & Zend Framework</tag>

After passing the string into htmlspecialchars(), it would become the following:

&lt;tag&gt;PHP &amp; Zend Framework&lt;/tag&gt;

Listing 4-20 shows how to use the method in the view.

**Listing 4-20.** *remove.phtml*

```php
<?php echo $this->doctype('XHTML1_STRICT'); ?>
<html xmlns="http://www.w3.org/1999/xhtml" xml:lang="en" lang="en">
<head>
  <?php echo $this->headTitle('LoudBite.com – Remove Artist'); ?>
</head>
<body>

  <?php echo $this->render('includes/header.phtml') ?>
  <h3>Remove Artist </h3>

  <table>
  <tr>
   <td>Artists - <i>Total Artists (<?php echo $this->totalArtist; ?>)</i></td>
  </tr>

  <?php foreach($this->artists as $artist){ ?>
  <tr>
   <td>
     <input type="checkbox" value="<?php echo $this->escape($artist['name'])?>"
         name="remove" /><?php echo $this->escape($artist['name'])?>
      <?php if($this->escape($artist['rating']) == 5){ ?> * <?php } ?>
   </td>
  </tr>
        <?php } ?>
  <tr><td><input type="submit" value="Remove"/></td></tr>
  </table>

</body>
</html>
```

Because the controller creates a Zend_View object by default, which can be accessed from the view using $this, you can also use the escape() function in the view with $this->escape(). This same process can be applied to the controller as well to escape any incoming user data (see Listing 4-21).

**Listing 4-21.** *ArtistController.php*

```php
public function saveArtistAction(){

  //Initialize variables
```

```
$artistName = $this->_request->getPost('artistName');
$genre     = $this->_request->getPost('genre');
$rating    = $this->_request->getPost('rating');
$isFav     = $this->_request->getPost('isFav');


//Clean up inputs
$artistName = $this->view->escape($artistName);
$genre      = $this->view->escape($genre);
$rating     = $this->view->escape($rating);
$isFav      = $this->view->escape($isFav);


//Save the input
}
```

Listing 4-21 updates the existing ArtistController.php file. You add the escape() method to escape all incoming data from the submitted add new artist form. The updated saveArtistAction() initializes the $artistName, $genre, $rating, and whether the artist is a favorite using the request object's getPost() method Finally, the input is saved, and a thank you page displays.

Because the default functionality of escape() is simply to convert the special characters, it provides you with some form of protection—but not enough. You want to extend the functionality of escape() and add a few more methods to clean the input.

## Creating Your Own escape() Function

Use the view setEscape() function, which accepts two types of parameters: a string value and an array value. By passing in a string value, you inform the view which method to use when escaping, as shown in Listing 4-22. When using an array, you are required to specify a class along with the method that will replace the default escape functionality.

*Listing 4-22.* *ArtistController.php*

```
public function saveArtistAction(){

    //Initialize variables
    $bandName = $this->_request->getPost('bandName');
    $genre    = $this->_request->getPost('genre');
    $rating   = $this->_request->getPost('rating');
    $isFav    = $this->_request->getPost('isFav');


    //Override default escape
    $this->view->setEscape('strip_tags');


    //Clean up inputs
```

```
$bandName = $this->view->escape($bandName);
$genre    = $this->view->escape($genre);
$rating   = $this->view->escape($rating);
$isFav    = $this->view->escape($isFav);

//Save the input
}
```

You want to restrict the user from entering any form of XHTML characters, so you change the escape() function to use the internal strip_tags() PHP function in the updated saveArtistAction(). Like the previous examples, initialize all the inputs using the request object's getPpost() method. After the inputs are retrieved, overwrite the default escape functionality using the setEscape() method and pass in the strip_tags parameter. This is the name of the function you want the escape() method to use instead of the htmlspecialchars() function. The strip_tags() function will take in a parameter and strip out all the HTML from it. For example, if a user enters Guns N' Roses into the artist name field, the return value will be Guns N' Roses when passed through the escape() function.

## Advanced Escape Functionality

If internal PHP functions aren't enough, you can also create your own escape() method and pass in the information to the setEscape() method, passing in an array as its parameter value. The setEscape() method accepts an array in which its first value contains the name of the class or an object, and the second value contains the method to call within the class.

Let's create an Escape class for this example that contains the doEnhancedEscape() method, as shown in Listing 4-23. The doEnhancedEscape() method accepts one string parameter and returns an escaped string. The body of the method initializes the $stringToEscape variable with the value of the passed-in value. It then passes the $stringToEscape string value through two functions: htmlentities() and strip_tags(). Finally, it returns the escaped value.

*Listing 4-23. Escape.php*

```php
<?php
class Escape {

    public function doEnhancedEscape ($string){

        $stringToEscape = $string;

        //Clean
        $stringToEscape = strip_tags($stringToEscape);
        $stringToEscape = htmlentities($stringToEscape, ENT_QUOTES, "UTF-8");

        return $stringToEscape;
    }
```

```
}
?>
```

Save the file in the APACHE_HOME/application/models/utils directory. Before using it, you need to make a change to the public/index.php file, as shown in Listing 4-24. The change will allow the Class to become available to you when you want to load in the controller:

***Listing 4-24.*** *Add Models Directory to index.php file*

```php
<?php

// Define path to application directory
defined('APPLICATION_PATH')
    || define('APPLICATION_PATH', realpath(dirname(__FILE__) . '/../application'));

// Define application environment
defined('APPLICATION_ENV')
    || define('APPLICATION_ENV', (getenv('APPLICATION_ENV') ?
      getenv('APPLICATION_ENV') : 'production'));

// Ensure library/ is on include_path
set_include_path(implode(PATH_SEPARATOR, array(
    realpath(APPLICATION_PATH . '/../library'),
    get_include_path(),
)).";".realpath(APPLICATION_PATH . '/models'));


/** Zend_Application */
require_once 'Zend/Application.php';

// Create application, bootstrap, and run
$application = new Zend_Application(
    APPLICATION_ENV,
    APPLICATION_PATH . '/configs/application.ini'
);


/** Routing Info **/
$FrontController = Zend_Controller_Front::getInstance();
$Router = $FrontController->getRouter();
```

```
$Router->addRoute("artiststore",
            new Zend_Controller_Router_Route(
                "artist/store",
                array
                ("controller" => "artist",
                 "action"     => "artistaffiliatecontent"
                )));
```

```
$application->bootstrap()
        ->run();
```

Now you use the new Escape class in the ArtistController.php file, as shown in Listing 4-25.

**Listing 4-25.** *ArtistController.php*

```php
/**
 * Save the artist into the system.
 *
 */
public function saveArtistAction()
{

  //Initialize variables
  $artistName = $this->_request->getPost('artistName');
  $genre    = $this->_request->getPost('genre');
  $rating   = $this->_request->getPost('rating');
  $isFav    = $this->_request->getPost('isFav');

  //Set new escape function to use.
  require "utils/Escape.php";
  $escapeObj = new Escape();
  $this->view->setEscape(array($escapeObj, "doEnhancedEscape"));

  //Clean up inputs
  $artistName = $this->view->escape($artistName);
  $genre    = $this->view->escape($genre);
  $rating   = $this->view->escape($rating);
```

```
$isFav    = $this->view->escape($isFav);

//Save the input
}
```

The updated saveArtistAction() method has now changed by including the new Escape class. You instantiated an Escape object and stored the object in the $escapeObj variable. With the object now created, the setEscape() method is called, passing it any array containing the $escapeObj object as the first element in the array and the name of the method containing the better escape sequence as the second parameter.

Let's now focus on easily creating forms by using the Zend_Form library.

# Creating Forms Using Zend_Form

An important part of the Web is the interaction that it allows between users and sites using forms. Forms are utilized by users to create accounts on a web site, fill out rating information, or enter data about themselves on an online application. Using Zend Framework's Zend_Form component, creating forms is now easy to do.

## Getting Started

When you create forms, you worry about what the user has entered into them. You also worry about the type of data submitted into the application and potentially causing havoc in the application. If this is your first site, you could create your own library to handle all the potential use cases, but after you begin creating additional applications you will wonder whether there is a faster way of creating forms, handling filters, and validating all user data that comes into the application.

The Zend_Form component allows you to create forms using an object-oriented approach, treating the form as an object and using each element as a type of Zend_Form_Element object. With a Zend_Form object, you can set all the typical properties that a form contains. It sets the method the form uses to submit the data, sets the action, and provides a way to set the name of the form. A complete list of setters is shown in Table 4-2 (each of these setters has a corresponding getter).

**Table 4-2.** *Zend_Form Setters*

| Setter | Description |
|---|---|
| setAction() | Sets the action attribute in the form tag. <form action='<value>'> Accepts single String value. |
| setMethod() | Sets the method attribute in the form tag. <form method='<value>'> Accepts single String value. (delete, get, post, put). Default is post. |
| setName() | Sets the name of the form. Cannot be empty. <form name='<value>'> |
| setEnctype() | Sets the form encoding type. <form enctype='<value>'> By default, the form encoding is set to application/x-www-form-urlencoded. |
| setAttrib() | Sets a single form attribute setAttrib(key, value). Can be used to add custom attributes to form tag <form key='<value>'>. |
| setDecorators() | Sets decorators that govern how the form is rendered. By default, the form is made up of <dl> elements that wrap each input. |
| setAttribs() | Sets multiple form attribute in one call. setAttribs(array(key, value)) Can be used to add custom attributes to form tag. <form key='<value>'> |
| setDescription() | Sets the description of the form. |

The setters outlined in Table 4-2 allow you to easily create a form. To show the Zend_Form component in action, you need to create a controller-action pair along with a view to display the form. Using the AccountController.php controller file, let's update newAction() to create a form that will replace the existing XHTML form version located in the view: views/scripts/account/new.phtml.

The controller shown in Listing 4-26 contains an updated newAction(). The action creates a form that will be displayed in the new.phtml view.

**Listing 4-26.** *AccountController.php: Updates*

```
/**
 * Account Sign Up.
 */
public function newAction(){

  //Create Form
  $form = new Zend_Form();
```

```
$form->setAction('success');
$form->setMethod('post');
$form->setDescription("sign up form");
$form->setAttrib('sitename', 'loudbite');

//Add the form to the view
$this->view->form = $form;

}
```

The code begins by instantiating a Zend_Form object: $form. You then set the form attributes, action, method, and description. Using Table 4-1 as a reference, you implement setMethod() and pass in one of four acceptable values: 'post'. You use the setAction() method to set the value of the action attribute. You also set the description of the form and implement a unique attribute (sitename) to demonstrate the use of the setAttrib() method. After the settings are set, you're finished creating the form using nothing but PHP. Initialize a view variable, form, with the Zend_Form object $form.

To display the form in your view, you can simply output the view variable $form using echo or use the Zend_Form method render(). The method can be used in both the view and in the controller, as long as you have a Zend_Form object to use. Let's display the form in the view by updating the views/scripts/account/new.phtml file with the code shown in Listing 4-27.

### Listing 4-27. new.phtml

```
<?php echo $this->doctype('XHTML1_STRICT'); ?>
<html xmlns="http://www.w3.org/1999/xhtml" xml:lang="en" lang="en">
<head>
  <?php echo $this->headTitle('LoudBite.com – Account Sign up'); ?>
</head>
<body>

  <?php echo $this->render("includes/header.phtml"); ?>
  <h3>Account Sign up</h3>
  <?php  echo $this->form; ?>

</body>
</html>
```

Load the URL http://localhost/account/new in your browser and take a look under the hood at the source code. You will see the XHTML shown in Listing 4-28.

**Listing 4-28.** *new.phtml Source Code*

```
<!DOCTYPE html PUBLIC "-//W3C//DTD XHTML 1.0 Strict//EN"
"http://www.w3.org/TR/xhtml1/DTD/xhtml1-strict.dtd">
<html xmlns="http://www.w3.org/1999/xhtml" xml:lang="en" lang="en">
<head>
  <title>LoudBite.com - Account Sign up</title>
</head>
<body>

<table width="100%" cellpadding="0" cellspacing="0">
<tr bgcolor="#eeeeee"><td><h1>LoudBite.com</h1></td></tr>
<tr><td>Sign Up | View All Artists | Add Artists | My Store</td></tr>
</table>
<br><br>

<h3>Account Sign up</h3>

<form enctype="application/x-www-form-urlencoded" action="success"
    method="post" sitename="loudbite">
<dl class="zend_form">
</dl>
</form>


</body>
</html>
```

The source code shown in Listing 4-28 displays in bold the markup that Zend_Form creates. Zend_Form sets the encoding type, action, method, and unique attribute site name. But this form still lacks a way for the user to add in data. You will now learn one way to add elements to the form.

# Adding Elements to a Form

Without the use of text fields, drop-down menus, check boxes, or other form elements a form is useless, and the data that the user provides can never be saved into the application. So you need a way to add form elements into the form.

The Zend_Form component provides the addElement() method to do just that—add elements to the form you are building. The method accepts three parameters: a required string or Zend_Form_Element object (covered later in this chapter), a second string representing the value of the name attribute in the element tag, and a final optional Zend_Config object.

119

A complete list of acceptable strings for the initial parameter is shown in Table 4-3. The table consists of all element types that Zend_Form supports in the Value column (for example, text, password, hidden, checkbox) and the resulting element in the Element Result column.

**Table 4-3.** *Acceptable addElement Values*

| Value | Element Result | Zend_Form_Element Object |
| --- | --- | --- |
| text | Text input field | Zend_Form_Element_Text |
| password | Password input field | Zend_Form_Element_Password |
| radio | Radio button | Zend_Form_Element_Radio |
| hidden | Hidden text field | Zend_Form_Element_Hidden |
| button | Form button | Zend_Form_Element_Button |
| checkbox | Check box | Zend_Form_Element_Checkbox |
| file | File upload field | Zend_Form_Element_File |
| hash | Hidden hash field that protects from cross site request forgery attacks | Zend_Form_Element_Hash |
| image | Image input type | Zend_Form_Element_Image |
| multicheckbox | Multicheck boxes | Zend_Form_Element_Multicheckbox |
| multiselect | Multiselect menu | Zend_Form_Element_MultiSelect |
| reset | Reset button | Zend_Form_Element_Reset |
| select | Select drop-down menu | Zend_Form_Element_Select |
| submit | Submit button | Zend_Form_Element_Submit |
| textarea | Test area | Zend_Form_Element_TextArea |

Using Table 4-3, let's now add two text fields and a single password field to the Account sign-up form you've been working with by updating the AccountController.php file, as shown in Listing 4-29.

***Listing 4-29.*** *AccountController.php*

```
/**
 * Account Sign Up.
 *
 */
public function newAction(){


  //Create Form
  $form = new Zend_Form();
  $form->setAction('success');
  $form->setMethod('post');
  $form->setDescription("sign up form");
  $form->setAttrib('sitename', 'loudbite');

  //Add Elements

  //Create Username Field.
  $form->addElement('text', 'username');
  $usernameElement = $form->getElement('username');
  $usernameElement->setLabel('Username:');

  //Create Email Field.
  $form->addElement('text', 'email');
  $emailElement = $form->getElement('email');
  $emailElement->setLabel('Email:');

  //Create Password Field.
  $form->addElement('password', 'password');
  $passwordElement = $form->getElement('password');
  $passwordElement->setLabel('Password:');

  $form->addElement('submit', 'submit');
  $submitButton = $form->getElement('submit');
  $submitButton->setLabel('Create My Account!');
```

```
//Add the form to the view
$this->view->form = $form;
}
```

Listing 4-29 not only demonstrates how to create and add form elements into the form but also demonstrates how to use setLabel() and getElement().

The getElement() method allows you to fetch a Zend_Form_Element_* object after adding a specific element to the form. (A list of all equivalent objects is also displayed in Table 4-3.) The method accepts a single string parameter as the name given to the element you created. Using the code shown in Listing 4-28, after creating the text type element 'username', the Zend_Form_Element_Text object is fetched.

Once the Zend_Form_Element_Text object is retrieved, you can use all its mutator methods. In this example, you use the setLabel() method. The method allows you to set the string the user will see next to the form element by passing in a single string parameter. Again take a look at Listing 4-29. After retrieving the Zend_Form_Element_Text object for the username field, you set the label as 'Username'. Continue with the code and do the same for both the email text field and the password text field.

If you now reload the http://localhost/account/new page, you will see Figure 4-10 as well as an updated source code.

*Figure 4-10. Zend_Form sign-up form*

# Formatting the Form

Continuing with the Zend_Form functionality, you now focus on element ordering and form decorating.

By default, the order of the elements is shown to the user in the same way as created in the code. Using the example shown in Listing 4-29, the username text field is initially created, followed by the email text field, the password text field, and finally the submit button. This same order is then shown in the view. To change the order, use the Zend_Form_Element setOrder() method.

The setOrder() method accepts a single integer parameter, from 1 to an arbitrary high number. The numerical value passed into the method represents the order in which the element will be displayed. If you set the value to 1 for the username text field, 2 for password, and 3 for email, the form will display the elements in that order. This is a great feature if you require your form to display each element in a different order based on previous user input on your site.

Open the AccountController.php file once again and make the modifications shown in Listing 4-30.

**Listing 4-30.** *Setting the Order in the AccountController*

```
/**
 * Account Sign Up.
 *
 */
public function newAction(){

  //Create Form
  $form = new Zend_Form();
  $form->setAction('success');
  $form->setMethod('post');
  $form->setDescription("sign up form");
  $form->setAttrib('sitename', 'loudbite');

  //Add Elements
  //Create Username Field.
  $form->addElement('text', 'username');
  $usernameElement = $form->getElement('username');
  $usernameElement->setLabel('Username:');
  $usernameElement->setOrder(1);

  //Create Email Field.
  $form->addElement('text', 'email');
  $emailElement = $form->getElement('email');
  $emailElement->setLabel('Email:');
  $emailElement->setOrder(3);
```

```
//Create Password Field.
$form->addElement('password', 'password');
$passwordElement = $form->getElement('password');
$passwordElement->setLabel('Password:');
$passwordElement->setOrder(2);

$form->addElement('submit', 'submit');
$submitButton = $form->getElement('submit');
$submitButton->setLabel('Create My Account!');
$submitButton->setOrder(4);


//Add the form to the view
$this->view->form = $form;


}
```

Reloading the URL http://localhost/account/new will give you an updated form with updated ordering.

---

■ **Note** A form usually loops through its elements and wraps them in its <form> tag in the order you specify. If you want to change this order, you can use setOrder(), as I have done here.

---

## Processing the Form

Submitting a form doesn't change when using the Zend_Form component; what does change is the level of complexity required to validate, filter, and process form submitted data. Let's now take a look at each of these steps using the Zend_Form component.

Start by validating all incoming data. To validate submitted data, the Zend_Form component contains the method isValid(). The method accepts only two values: $_POST or $_GET. This value is determined by the way in which you're submitting data to the action. In the context of this section, you're submitting data using a form with the method attribute set to post; therefore you set the value to $_POST.

Unlike the traditional approach of validating a form, in which all incoming data must be initially fetched using the request object and then the data is validated using either a set of regular expression or filters you created, Zend Framework uses isValid() to check each form element's validator and filter settings to determine whether the submitted data meets the requirements. If one of the values fails to meet these settings, isValid() returns false. If the validation is a success, you can retrieve the values of the submitted content using either the getValue() or getUnfilteredValue() methods.

Both the getValue() and getUnfilteredValue() methods accept the name of the element to retrieve, except that the getUnfilteredValue() method returns the submitted string prior to filtering. Let's create a quick example and update the complete sign-up process in the AccountController.php file, as shown in Listing 4-31.

*Listing 4-31. Creating and Processing a Form: Updated and New Actions*

```
/**
 * Create the sign up form.
 */
private function getSignupForm()
{

    //Create Form
    $form = new Zend_Form();
    $form->setAction('success');
    $form->setMethod('post');
    $form->setAttrib('sitename', 'loudbite');

    //Add Elements
    //Create Username Field.
    $form->addElement('text', 'username');
    $usernameElement = $form->getElement('username');
    $usernameElement->setLabel('Username:');
    $usernameElement->setOrder(1)->setRequired(true);

    //Create Email Field.
    $form->addElement('text', 'email');
    $emailElement = $form->getElement('email');
    $emailElement->setLabel('Email:');
    $emailElement->setOrder(3)->setRequired(true);

    //Create Password Field.
    $form->addElement('password', 'password');
    $passwordElement = $form->getElement('password');
    $passwordElement->setLabel('Password:');
    $passwordElement->setOrder(2)->setRequired(true);

    $form->addElement('submit', 'submit');
    $submitButton = $form->getElement('submit');
    $submitButton->setLabel('Create My Account!');
    $submitButton->setOrder(4);
```

```
    return $form;
}

/**
 * Process new account form.
 *
 */
public function successAction()
{

    $form = $this->getSignupForm();

    //Check if the submitted data is POST type
    if($form->isValid($_POST)){

        $email      = $form->getValue("email");
        $username = $form->getValue("username");
        $password = $form->getValue("password");

        //Save the user into the system.

    }else{

        throw new Exception("Whoops.  Wrong way of submitting your
        information.");

    }

}

/**
 * Account Sign Up.
 *
 */
public function newAction()
{

    //Get the form.
    $form = $this->getSignupForm();
```

```
//Add the form to the view
$this->view->form = $form;
}
```

Listing 4-31 contains three actions, two of which contain updates and a new method called getSignupForm(). The new method is set to private because it's a method required only by the class, not an action that a user can request. Unlike Listing 4-30, you do not create the sign-up form in newAction(). Instead the sign-up form is created within the new method to promote reusability while working with the form in newAction() and successAction(). The form itself has been slightly modified. The setRequired() method is introduced, which sets the form element as data the user must populate. This is one of the many types of validators you can use for each element additional validators will be covered later in this chapter.

Turn your attention to newAction(); all form creation logic is removed and the getSignupForm() method is called to fetch an instance of the form. You pass this instance into the form view variable to use in the view. After the user submits the form, you fetch an instance of the form using the newly created method, getSignupForm(), and check whether the submitted $_POST values pass validation using the isValid() method. If the submitted data is valid, you retrieve the data using the getValue() method before saving the content to the database (covered in Chapter 5). In this example, if the data is not valid, you throw an exception that isn't helpful to the user. You need a way to handle user errors properly.

# Error Handling

Your users aren't perfect; they will make mistakes. They might click submit on the sign-up form, but the e-mail address, username, and password might be missing. Validating the form will fail because of the missing values, and users will be left wondering what happened when they reach an exception error page. Developers need a graceful way to display the form again to users, display the errors, and allow users to correct their mistakes.

The Zend_Form object contains two methods to retrieve any errors that arise when the user submits the data: getMessages() and getErrors(). The getMessages() method returns only information regarding the failed elements as a key-value pair, where the key is the element containing the errors, and the value is a key-value array where the key is the abbreviated error and the value is the full error message. This array can contain many entries if the element fails for one or more validations.

The getErrors() method, on the other hand, returns a key-value array with every key representing the name of the element with the form. The key-value array returns every form element as a key, even if there are no errors with the data submitted for that element. The value contains an array with abbreviated error messages within its elements.

Let's update the sign-up process and add error handling to it. Open the AccountController.php file and update the code, as shown in Listing 4-32.

***Listing 4-32.*** *AccountController.php: Updates*

```php
/**
* Process Sign up Form.
*
*/
public function successAction()
{

  $form = $this->getSignupForm();

  //Check if the submitted data is POST type
  if($form->isValid($_POST)){

    $email    = $form->getValue("email");
    $username = $form->getValue("username");
    $password = $form->getValue("password");

    //Save the user into the system.

  }else{

    $this->view->errors = $form->getMessages();
    $this->view->form = $form;

  }

}
```

The code shown in Listing 4-32 is the updated successAction() method. This example focuses on submitted data that is invalid. Look at the else statement. It contains two lines of code: the initial line retrieves any error messages created by the form, and the subsequent line places the form into a view variable. Now you need to make the updates to the view.

Open the views/scripts/accounts/success.phtml file and update the file, as shown in Listing 4-33.

*Listing 4-33. success.phtml: Updates*

```php
<?php echo $this->doctype('XHTML1_STRICT'); ?>
<html>
<head>
    <?php echo $this->headTitle('LoudBite.com – Account Sign up success'); ?>
</head>
<body>

<?php echo $this->render("includes/header.phtml"); ?>

<h3>Account Sign up</h3>

<?php
if($this->errors){

  echo $this->form;

}else{

  echo "Thank you!  You are one step closer
  to becoming a full member.";

}
?>
</body>
</html>
```

The updates made to the view shown in Listing 4-33 checks whether the error variable contains information using an if statement. If the error variable contains values, as in this case, it redisplays the form so the user can have a chance to correct the mistakes. If there are no errors, the success message displays, and the user can continue. That's it! Load the sign-up page again, http://localhost/account/new, and sign up for an account, leaving the password field empty. You will see Figure 4-11.

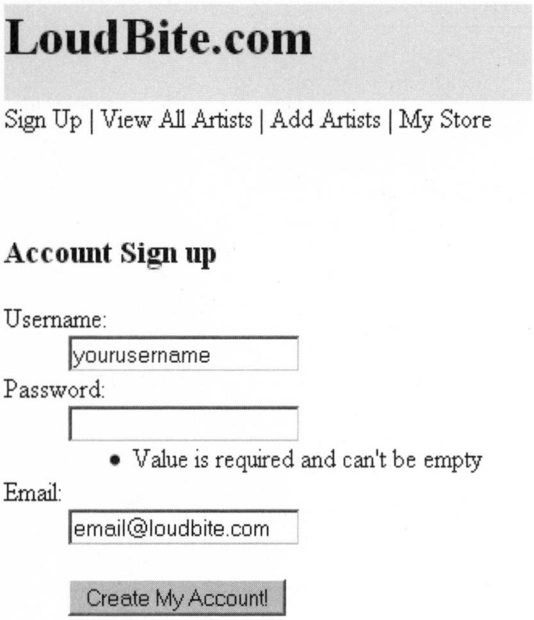

## LoudBite.com

Sign Up | View All Artists | Add Artists | My Store

### Account Sign up

Username:

> yourusername

Password:

> - Value is required and can't be empty

Email:

> email@loudbite.com

> Create My Account!

**Figure 4-11.** *Displaying* error *messages*

## Adding Validation and Filtering

You know that form-submitted data can be validated by using Zend_Form; you also know that there are setters such as the setRequired() method, which enables you to set a form element as a required form field the user must populate. Now let's see the complete collection of validators and filters that Zend_Form contains.

Why validate? Validation allows you to check whether the user really did submit data that is properly formatted and meets your application requirements. For example, you might require the username to be all lowercase, contain no numbers, and have a length between 4 and 16 characters. If the user submits the string "12", the data is useless and should not be saved into your application.

Using the Zend_Validate component you can check for such things. The Zend_Validate component contains a list of built-in validators you can use (see Table 4-4).

***Table 4-4.*** *Built-in Validators*

| Validator | Description |
| --- | --- |
| Zend_Validate_Alnum | Allows only alphanumeric characters. |
| Zend_Validate_Alpha | Allows only alphabetic characters. |
| Zend_Validate_Barcode | Validated barcode. |
| Zend_Validate_Between | Validates ranges: min/max values. |
| Zend_Validate_Ccnum | Validates entered credit card value to match Luhn algorithm. |
| Zend_Validate_Date | Allows valid dates in 0000-00-00 format. |
| Zend_Validate_Digits | Allows only digits. |
| Zend_Validate_EmailAddress | Allows valid e-mail address formats. |
| Zend_Validate_Float | Allows only float values. |
| Zend_Validate_GreaterThan | Allows values greater than a certain value. |
| Zend_Validate_Hex | Allows only hex values. |
| Zend_Validate_Hostname | Checks for valid host. |
| Zend_Validate_Int | Allows only integer values. |
| Zend_Validate_Ip | Checks for valid IP address. |
| Zend_Validate_LessThan | Allows the value to be less than the given value. |
| Zend_Validate_NotEmpty | Checks that the value is not empty. |
| Zend_Validate_Regex | Checks value against specified regular expression. |
| Zend_Validate_StringLength | Checks that the string is given between min and max length. |

To add a validator to a form element, you need the addValidator() method provided by the each Zend_Form_Element object. The method accepts a Zend_Validate_* object (shown in Table 4-4) .

Adding a filter to a form element can be done by using the Zend_Form_Element object's method addFilter(). The method accepts a single Zend_Filter object (see Table 4-5).

**Table 4-5.** *Zend_Filter Objects*

| Filter Object | Description |
| --- | --- |
| Zend_Filter_Alnum | Returns only alphanumeric characters. |
| Zend_Filter_Alpha | Returns only alphabetic characters. |
| Zend_Filter_Basename | Returns the base name of the file. |
| Zend_Filter_Digits | Returns only the digits in a string. |
| Zend_Filter_Dir | Returns the directory name. |
| Zend_Filter_HtmlEntities | Encodes the string and returns the encoded value of the string. |
| Zend_Filter_Int | Returns only int values. |
| Zend_Filter_StripNewlines | Removes \n markers from the string. |
| Zend_Filter_StringToLower | Converts the string to lowercase values. |
| Zend_Filter_StringToUpper | Converts the string to uppercase values. |
| Zend_Filter_StringTrim | Strips whitespace from the string. |
| Zend_Filter_StripTags | Strips HTML tags from the string. |

Let's expand the sign-up form to add both a filter and a validator to the three form elements in the sign-up form (see Listing 4-34).

***Listing 4-34.*** *Adding Validators and Filters to Sign-up Form*

```
/**
 * Create the sign up form.
 */
private function getSignupForm(){

    //Create Form
    $form = new Zend_Form();
    $form->setAction('success');
    $form->setMethod('post');
    $form->setAttrib('sitename', 'loudbite');

    //Add Elements
    //Create Username Field.
    $form->addElement('text', 'username');
    $usernameElement = $form->getElement('username');
    $usernameElement->setLabel('Username:');
    $usernameElement->setOrder(1)->setRequired(true);

    //Add validator
    $usernameElement->addValidator(
                new Zend_Validate_StringLength(6, 20)
            );
    //Add Filter
    $usernameElement->addFilter(new Zend_Filter_StringToLower());
    $usernameElement->addFilter(new Zend_Filter_StripTags());

    //Create Email Field.
    $form->addElement('text', 'email');
    $emailElement = $form->getElement('email');
    $emailElement->setLabel('Email:');
    $emailElement->setOrder(3)->setRequired(true);

    //Add Validator
    $emailElement->addValidator(new Zend_Validate_EmailAddress());
    //Add Filter
    $emailElement->addFilter(new Zend_Filter_StripTags());
```

```
//Create Password Field.
$form->addElement('password', 'password');
$passwordElement = $form->getElement('password');
$passwordElement->setLabel('Password:');
$passwordElement->setOrder(2)->setRequired(true);

//Add Validator
$passwordElement->addValidator(
            new Zend_Validate_StringLength(6,20)
        );
//Add Filter
$passwordElement->addFilter(new Zend_Filter_StripTags());

$form->addElement('submit', 'submit');
$submitButton = $form->getElement('submit');
$submitButton->setLabel('Create My Account!');
$submitButton->setOrder(4);

return $form;


}
```

The code shown in Listing 4-34 is an update to the getSignupForm() method. As before, you start by instantiating a Zend_Form object and setting the form's attributes. Aside from creating the form elements, you used the addValidator() and addFilter() methods. You set a validator to check whether the submitted data is at least 6 characters (and at most 20 characters) long for the username text field. You also set a filter on the username text field to remove any HTML and set the data to lowercase by passing in a Zend_Validate_* object into the addFilter() method. Likewise, you set a validator on the email form element to check whether the data submitted follows an e-mail format and filters any HTML tags. Finally, you add another validator and filter to the password form element.

Pull up the account sign-up form once more by loading the URL http://localhost/account/new and try submitting erroneous data to see the validators in action.

You can now validate, filter, and process submitted content. Let's look at additional form elements you can create using Zend_Form.

## Creating Form Element Objects

As shown in the previous sections, creating form elements using the Zend_Form component is easy and fun. In this section, you'll create the majority of the available form elements and implement them in the LoudBite application.

Take a look at Table 4-5. Each of the Zend_Form_Element objects contain setters that enable you to set the name, set the label, and determine whether the field should be required (among other things).

**Table 4-6.** *Zend_Form_Element Setters*

| Setter | Description |
| --- | --- |
| setName() | Sets the name of the element. |
| setLabel() | Sets the label of the element. |
| setOrder() | Sets the order the element will be shown on the form. |
| setValue() | Sets the default value that will be shown on the element when the form renders. |
| setDescription() | Sets the description of the element. |
| setRequired() | Identifies whether the element is required. |
| setAllowEmpty() | Identifies whether the element can be empty. |
| setAutoInsertNotEmptyValidator() | Sets whether the element will be marked as not empty when it is required. If it is marked as not empty, no other validators will run, and the user will be told. |
| setAttrib() | Sets any attribute on the element. |
| setAttribs() | Sets multiple attributes for the element. |

## Creating Textarea Fields

Let's create a textarea, a widely used form element that allows developers to create an input field in which the user has ample amount of space to type in any number of characters. This is a great field if you want the user to type in large amounts of data, such as a personal biography or a short story. To add the element to the form, you use the Zend_Form_Element_TextArea class.

Let's use the new Zend_Form_Element_TextArea class to create the update form. The new action will create the update form that enables users to update their personal content stored in the application. You'll also add a new textarea field, About Me, in which users can enter data about themselves to display on their profile page.

Before creating the new action, you must create a new class that abstracts the way in which the application's password, username, and email text fields are created. The new class enables you to create these fields, along with their validators and filters, in a single location and share them between the sign-up and update forms. Create a new file called Elements.php and save it inside a new directory: application/models/Form. The complete code is shown in Listing 4-35.

**Listing 4-35.** *Form/Elements.php class*

```php
<?php
/**
 * Loudbite.com Form Elements.
 *
 */
class Elements
{

    /**
     * Create email text field
     *
     * @return Zend_Form_Element_Text
     */
    public function getEmailTextField()
    {

        //Create Text Field Object.
        $emailElement = new Zend_Form_Element_Text('email');
        $emailElement->setLabel('Email:');
        $emailElement->setRequired(true);

        //Add Validator
        $emailElement->addValidator(new Zend_Validate_EmailAddress());

        //Add Filter
        $emailElement->addFilter(new Zend_Filter_HtmlEntities());
        $emailElement->addFilter(new Zend_Filter_StripTags());

        return $emailElement;

    }


    /**
     * Create password text field
     *
     * @return Zend_Form_Element_Password
```

```
 */
public function getPasswordTextField()
{

    //Create Password Object.
    $passwordElement = new Zend_Form_Element_Password('password');
    $passwordElement->setLabel('Password:');
    $passwordElement->setRequired(true);

    //Add Validator
    $passwordElement->addValidator
            (
             new Zend_Validate_StringLength(6,20)
            );

    //Add Filter
    $passwordElement->addFilter(new Zend_Filter_HtmlEntities());
    $passwordElement->addFilter(new Zend_Filter_StripTags());

    return $passwordElement;

}


/**
 * Create username text field.
 *
 * @return Zend_Form_Element_Text
 */
public function getUsernameTextField()
{

    $usernameElement = new Zend_Form_Element_Text('username');
    $usernameElement->setLabel('Username:');
    $usernameElement->setRequired(true);

    //Add validator
    $usernameElement->addValidator
            (
             new Zend_Validate_StringLength(6, 20)
```

```
                        );

    //Add Filter
    $usernameElement->addFilter(new Zend_Filter_StripTags());
    $usernameElement->addFilter(new Zend_Filter_HtmlEntities());
    $usernameElement->addFilter(new Zend_Filter_StringToLower());

    return $usernameElement;

  }

}
```

The code shown in Listing 4-35 is the class Elements, which contains three public methods: getUsernameTextField(), getPasswordTextField(), and getEmailTextField(). Each of these methods creates a Zend_Form_Element object, sets the validators as well as any filters, and returns the object. The code is taken from the account sign-up form created earlier. Now open the AccountController.php file and create the update profile form, as shown in Listing 4-36.

***Listing 4-36.*** *Creating an Update Profile Form*

```
/**
 * Update Form
 */
private function getUpdateForm(){

  //Create Form
  $form = new Zend_Form();
  $form->setAction('update');
  $form->setMethod('post');
  $form->setAttrib('sitename', 'loudbite');

  //Load Elements class
  require "Form/Elements.php";
  $LoudbiteElements = new Elements();

  //Create Username Field.
  $form->addElement($LoudbiteElements->getUsernameTextField());

  //Create Email Field.
  $form->addElement($LoudbiteElements->getEmailTextField());
```

```
//Create Password Field.
$form->addElement($LoudbiteElements->getPasswordTextField());

//Create Text Area for About me.
$textAreaElement = new Zend_Form_Element_TextArea('aboutme');
$textAreaElement->setLabel('About Me:');
$textAreaElement->setAttribs(array('cols' => 15,
                        'rows' => 5));

$form->addElement($textAreaElement);

//Create a submit button.
$form->addElement('submit', 'submit');
$submitElement = $form->getElement('submit');
$submitElement->setLabel('Update My Account');

    return $form;

}

/**
 * Update the User's data.
 *
 */
public function updateAction()
{

//Check if the user is logged in
//Fetch the user's id
//Fetch the users information

//Create the form.
$form = $this->getUpdateForm();

//Check if the form has been submitted.
//If so validate and process.
if($_POST){

    //Check if the form is valid.
```

```
        if($form->isValid($_POST)){

            //Get the values
            $username = $form->getValue('username');
            $password = $form->getValue('password');
            $email    = $form->getValue('email');
            $aboutMe  = $form->getValue('aboutme');

            //Save.

        }
        //Otherwise redisplay the form.
        else{

            $this->view->form  = $form;

        }

    }
    //Otherwise display the form.
    else{

        $this->view->form = $form;

    }

}
```

Listing 4-36 contains the action updateAction() and a new private method: getUpdateForm(). The new private method creates the update form using the Elements class you created and also creates a new textarea form element by instantiating the Zend_Form_Element_Textarea, setting its label to About Me:, setting the cols and rows attributes using setAttribs(), and adding the element to the form. Once the form has been complete, you can return the Zend_Form object stored within the $form variable.

The second method, updateAction(), is the action called by the user to view the update form and when submitting any updates. The action begins by fetching the update form from the getUpdateForm() method. Because this action will also support both creating the form and processing any submitted data, you have to determine whether the form has been submitted. You do this by checking whether the $_POST variable has been set; if it is, validate the form. If the form has not been submitted, you know the user has just arrived and simply wants to see the form to begin the edits.

You now need a view for your updateAction() method: create a file under the views/scripts/account/ directory and save the file with the XHTML shown in Listing 4-37.

*Listing 4-37. New update.phtml Page*

```
<?php echo $this->doctype('XHTML1_STRICT'); ?>
<html xmlns="http://www.w3.org/1999/xhtml" xml:lang="en" lang="en">
<head>
  <?php echo $this->headTitle('LoudBite.com – Update Info'); ?>
</head>
<body>

<?php echo $this->render('includes/header.phtml') ?>

  <h3>Update My Profile</h3>
  <?php echo $this->form; ?>

</body>
</html>
```

If you load the update form http://localhost/account/update and fill out the form, you will go through the complete update process, but your data will not be saved.

## Creating Password Fields

Password support comes standard in Zend Framework with the Zend_Form_Element_Password object. Aside from the setters in Table 4-2, the object contains an additional function that allows you to toggle between hiding users' passwords as they type: setObscureValue:

setObscureValue(boolean)

The function accepts a Boolean value: true if you want to hide the data and false if you don't. By default, it's set to true.

## Creating Hidden Text Fields

The hidden form element is a text field that does not display for the user, but can contain valuable information in its value attribute. The Zend_Form component creates hidden text fields using the Zend_Form_Element_Hidden class with the setters shown in Table 4-5.

You can set the Zend_Form_Element_Hidden value property with setValue(), which accepts a string representing the value you want the attribute to contain.

## Creating Radio Buttons

Radio buttons allow the user to select a single value from a set of possible values. If you wanted to create a rating system, you could display a set of radio buttons with the values 1–5 and allow the user to select one and only one value.

141

The Zend_Form_Element_Radio class contains additional setters that are required for a successful implementation (see Table 4-7).

*Table 4-7.* *Zend_Form_Element_Radio Setters*

| Function | Description |
| --- | --- |
| addMultiOption() | Adds an option and value of the option to display as a radio option. |
| addMultiOptions() | Adds a set of options and values to display as radio options. |
| setMultiOptions() | Overwrites existing options. |

## Creating Check Boxes

Check boxes allow users to select multiple values from many options. They are represented as Zend_Form_Element_Checkbox objects or Zend_Form_Element_MultiCheckbox objects if you want the user to have the option to select two or more values. For the Zend_Form_Element_Checkbox, the default value for a checked item is 1, and the default value for an unchecked item is 0.

Table 4-8 shows the key methods of Zend_Form_Element_Checkbox.

*Table 4-8.* *Zend_Form_Element_Checkbox Methods*

| Method | Description |
| --- | --- |
| setCheckedValue() | Sets the value for the checked value. |
| setUncheckedValue() | Sets the value for the unchecked value. |

The Zend_Form_Element_MultiCheckbox contains the setters shown in Table 4-9.

*Table 4-9.* *Zend_Form_Element_MultiCheckbox Setters*

| Method | Description |
| --- | --- |
| addMultiOption() | Adds an option and value of the option to display as a radio option. |
| addMultiOptions() | Adds a set of options and values of the options to display as radio options. |
| setMultiOptions() | Overwrites existing options. |

## Creating Select Menus and Multiselect Menus

Standard select menus allow the user to select only one option, whereas multiselect menus allow users to select multiple options. Standard select menus are represented by Zend_Form_Element_Select;

multiselect menus are represented by Zend_Form_Element_Multiselect. They both have the setters shown in Table 4-8.

Let's now update the ArtistController.php file and focus on the newAction() method. You will implement all the input fields covered up to his point, as shown in Listing 4-38.

*Listing 4-38. Updating newAction() with Zend_Form_Element Objects*

```
/**
 * Create Add Artist Form.
 *
 * @return Zend_Form
 */
private function getAddArtistForm()
{

  $form = new Zend_Form();
  $form->setAction("saveartist");
  $form->setMethod("post");
  $form->setName("addartist");

  //Create artist name text field.
  $artistNameElement = new Zend_Form_Element_Text('artistName');
  $artistNameElement->setLabel("Artist Name:");

  //Create genres select menu
  $genres = array("multiOptions" => array
  (
      "electronic"       => "Electronic",
      "country"          => "Country",
      "rock"             => "Rock",
      "r_n_b"            => "R & B",
      "hip_hop"          => "Hip-Hop",
      "heavy_metal"      => "Heavy-Metal",
      "alternative_rock" => "Alternative Rock",
      "christian"        => "Christian",
      "jazz"             => "Jazz",
      "pop"              => "Pop"
  ));

  $genreElement = new Zend_Form_Element_Select('genre', $genres);
  $genreElement->setLabel("Genre:");
```

```php
$genreElement->setRequired(true);

//Create favorite radio buttons.
$favoriteOptions = array("multiOptions" => array
(
    "1" => "yes",
    "0" => "no"
));


$isFavoriteListElement = new Zend_Form_Element_Radio('isFavorite',
                        $favoriteOptions);
$isFavoriteListElement->setLabel("Add to Favorite List:");
$isFavoriteListElement->setRequired(true);

//Create Rating raio button
$ratingOptions = array("multiOptions" => array
 (
    "1" => "1",
    "2" => "2",
    "3" => "3",
    "4" => "4",
    "5" => "5"
));

$ratingElement = new Zend_Form_Element_Radio('rating', $ratingOptions);
$ratingElement->setLabel("Rating:");
$ratingElement->setRequired(true)->addValidator(new Zend_Validate_Alnum(false));

//Create submit button
$submitButton = new Zend_Form_Element_Submit("submit");
$submitButton->setLabel("Add Artist");

//Add Elements to form
$form->addElement($artistNameElement);
$form->addElement($genreElement);
$form->addElement($isFavoriteListElement);
$form->addElement($ratingElement);
$form->addElement($submitButton);
```

```
    return $form;

}

/**
 * Add an artist to the database.
 *
 */
public function newAction()
{

    //Check if the user is logged in.
    //Set the view variables
    $this->view->form = $this->getAddArtistForm();

}
```

Listing 4-38 contains two methods: getAddArtistForm() and newAction(). The getAddArtistForm() method creates the form that is used by the user to add a new artist into the system. You start by creating an instance of Zend_Form and setting the action to saveartist, the method to post, and the form name to addartist. You then create, but not add, individual Zend_Form_Element objects. The initial element you create is a text field by instantiating Zend_Form_Element_Text, setting the name attribute to artistName, and the label. Next you create a select menu by creating an array called $genres. The $genres array contains the key multiOptions and an additional array as its value. The secondary array contains both the value that is stored as the array key and the value a user will see as the value of the key. Using the $genres variable, pass it into the Zend_Form_Element_Select constructor along with an element's name as its initial parameter, set the label, and finally set the select menu as required.

Next, create radio buttons. As you did with the select menu, you start by creating an array containing the value a user will save as the key and the value the user will see next to the radio button. You then create the radio button using the class Zend_Form_Element_Radio, passing in isFavorite as the name of the element and $favoriteOptions as the second parameter, set the label, and set the field to be required. Setting up the rating radio buttons is much the same, so you can skip this portion and head to the end, where you add each element created using the Zend_Form method addElement() and finally return the form.

The second method, newAction(), simply creates an instance of the add artist form and saves it as a view variable: $form. Now, load the URL http://localhost/artist/new to see the newly created form.

## File Uploading

File uploading elements for a form are also available. With the Zend_Form_Element_File class, you can transform a simple XHTML form into a file uploading tool that allows users to upload anything from MP3 files to images onto your server.

The Zend_Form_Element_File class contains additional setters and validators you can use to control such things as the destination of the file as well as the types of files a user is allowed to upload (see Table 4-10).

**Table 4-10.** *Zend_Form_Element_File Methods*

| Function | Description |
|---|---|
| setDestination() | Sets the path to the destination where the files will be saved. |
| setMultiFile() | Sets the total number of files to upload. |
| setMaxFileSize() | Sets the maximum file size. |
| isUploaded() | Determines whether the file has been uploaded. |
| isReceived() | Determines whether the file has been received by the server. |
| isFiltered() | Determines whether any filtering has been done to the file. |
| addValidator() | Adds constraints to the file upload. Acceptable values: count, size, extension. |

Using the methods in Table 4-10, let's update the account update form to allow users the ability to add an avatar to their profile page. First you need a place to store the images. Create a folder called users in your public directory. This folder will be the final destination for any user-uploaded avatar. The folder will contain only one profile image per user, and each image will be renamed to the user's unique ID as soon as the file has been uploaded.

**Listing 4-39.** *Updated getUpdateForm()*

```
/**
 * Update Form
 */
private function getUpdateForm()
{

    //Create Form
    $form = new Zend_Form();
    $form->setAction('update');
    $form->setMethod('post');
    $form->setAttrib('sitename', 'loudbite');
    $form->setAttrib('enctype', 'multipart/form-data');

    //Load Elements class
    require "Form/Elements.php";
    $LoudbiteElements = new Elements();
```

```
//Create Username Field.
$form->addElement($LoudbiteElements->getUsernameTextField());

//Create Email Field.
$form->addElement($LoudbiteElements->getEmailTextField());

//Create Password Field.
$form->addElement($LoudbiteElements->getPasswordTextField());

//Create Text Area for About me.
$textAreaElement = new Zend_Form_Element_TextArea('aboutme');
$textAreaElement->setLabel('About Me:');
$textAreaElement->setAttribs(array('cols' => 15,
                    'rows' => 5));
$form->addElement($textAreaElement);

//Add File Upload
$fileUploadElement = new Zend_Form_Element_File('avatar');
$fileUploadElement->setLabel('Your Avatar:');
$fileUploadElement->setDestination('../public/users');
$fileUploadElement->addValidator('Count', false, 1);
$fileUploadElement->addValidator('Extension', false, 'jpg,gif');
$form->addElement($fileUploadElement);

//Create a submit button.
$form->addElement('submit', 'submit');
$submitElement = $form->getElement('submit');
$submitElement->setLabel('Update My Account');

return $form;


}
```

The bold code shown in Listing 4-39 contains the updated getUpdateForm() method, which contains the code to add an additional element to the form and sets the form enctype attribute. You use the Zend_Form_Element_File class to create a file upload input field. You set the label, the destination, a validator indicating the maximum number of files to upload, and a validator to restrict the user in uploading any file not of type jpg or gif. Finally, add the element to the form. With the form created, you need to update the updateAction() method. As it is now, the updateAction() method will not save the file. Listing 4-40 contains the updated code.

***Listing 4-40.*** *Updating Form with File Upload*

```
/**
 * Update the User's data.
 *
 */
public function updateAction()
{

    //Check if the user is logged in
    //Fetch the user's id
    //Fetch the users information

    //Create the form.
    $form = $this->getUpdateForm();

    //Check if the form has been submitted.
    //If so validate and process.
    if($_POST){

        //Check if the form is valid.
        if($form->isValid($_POST)){

            //Get the values
            $username = $form->getValue('username');
            $password = $form->getValue('password');
            $email    = $form->getValue('email');
            $aboutMe  = $form->getValue('aboutme');

            //Save the file
            $form->avatar->receive();

            //Save.

        }
        //Otherwise redisplay the form.
        else{

            $this->view->form  = $form;
```

```
    }


}
//Otherwise display the form.
else{

    $this->view->form = $form;


    }


}
```

Listing 4-40 contains a single update to the method. The bold line moves the uploaded file from the PHP tmp directory to the destination folder specified in the setDestination() method. Now load the URL http://localhost/account/update and upload an avatar. As a test, open the destination folder public/user to verify that the file you uploaded is present.

Uploading multiple files is done much the same way. If you require the user to upload multiple files, use the Zend_Form_Element_File::setMultiFile() method, passing in the correct number of files a user can upload.

## Implementing CAPTCHA

CAPTCHA, which stands for Completely Automated Public Turing Test to Tell Computers and Humans Apart, is an easy way to determine whether the user submitting a form is a human, a web crawler, or a spambot.

CAPTCHAs come in many forms. Some use images and ask a simple question the user must answer to successfully submit the form, and some ask you to click the speaker icon to listen to something. These often-annoying features serve a purpose; they reduce the amount of spam, junk messages, and phony accounts created on a site.

The Zend_Form component contains an easy-to-use class that allows you to implement a CAPTCHA on the site using Zend_Form_Element_Captcha. This class contains four types of available CAPTCHAs:

- Images-based

- Dumb (user types word displayed backward)

- Figlet

- ReCaptcha

Zend_Form_Element_Captcha also contains an additional set of setters to use (see Table 4-11).

*Table 4-11. Zend_Form_Element_Captcha Setters*

| Function | Description |
|---|---|
| setExpiration() | Determines how long a CAPTCHA image should reside in the server (accepts time in seconds). |
| setGcFreq() | Determines how often garbage collection is run (the default is 1/*<value you set>*). |
| setFont() | Sets the font to use. |
| setFontSize() | Sets the font size to use. |
| setHeight() | Sets the image height used for CAPTCHA. |
| setWidth() | Sets the width of the image used for CAPTCHA. |
| setImgDir() | Sets the image directory that holds the images to use for CAPTCHA. |
| setImgUrl() | Sets the image path to use for the CAPTCHA. |
| setSuffix() | Sets the file name suffix for the images (the default is .png). |

Let's add a CAPTCHA to the sign-up process to demonstrate its use (see Listing 4-41).

*Listing 4-41. Using a CAPTCHA*

```
/**
 * Create the sign up form.
 */
private function getSignupForm()
{

  //Create Form
  $form = new Zend_Form();
  $form->setAction('success');
  $form->setMethod('post');
  $form->setAttrib('sitename', 'loudbite');

  //Add Elements
  require "Form/Elements.php";
  $LoudbiteElements = new Elements();
```

```
//Create Username Field.
$form->addElement($LoudbiteElements->getUsernameTextField());

//Create Email Field.
$form->addElement($LoudbiteElements->getEmailTextField());

//Create Password Field.
$form->addElement($LoudbiteElements->getPasswordTextField());

//Add Captcha
$captchaElement = new Zend_Form_Element_Captcha
(
'signup',
array('captcha' => array(
    'captcha' => 'Figlet',
    'wordLen' => 6,
    'timeout' => 600))
);
$captchaElement->setLabel('Please type in the
  words below to continue');

$form->addElement($captchaElement);
$form->addElement('submit', 'submit');
$submitButton = $form->getElement('submit');
$submitButton->setLabel('Create My Account!');

return $form;

}
```

Before loading the URL, let's go through Listing 4-41. The code shown replaced the creation of the username, password, and email fields with your application-specific Elements class, and created the new CAPTCHA form element. To create the CAPTCHA element, you instantiated a Zend_Form_Element_Captcha, assigned its name attribute to sign up, and configured the CAPTCHA using the constructor's second parameter. The second parameter was passed an array in which you set the type of CAPTCHA to use (Figlet), set the length of the word to 6, and set the length of time to the word presented to the user is valid for. You set the label, add the CAPTCHA to the form, add a submit button, and finally return the newly updated form. Now, load the updated sign-up form by visiting the URL http://localhost/account/new. You should see the figure displayed in Figure 4-12.

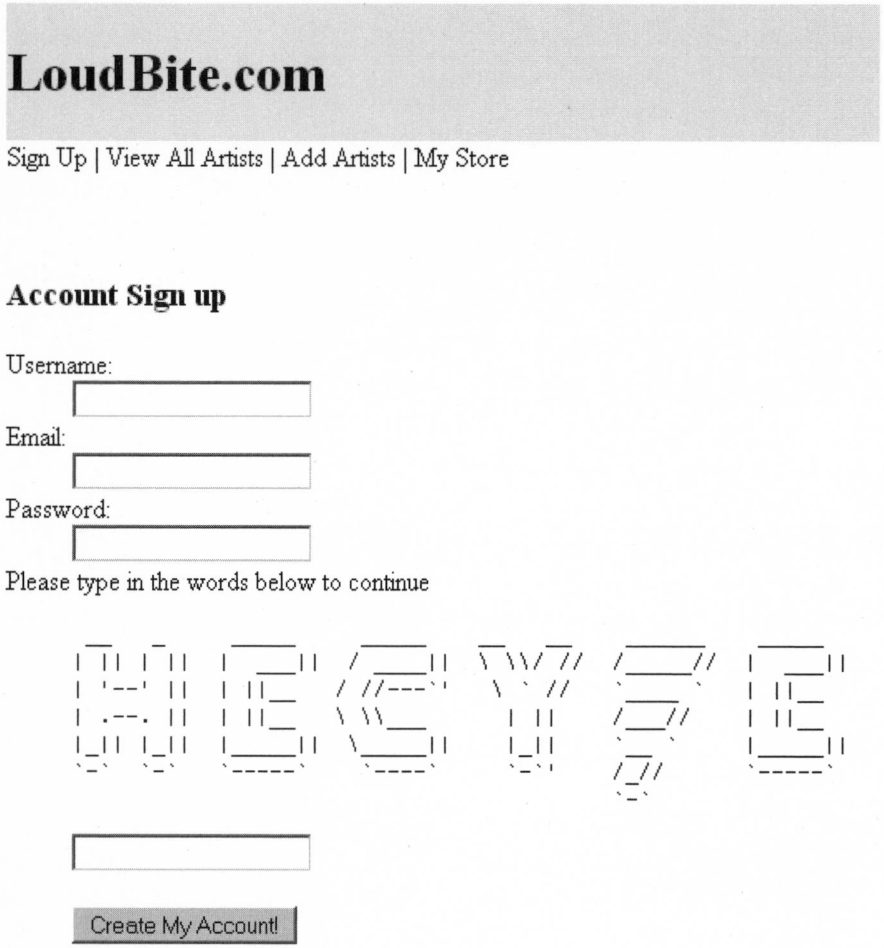

# LoudBite.com

Sign Up | View All Artists | Add Artists | My Store

## Account Sign up

Username:

Email:

Password:

Please type in the words below to continue

Create My Account!

*Figure 4-12.* CAPTCHA display on sign-up form

# Summary

This chapter was an in-depth look at what the view in the MVC pattern accomplishes in terms of providing loosely coupled designs and showed how Zend Framework uses Zend_View. The chapter also went over how to initialize variables for later use in the view, embed PHP, and manipulate the default directory structure of Zend Framework.

Forms were also a topic in this chapter. You learned how to create a form using the Zend_Form component, how to use and add Zend_Form_Element objects to the form, process any submitted data, and validate and filter the data using Zend_Validate and Zend_Filter. You also learned how to upload files using Zend_Form_Element_File and create and implement a CAPTCHA using Zend_Form_Element_Captcha.

■■■

# CHAPTER 5

# Database Communication, Manipulation, and Display

One sure way to enhance the application is by saving user-generated content in some way, which will completely change the way users interact with the application. From saving favorite artists to personalizing profile pages, a database enhances an application in more ways than you can imagine.

This chapter covers database functionality from the initial point of the setup to effectively displaying the result set. The chapter will answer questions such as the following:

- What is the Zend_Db component?

- What is needed to use the Zend_Db component?

- What is PDO, anyway?
  This chapter also covers the following topics:

- How to create a connection to the database for the first time

- How to retrieve and manipulate data within the database

- How to use Zend_Db_Exception to handle any errors you might encounter

- How the Zend_Db component handles security issues and what those issues are

- How to make database queries transactional and why it's beneficial to use transactions

- How to display the data using Zend_Paginator and its pagination features

Finally, you'll move into the more advanced features of the application by learning how to construct basic-to-advanced SQL statements using the object-oriented approach of the Zend_Db_Select object. You'll be amazed how easy it is to create an application that runs complex SQL statements without writing a single line of SQL.

## Getting Started

Before diving into the code, review the tables you'll work with throughout this chapter. The better part of this chapter deals with the three tables from Chapter 2. If you aren't familiar with them, don't worry; you'll take another quick look at the entity relationship diagram (ERD). If you don't need a refresher, skip ahead to the "Installing PDO" section later in this chapter. If you haven't read Chapter 2 and want to use the code directly, refer to the Data Definition Language (DDL)_the SQL statements defining the data structures_in that chapter to construct the database on your system.

The application contains three tables, as shown in Figure 5-1. The accounts table contains all the accounts in the system. User details are stored here: e-mail, password, username, and so on.

The accounts_artists join table allows users to identify themselves as fans of one or more artists stored in the artists table. Using the ID of the user stored in the accounts table along with the ID of the artist stored in the artists table, you can associate an account with an artist and store the date when the user became a fan of the artist.

The artists table contains a list of artists in the system. Users enter each of the artists in this table, which cannot have any duplicates, and an artist can belong to only one genre. The table contains the artist name, genre, date the record was created, and unique ID of the record.

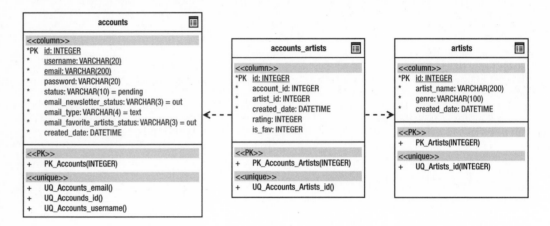

**Figure 5-1.** *LoudBite database ERD*

You now have an overall understanding of the database that powers the next couple of examples. Let's head over to the next section and get to work.

## Installing PDO

Out of the box, Zend Framework's database support works, but it requires an additional piece to function properly when using it with PHP's PDO.

What's PDO, how do you get it, and how can you install it? PDO, which stands for PHP Data Object, is an extension that requires and is included with all PHP 5 installations. PDO allows a PHP developer using different relational database management systems (RDBMSs) to access data in a universal way. If the system used MySQL without the PDO extension, you would execute a query by calling the PHP function mysql_query(). On the other hand, if you used an Oracle database you would need to call the equivalent query execution function oracle_execute(). Using PDO, the call you make to query a table in MySQL is the same for Oracle and Postgres. But don't get it confused with a data abstraction layer; it does not write SQL in any way. You'll leave that piece of the puzzle up to Zend Framework, as you'll see later in the chapter.

There are two ways to install the PDO extension. You can use PECL or you can pull up your sleeves and get dirty editing the php.ini file, which you'll do. Because you want to become an expert at this, take the php.ini path. For starters, you need to make sure that the .dll or.so files that you need were installed during the initial installation process. Open the directory PHP_HOME/ext and see if the following files are present:

- php_pdo.dll for Windows and pdo.so for Unix-based systems

- php_pdo_mysql.dll (if you're not using MySQL, check for your appropriate .dll file)

If you do not see the files, don't panic. Open the PHP installation zip file, or download it again from the PHP site, and extract the files from the ext drectory to PHP_HOME/ext on the computer. After all the files are extracted to the location, you're one step closer to installing PDO.

Open the php.ini file and search for the following lines:

- extension=php_pdo.dll for Windows and pdo.so for Unix

- extension=php_pdo_mysql.dll

Uncomment the lines (if you are not using MySQL, uncomment the proper extension) by removing the ; from the front of the line. Save your changes and restart Apache. Congratulations, you now have PDO!

# Connecting to a Database

You should now have both PDO and Zend Framework installed. Let's open a direct connection to the database to get things started. Create or open the AccountController.php file located in application/controllers and create a new action: testConnAction. The new action will demonstrate how to connect to the database for the first time and will use ViewRenderer setNoRender() to halt the use of a view. Copy the code shown in Listing 5-1 and load the URL http://localhost/account/test-conn.

**Listing 5-1.** *AccountController.php:testConnAction*

```
/**
 * Test our connection
 */
public function testConnAction()
{

  try{

    $connParams = array("host"     => "localhost",
             "port"     => "<Your Port Number>",
             "username" => "<Your username>",
             "password" => "<Your password>",
             "dbname"   => "loudbite");

    $db = new Zend_Db_Adapter_Pdo_Mysql($connParams);

  }catch(Zend_Db_Exception $e){
    echo $e->getMessage();
  }
```

```
echo "Database object created.";

//Turn off View Rendering.
$this->_helper->viewRenderer->setNoRender();
}
```

The code to create an instance of a database connection uses one of many Zend_Db_Adapter classes shown as follows:

- Zend_Db_Adapter_Pdo_Mysql

- Zend_Db_Adapter_Pdo_Ibm

- Zend_Db_Adapter_Pdo_Mssql

- Zend_Db_Adapter_Pdo_Oci

- Zend_Db_Adapter_Pdo_Pgsql

- Zend_Db_Adapter_Pdo_Sqlite

Depending on the RDBMS you are using, you can instantiate the proper adapter. In this case, use the Zend_Db_Adapter_Pdo_Mysql class because you are using the MySQL RDBMS.

The Zend_Db_Adapter_Pdo_Mysql class indirectly extends the Zend_Db_Adapter_Abstract class and pulls in much of its functionality to execute queries on a database. The class accepts one parameter within its constructor: a key-value pair array or a Zend_Config object. You're using the array that contains key-value pairs. The keys in the array are any of the parameters found in Table 5-1, and the value portion contains the desired value for the parameter.

***Table 5-1.*** *Connection Parameters*

| Parameter | Description |
| --- | --- |
| dbname | Name of the database to use. |
| username | Username with access to the database. |
| password | Password for the username that contains access to the database. |
| host | IP address of the host to access; localhost can also be used. The default is localhost. |
| port | Port number the database is running on. |
| persistent | Determines whether the connection should be persistent. True or False values accepted (the default is False). |

| | |
|---|---|
| protocol | Network protocol (the default is TCPIP). |
| caseFolding | Type of style used for identifiers. |

In this example, you use five parameters: host, port, username, password, and dbname. The host parameter accepts only IP addresses, but makes an exception when using the keyword localhost, which will resolve to the IP address 127.0.0.1. You also set the port number to 3306 because MySQL runs on port 3306 by default. You might want to check which port number the installation is running on. The username parameter was also set to the username you used to access the database, the password parameter to the password you used to access the database, and the database name to loudbite.

Store the connection information into the $connParams variable and instantiate a Zend_Db_Adaptor_Pdo_Mysql object by passing in the $connParams variable into the constructor. Store the object into the $db variable and you're done. Now any time within the connection scope you can refer to the $db object and can quickly utilize the database.

The example created an instance of the database, not a connection; it is not until you query the database that the connection is created, as Figure 5-2 demonstrates. When you instantiate a Zend_Db object, it's like arriving at the door to the database's house and waiting for a cue to open the door. In this case, the cue is a database query. It is then that any errors connecting to the database appear.

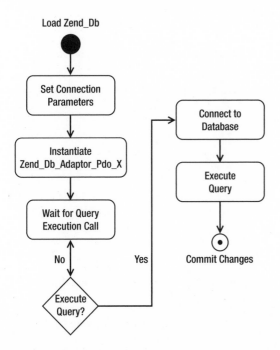

*Figure 5-2. Database initialization and connection process*

At this point, create a reusable database connection file, a model that will allow you to set the database information in a single location and instantiate a Zend_Db_Adapter_Pdo_Mysql object throughout the application.

Create or add the application/models/Db directory and create a new file called Db_Db.php. The file contains a single conn() method that will return a Zend_Db_Adapter object, as shown in Listing 5-2.

***Listing 5-2.*** *Db_Db. php*

```php
<?php
/**
 * Database handler.
 *
 */
class Db_Db
{

  public static function conn(){

    $connParams = array("host"     => "localhost",
                "port"     => "<Your Port Number>",
                "username" => "<Your username>",
                "password" => "<Your password>",
                "dbname"   => "loudbite");

    $db = new Zend_Db_Adapter_Pdo_Mysql($connParams);
    return $db;

  }
}
```

With the reusable database model and an introduction on how to connect to a database, you've arrived at the door to the database's house. Knock on the door by creating queries to insert data into the database.

# Inserting Data

What's the use of a database if you can't save data into it? As a developer, you want to save data that will continue to exist even if the user decides to use it at a future date or leaves the site.

The Zend_Db component opens up functionality that allows you to insert data into a table as easily as creating a simple array, but also allows you to create SQL statements to have complete control over what is executed. You'll look at each one of these approaches.

In the first approach, you create the complete SQL statement; in the second approach, you supply all the necessary information to save, along with the table name you want to save the data into.

# Using Plain Old SQL (POSQL)

The initial way of saving content into the database is the tried-and-true method of creating the full INSERT statement and then using the data-access layer supplied by PDO to execute the statement. To execute the INSERT statements, you use the query() method.

The query() method accepts two parameters:

- The initial parameter is a string value containing the full SQL statement you want to execute. The SQL statement can contain a placeholder values represented as a question mark (?). The ? will be replaced with the escaped values or data-binding values contained in the second parameter of the query() function.

- The second optional parameter is a mixed type. It can be either a string value or an array containing elements you want to replace the ? with in the SQL statement. Before replacing the placeholders with the values, Zend_Db escapes the values with quotes.

Let's create a test action to insert a couple of rows into the accounts table using a complete INSERT statement along with the query functionality. Open the AccountController.php file and add a new action: testInsertAction().

Listing 5-3 creates a Zend_Db_Adapter_Pdo_Mysql object by creating a database object using the model Db_Db.php you created in the beginning of this chapter. You create three INSERT SQL statements, each of which inserts a new account into the accounts table. Each INSERT statement contains the username, e-mail, password, status, and created date information.

***Listing 5-3.*** *Using Full SQL INSERT Statements: testInsertAction()*

```
/**
* Test Insert
*/
public function testInsertAction()
{

  try {

    //Create a DB object
    require_once "Db/Db_Db.php";
    $db = Db_Db::conn();

    //DDL for initial 3 users
    $statement  = "INSERT INTO accounts(
            username, email, password,status, created_date
          )
        VALUES(
          'test_1', 'test@loudbite.com', 'password',
          'active', NOW()
```

```
                )";

    $statement2 = "INSERT INTO accounts(
            username,email,password,status,created_date
            )
            VALUES(
            'test_2', 'test2@loudbite.com', 'password',
            'active', NOW()
            )";

    $statement3 = "INSERT INTO accounts(
            username,email,password,status,created_date
            )
            VALUES (
            ?, ?, ?, ?, NOW()
            )";

    //Insert the above statements into the accounts.
    $db->query($statement);
    $db->query($statement2);

    //Insert the statement using ? flags.
    $db->query($statement3, array('test_3', 'test3@loudbite.com',
    'password', 'active'));

    //Close Connection
    $db->closeConnection();

    echo "Completed Inserting";

}catch(Zend_Db_Exception $e){
  echo $e->getMessage();
}

//Supress the View.
$this->_helper->viewRenderer->setNoRender();


}
```

Each statement is constructed the same way except for the third statement, which excludes the values in the statement. Instead you can use the placeholder flag ?. Zend_Db will replace these markers with the proper data-binding value supplied in the second parameter when you query the database.

Using the query() method to run the statements, pass in the variables containing $statement[1–3]. The final query call uses the optional second parameter. It contains an array with each element representing the value for each of the placeholder markers. When the query creates the statement, it places each of the elements into the proper position in the statement. The first element will replace the first marker, the second element in the array will replace the second marker in the statement, and so on. The final statement when executed will look like this:

INSERT INTO Accounts (username, email, password, status, created_date) VALUES

('test_3', 'test3@loudbite.com', 'password', 'active', NOW())

Finally, close the connection by calling the closeConnection() method on the Zend_Db_Adapter_Pdo_Mysql object.

Open the browser and run the new action by visiting the URL http://localhost/account/test-insert. If all went well, you should see no errors and should see only the Completed Inserting string. Check the database table and make sure that you see the three new accounts.

## Inserting Data Without SQL

You now have three records in the database, but you might be wondering how this is any different from not using Zend Framework. It's not; I just wanted to show you that Zend Framework allows developers who are savvy enough to create optimal SQL statements to continue using and executing them.

An easier way to insert data into the database tables is one that does not require a single line of SQL. No, this isn't a joke. Using the insert() method provided by the Zend_Db_Adapter_Abstract object allows you to bypass the traditional creation of SQL in the PHP code and just worry about the creation of a key-value array.

The insert() function accepts two parameters:

• The initial parameter is a string and is the name of the table you want to insert the data into.

• The second parameter is an array. It must contain key-value pairs, in which the key is the column name in the table, and the value is the data you want stored into the column.

Let's update the code created in Listing 5-3 to use the insert() method. Open the AccountController.php file and create a new action, testInsertMethodAction(), as shown in Listing 5-4.

**Listing 5-4.** *Using the insert() Method: testInsertMethodAction()*

```
/**
* Test Insert Method
* Insert data into table using insert()
*/
public function testInsertMethodAction()
{

  try{

    //Create a DB object
    require_once "Db/Db_Db.php";
```

```php
        $db = Db_Db::conn();

     //Data to save.
     $userData1 = array("username"   => 'test_4',
                "email"      => 'test4@loudbite.com',
                "password"   => 'password',
                "status"     => 'active',
                "created_date" => '0000-00-00 00:00:00');

     $userData2 = array("username"   => 'test_5',
                "email"      => 'test5@loudbite.com',
                "password"   => 'password',
                "status"     => 'active',
                "created_date"=> '0000-00-00 00:00:00');

     $userData3 = array("username"   => 'test_6',
                "email"      => 'test6@loudbite.com',
                "password"   => 'password',
                "status"     => 'active',
                "created_date"=> '0000-00-00 00:00:00');

     //Insert into the Accounts.
     $db->insert('accounts', $userData1);
     $db->insert('accounts', $userData2);
     $db->insert('accounts', $userData3);

     //Close Connection
     $db->closeConnection();

     echo "Completed Inserting";

    }catch(Zend_Db_Exception $e){
     echo $e->getMessage();
    }

   //Supress the View
   $this->_helper->viewRenderer->setNoRender();


 }
```

Referencing Listing 5-4, create an instance of the Zend_Db_Adapter_Pdo_Mysql class by instantiating the database model created earlier. Unlike Listing 5-3, you don't write any INSERT statements. Instead, you create three key-value arrays, each containing keys representing the columns in the accounts database table and the values representing the data you want to save in each column. You store the data into the $userData1, $userData2, and $userData3 variables.

After the data to save is initialized, use insert(), passing in the table name accounts as its first parameter and the array containing the data as its second parameter. Finally, close the connection; if everything went well, you should see the text Completed Inserting when visiting the URL http://localhost/account/test-insert-method.

Without the SQL statements, the code is much cleaner and lets you focus on the business logic and not worry whether the statement is optimal.

There is one thing to notice in the arrays created in Listing 5-4. Notice the way in which you saved the dates using the literal string 0000-00-00. If you tried to use the NOW() database expression, PHP would think it was calling a PHP function somewhere in the controller code. You need a way to tell PHP that the database expression is a database function, not a PHP function.

# Database Expressions

Database expressions are used extensively and even required when you begin creating complex SQL statements. Typical expressions include NOW(), COUNT(), LOWER(), and SUB(), just to name a few. You can review the RDBMS's documentation for a complete list of expressions you can use.

When it comes to Zend_Db, these expressions pose a problem. If you use a Zend_Db_Adaptor and try to pass in the literal string NOW() as an example, the PHP script will fail before it reaches the insert() method with the error message Call to undefined function NOW(). At this point, NOW() in the code is seen as just another PHP function, not a database expression. You need a way to tell PHP to ignore the database expression call and allow the database to handle the function. The Zend_Db_Expr class lets you do just that.

Listing 5-5 demonstrates the functionality of the Zend_Db_Expr class. Apart from that, the code inserts only one user. You use the insert() method and pass in two parameters: the name of the table, accounts, and a key-value pair array. The important difference is how you treat the NOW() database expression. You create a new instance of the Zend_Db_Expr class and using its constructor you pass in the expression as a string: "NOW()".

**Listing 5-5.** *Zend_Db_Expr Usage: testExpressionAction*

```
/**
 * Test Expression
 * Using Database Expressions.
 */
public function testExpressionAction()
{

  try{

    //Create a DB object
    require_once "Db/Db_Db.php";
    $db = Db_Db::conn();
```

```
//Data to save.
$userData = array("username"    => 'test_7',
                  "email"       => 'test7@loudbite.com',
                  "password"    => 'password',
                  "status"      => 'active',
                  "created_date"=> new Zend_Db_Expr("NOW()"));

//Insert into the accounts.
$db->insert('accounts', $userData);

//Close Connection
$db->closeConnection();

echo "Completed Inserting";

}catch(Zend_Db_Exception $e){
  echo $e->getMessage();
}

//Supress the View
$this->_helper->viewRenderer->setNoRender();

}
```

Pull up the browser and enter the URL http://localhost/account/test-expression to run the action. When the action finishes, open the database and take a look at the records currently saved in the accounts table. You should see a new user with an accurate date in the created_date column for the account.

Zend_Db_Expr contains only two methods: its constructor and the __toString() method. The constructor accepts a single parameter as a string. The string is a database expression such as NOW(), SUM(), or COUNT(), and can be used during the calls to insert() and update(). (You'll learn more in the "Updating Records" section.)

## Escaping Values

With the ability to save data into the database, it's only logical to become paranoid about what the user is saving into the tables. Can you trust users to save data into the database with your best interest at heart? You must be cautious that the user does not try to use any number of SQL injection techniques when storing data in the tables.

### Brief Background: SQL Injection

*SQL injection*, a vulnerability that affects many RDBMSs, permits the user to inject a SQL statement into a predefined SQL statement that will execute in the database. Let's take a quick look at a small test case.

Suppose that the user decided to sign up for the application and entered the following into the username field without any filtering or cleanup:

user'DELETE * FROM Accounts

The single quote after user would halt the predefined INSERT statement and execute the DELETE statement injected into the code by the user. This will cause the accounts table to remove all the records currently stored in it. This vulnerability can be extremely dangerous to the application, so Zend Framework provides a method to guard you from this exploit.

## Escaping User Data

To counter the attack, Zend Framework has supplied you with two methods to escape single quotes. Using quote() and quoteInto(), you can add slashes into the user-supplied data. Any data the user decides to pass into the database containing a single quote will be escaped by placing a backslash in front of the single quote.

The quote() method accepts two parameters. The initial value can be a string, an array with each element containing the value you want to escape, a Zend_Db_Expr object, or a Zend_Db_Select object (covered in the "Object Oriented Select Statements" section later in the chapter).

By default, the method returns a single quoted value. If you passed the "this is a test" parameter, the returned string would be "'this is a test'". The value is returned in this fashion because of the way some RDBMSs require data to be passed into the INSERT or UPDATE statement. Each of the data values is required to be surrounded by single quotes. This is seen in the INSERT statements created in Listing 5-3.

There are times when the database table does not allow values to save as strings_for example, when saving INTEGER values. In such cases you use the second parameter to specify the SQL data type to use. By default, the second parameter is set to null, but you can overwrite it by using the following values:

- INTEGER

- FLOAT

- BIGINT

Using the example shown in Listing 5-3 you'll display the full cycle of a string containing a ' by seeing it before it's filtered and after the string is passed through quote(). Open the AccountController.php file and create a new action, testQuoteAction(), as shown in Listing 5-6.

**Listing 5-6.** *Quoting Strings: testQuoteAction()*

```
/**
 * Test Quote
 */
public function testQuoteAction()
{

  try {

    //Create Db object
    require_once "Db/Db_Db.php";
    $db = Db_Db::conn();
```

167

```
$username = "testing ' user";
$usernameAfterQuote = $db->quote($username);

echo "BEFORE QUOTE: $username<br>";
echo "AFTER QUOTE: $usernameAfterQuote<br>";

//DDL for initial 3 users
echo $statement  = "INSERT INTO accounts(
    username, email, password, status, created_date
    )
    VALUES(
    $usernameAfterQuote, 'test8@loudbite.com', 'password',
    'active', NOW()
    )";

//Insert the above statements into the accounts.
$db->query($statement);

//Close Connection
$db->closeConnection();

echo "Successfully inserted.";

}catch(Zend_Db_Exception $e){
  echo $e->getMessage();
}

//Supress the View.
$this->_helper->viewRenderer->setNoRender();
}
```

You instantiate the $db object and call the quote() method on the $username data. After these calls, you echo each of the returned values to see the resulting string. Pull up the action in the browser so you can see how quote() treats the values using the URL http://localhost/account/test-quote.

Before the string is passed through quote(), the username is set as testing ' user. The username at this point is not saved, but you need to pass it through quote(). After you use quote(), the username is returned as 'testing \' user'. The username containing the backslash is now ready and safe to save into the database.

---

■ **Note** You can also use the filtering techniques covered in Chapter 4 to filter out any unwanted characters or data when saving the data to the database.

---

## Escaping by Using quoteInto()

The second method that allows you to quote values is quoteInto(). The method is primarily used when using the ? placeholder.

The quoteInto() method accepts four parameters and returns a SQL safe string:

- The initial parameter contains the string with any number of placeholder question marks. It can be a complete SQL statement or a partial statement such as username=?.

- The second parameter is the data-binding value you want to replace the ? with. If there is more than a single placeholder value to replace, use an array with each element representing the data-binding value.

- The optional third parameter is a SQL data type.

- The optional fourth parameter is the number of placeholders that need to be replaced.

Additional quote methods are shown in Table 5-2, including methods to escape unique table names that use SQL operators such as Limit and Order to identify tables and columns.

*Table 5-2.* DB Quote Method

| Method | Description |
| --- | --- |
| quoteIdentifier | Allows the use of SQL restricted words such as order or limit as SQL identifiers.<br>quoteIdentifier(string\|array\|Zend_Db_Expr, Boolean)<br>Example:<br>$name = $db->quoteIdentifier("limit");<br>//SELECT * FROM "limit";<br>$query = "SELECT * FROM ".$name.";"<br>Case-sensitive |
| quoteColumnAs | Allows the use of SQL restricted words as column SQL identifiers.<br>quoteColumnAs(string\|array\|Zend_Db_Expr, string column alias, Boolean Use AUTO_QUOTE_IDENTIFIERS?)<br>Example:<br>$column = $db->quoteColumnAs("order", "a", true);<br>//SELECT `order` AS `a` FROM Acounts<br>$query = "SELECT ".$column." FROM Acounts";<br>Case-sensitive |

*(Continued)*

| | |
|---|---|
| quoteTableAs | Allows the use of SQL restricted words as table name SQL identifiers.<br>quoteIdentifier(string\|array\|Zend_Db_Expr, string table alias, Boolean Use<br>AUTO_QUOTE_IDENTIFIERS?)<br>Example:<br>$table = $db->quoteTableAs("order", "a", true);<br>//SELECT order_name FROM "order" AS "a"<br>$query = "SELECT order_name FROM ".$table.";";<br>Case-sensitive |

## Last Inserted ID

Database tables use primary keys, which often contain an autoincremental value, typically a numerical value to uniquely identify a record in the table. Using the primary key you can associate other information to the record, so it's important that you have an easy way of retrieving the primary key.

Zend Framework provides you with two methods that provide such effortless functionality: the lastInsertId() and lastSequenceId() methods that will retrieve the last-generated ID for a table (depending on the RDBMS). To use the methods, the primary key for the database table must be set to autoincrement and must be an int type.

The lastInsertId() method accepts two parameters:

- The initial parameter is a string representing the name of the table.

- The second parameter is a string and is the name of the column that contains the primary key.

The method lastInsertId is used only if the RDBMS follows the standard sequence-naming format. An example of the sequence-naming format is this: if you supply lastInsertId() with the parameters, artists, and id, you'll have a sequence called artists_id_seq within the RDBMS.

If you have an RDBMS that supports sequences, yet does not conform to the format supported by default, you can use lastSequenceId().This method allows the use of a specific sequence name to be specified by passing in a single string parameter to the method.

Unfortunately, MySQL and MsSQL do not support sequences, so they ignore the parameters in both lastInsertId and lastSequenceId, and return the last inserted ID for the specific database query.

Let's add another account into the account table and use lastInsertId() to fetch the account's unique ID by creating a new action, the testLastInsertAction, in the AccountController.php file.

Using the code shown in Listing 5-5 and updating the user information, add the extra lines of code shown in bold to retrieve the ID of the account that was created.

In Listing 5-7, you insert the new user into the table and immediately call lastInsertId(). Calling the method returns 9, the autoincrement value for the new record. The call is available only immediately after an insert and cannot be used with other instances of a database connection.

***Listing 5-7.*** *Retrieving the ID for the New Record*

```
/**
 * Test Last Insert
 */
public function testLastInsertAction()
```

```
{

    try {

        //Create Db object
        require_once "Db/Db_Db.php";
        $db = Db_Db::conn();

        //Data to save.
        $userData = array("username"    => 'testinguser9',
                    "email"        => 'test9@loudbite.com',
                    "password"     => 'password',
                    "status"       => 'active',
                    "created_date" => new Zend_Db_Expr("NOW()"));

        $db->insert('accounts', $userData);

//Retrieve the id for the new record and echo
$id = $db->lastInsertId();
echo "Last Inserted Id: ".$id."<br>";

        //Close Connection
        $db->closeConnection();

        echo "Successfully Inserted Data";

    }catch(Zend_Db_Exception $e){
        echo $e->getMessage();
    }

    //Supress the View.
    $this->_helper->viewRenderer->setNoRender();

}
```

You're now ready to apply the techniques covered so far into the application, enhancing the sign-up form and creating the add artist page.

## LoudBite Sign-up Page

Open up the AccountController.php file and look at successAction(). The action takes the user-supplied data, cleans it up, and then does nothing. You need to fill in that void now. Right after the user's data is cleaned, you need to add in the functionality to save the data. Using the techniques you learned, let's create the insert functionality.

The updated successAction() is shown in Listing 5-8. The action is triggered after the user submits the form to add a new account and is the action that enters a new user into the system.

***Listing 5-8.*** *AccountController.php: SuccessAction*

```
/**
* Process Sign up Form.
*
*/
public function successAction()
{

  $form = $this->getSignupForm();

  //Check if the submitted data is POST type
  if($form->isValid($_POST)){

    $email    = $form->getValue("email");
    $username = $form->getValue("username");
    $password = $form->getValue("password");

    //Create Db object
    require_once "Db/Db_Db.php";
    $db = Db_Db::conn();



    //Create the record to save into the Db.
    $userData = array("username"   => $username,
              "email"      => $email,
              "password"   => $password,
              "status"     => 'pending',
              "created_date" => new Zend_Db_Expr("NOW()"));

    try{

      //Insert into the accounts.
      $db->insert('accounts', $userData);

      //Get the Id of the user
      $userId = $db->lastInsertId();
```

```
    //Send out thank you email. We'll get to this. Chapter 6.

  }catch(Zend_Db_Exception $e){

    $this->view->form   = $form;

  }

}else{

  $this->view->errors = $form->getMessages();
  $this->view->form = $form;

}

}
```

Reviewing the action, begin by ensuring that the form has no errors, and the form values meet the required formats. If there are no errors, initialize the $username, $email, and $password variables using the Zend_Form object's getValue(). You then create an instance of the Zend_Db_Adapter_Pdo_Mysql object using the database model. After you have the database object, initialize the data you will save into the database using the $userData variable. You will then pass in accounts and the $userData variable into the insert() method. I also recommend that you wrap the logic in try-catch just in case there are any issues with the insert. If there are no errors, return the unique user ID using lastInsertId() and eventually send out the verification e-mail (covered in Chapter 6).

Open the sign-up form in the browser http://localhost/account/new, fill out the form, and click Create My Account. If there are no database errors, you are now one of the first real users in the application.

## LoudBite Add Artist

Now open the ArtistController.php file. You'll update saveArtistAction() to actually save the user's artist. The new saveArtistAction() method should take the user's artist information, ensure that the entered data is valid, and save the data into the database for the specific user. For this example, because the login page has yet to be created, you need to create a static account ID and set it to the ID for the account you finished adding using the updated sign-up form. It should be 10. Using lastInsertId(), you'll link the artist to the account specified by the static value.

Let's start by updating the add artist form you created in Chapter 4. You're going to focus on the saveArtistAction() method. Update the method as shown in Listing 5-9.

**Listing 5-9.** *ArtistController.php: saveartistAction()*

```
/**
 * Save Artist to Db
 *
```

```
    */
public function saveArtistAction()
{

    //Create instance of artist form.
    $form = $this->getAddArtistForm();

    //Check if there were no errors
    if($form->isValid($_POST)){

        //Initialize the variables
        $artistName = $form->getValue('artistName');
        $genre      = $form->getValue('genre');
        $rating     = $form->getValue('rating');
        $isFav      = $form->getValue('isFavorite');

        //Set the temporary account id to use.
        $userId     = 10;

        try{

            //Create a db object
            require_once "Db/Db_Db.php";
            $db = Db_Db::conn();



            //Initialize data to save into DB
            $artistData = array("artist_name"  => $artistName,
                        "genre"        => $genre,
                        "created_date" =>
                        new Zend_Db_Expr("NOW()"));

            //Insert the artist into the Db
            $db->insert('artists', $artistData);

            //Fetch the artist id
            $artistId = $db->lastInsertId();

            //Initialize data for the account artists table
            $accountArtistData = array("account_id"  => $userId,
```

```
                    "artist_id"    => $artistId,
                    "rating"       => $rating,
                    "is_fav"       => $isFav,
                    "created_date" =>
                    new Zend_Db_Expr("NOW()"));

        //Insert the data.
        $db->insert('accounts_artists', $accountArtistData);

    }catch(Zend_Db_Exception $e){

        echo $e->getMessage();

    }

    }else{

    $this->view->errors = $form->getMessages();
    $this->view->form = $form;

    }

}
```

Listing 5-9 contains updates for the saveArtistAction() method, which is executed after the user fills out the artist information and submits the form. Reviewing the code, the action verifies whether the form values are valid; initializes and sets the variables $artistName, $genre, $rating, and $isFav; and initializes a Zend_Db Adapter_Pdo_Mysql object using the database model. You then create the array that contains the data to save into the artists table and insert the data into the table using the insert() method. If there are no errors, continue down the code by calling lastInsertId() and associate the artist to the user specified by the $userId using the returned ID. Finally, you create a new array, $accountArtistData, which holds the user's properties for the artist, the rating, the user's ID, the ID of the artist, and the flag if the user considers the artist to be a favorite.

Pull up the browser and load the http://localhost/artist/new page. Fill out the form, click Add Artist, and watch the thank you page come up.

You're done with inserting data. Now you'll focus your attention on fetching and displaying the data the users saved in the database.

# Fetching and Displaying Records

You're now open for business. Even if it's not much, users can become members of the application and add artists to the system. You can now focus on fetching the data stored in the tables.

Like the insert() method, the Zend_Db component contains fetch methods that make the task of fetching data easy. But unlike insert(), you are required to create your own SELECT statements to use in one of the six fetch methods you can use. Table 5-3 contains six fetch methods that allow you to retrieve data from a database table.

***Table 5-3.** Available Fetch Methods*

| Method | Description |
| --- | --- |
| fetchAll() | Returns all records for the supplied SELECT statement. Default returns an associated array. Fetch mode can be changed using the setFetchMode() method. fetchAll(string <select statement>\|Zend_Db_Select, mixed <Data bind values>, mixed <Fetch Modes Values> ) |
| fetchAssoc() | Returns all records for the supplied SELECT statement as an associated array. Ignores any mode that setFetchMode() is set to. fetchAssoc(string <select statement>\|Zend_Db_Select, mixed <Data bind values>) |
| fetchCol() | Returns the values for the initial column, regardless of the number of columns specified to retrieve within the SELECT statement. fetchCol(string <select statement>\|Zend_Db_Select, mixed <Data bind values>) |
| fetchRow() | Returns the values for the first row, regardless of the number of rows returned by the SELECT statement provided. fetchRow(string <select statement>\|Zend_Db_Select, mixed <Data bind values>, mixed <Fetch Modes Values> ) |
| fetchPairs() | Returns the initial two columns, regardless of the number of columns specified in the SELECT statement. fetchPairs(string <select statement>\|Zend_Db_Select, mixed <Data bind values>) |
| fetchOne() | Returns the first row and its initial column provided by the SELECT statement. fetchOne(string <select statement>\|Zend_Db_Select, mixed <Data bind values>) |

## Using fetchAll()

Now that there are a few records in the accounts table, you can use the data to work out a few examples in this section. The first example will use the fetchAll() method, which accepts three parameters:

- The initial parameter is a SQL SELECT statement passed in as a string type or a Zend_Db_Select object.

- The second parameter is an optional mixed type. It specifies the data binding values for the placeholders within the SQL statement.

- Although the third parameter is also optional, it can allow you to set a FETCH_MODE type. The fetch mode can also be set by using the setFetchMode() method.
  Table 5-4 outlines additional fetch mode settings.

**Table 5-4.** *Fetch Mode Options*

| Fetch Mode | Description |
|---|---|
| Zend_Db::FETCH_ASSOC | Returns data as an associated array. Keys are the names of the columns. |
| Zend_Db::FETCH_NUM | Returns the data as an array. Keys are numbered incrementally. |
| Zend_Db::FETCH_BOTH | Returns the data as an array. Each key is represented twice in the array: once as the name of the column and the other as a numerical value. |
| Zend_Db::FETCH_COLUMN | Returns data as an array. Keys are the index in the array; values are the content in the first column in the SELECT statement. |
| Zend_Db::FETCH_OBJ | Returns data as array of objects. Columns are properties in the stdClass object. |

Let's use the fetchAll() method in an example. Listing 5-10 implements the first fetch method covered. The code creates an instance of the database object by using the Db_Db model created earlier in this chapter. You then create the SELECT statement that will retrieve all the active accounts in the system and will be the statement that you supply to fetchAll(). You pass the statement as the initial parameter in the fetchAll() method and leave the other two parameters empty. When the fetchAll() method is invoked, it returns an array containing the records. You then set this data as the $members variable to display within the view.

Open the AccountController.php file and create the viewAllAction() action. The action will handle the fetching and displaying of accounts.

**Listing 5-10.** *AccountController.php: Fetching Data Using fetchAll()*

```
/**
 * View All Accounts.
 *
 */
public function viewAllAction()
{

  //Create Db Object
  require_once "Db/Db_Db.php";
  $db = Db_Db::conn();

  try{

    //Create the SQL statement to select the data.
    $statement = "SELECT id, username, created_date
```

```
            FROM accounts
            WHERE status = 'active'";

    //Fetch the data
    $results = $db->fetchAll($statement);

    //Set the view variable.
    $this->view->members = $results;

  }catch(Zend_Db_Exception $e){

    echo $e->getMessage();

  }
}
```

Let's now take a look at the view. In the view, you will loop through the result set and print each of the records using a foreach loop after validating that there are active accounts in the system. If there are no accounts, the following message displays: There are no active accounts.

Create the view-all.phtml file and save it under the /views/scripts/account/ directory with the code shown in Listing 5-11.

**Listing 5-11.** *Viewall Accounts View*

```php
<?php echo $this->doctype('XHTML1_STRICT'); ?>
<html xmlns="http://www.w3.org/1999/xhtml" xml:lang="en" lang="en">
<head>
  <?php echo $this->headTitle('LoudBite.com – View All Accounts'); ?>
</head>
<body>

<?php echo $this->render("includes/header.phtml"); ?>
<h2>Active User List</h2>

<table width="300" border="1">

<?php if($this->members){ ?>

  <tr align="center">
    <td><b>Member Name</b></td>
    <td><b>Date Joined</b></td>
  </tr>
```

```php
<?php
foreach($this->members as $member){
?>

  <tr>
    <td><a href='/<?php echo urlencode($member['username'])?>'>
      <?php echo $member['username']?>
      </a></td>
    <td><?php echo $member['created_date']?></td>
  </tr>
<?php
  }

}else{
?>
  <tr>
    <td>There are no active members in the system.</td>
  </tr>

<?php
}
?>

</table>
</body>
</html>
```

Save the code and open the URL http://localhost/account/viewall. You should now see a page that looks like Figure 5-3.

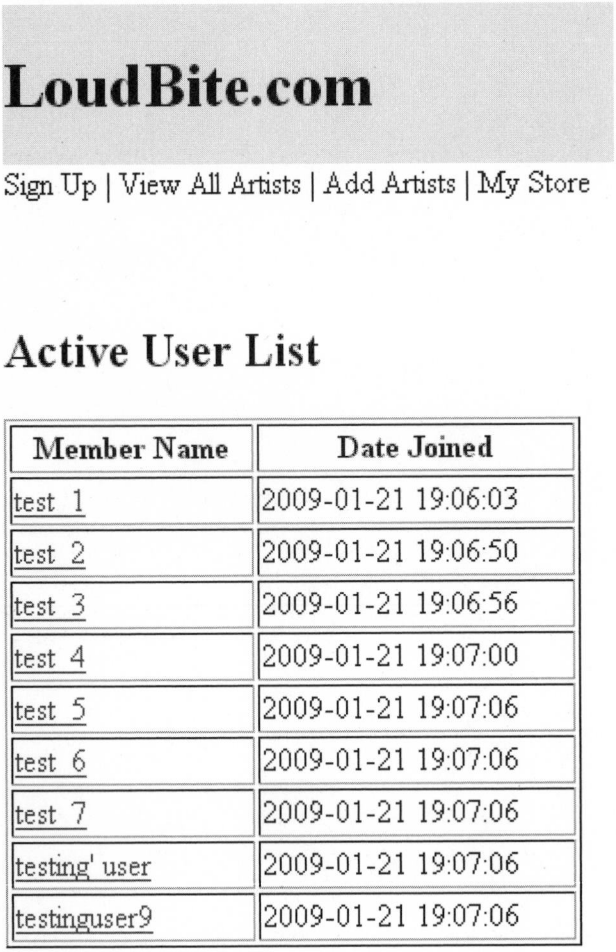

# LoudBite.com

Sign Up | View All Artists | Add Artists | My Store

## Active User List

| Member Name | Date Joined |
|---|---|
| test_1 | 2009-01-21 19:06:03 |
| test_2 | 2009-01-21 19:06:50 |
| test_3 | 2009-01-21 19:06:56 |
| test_4 | 2009-01-21 19:07:00 |
| test_5 | 2009-01-21 19:07:06 |
| test_6 | 2009-01-21 19:07:06 |
| test_7 | 2009-01-21 19:07:06 |
| testing' user | 2009-01-21 19:07:06 |
| testinguser9 | 2009-01-21 19:07:06 |

**Figure 5-3.** *LoudBite active user list page*

## USING VARIABLES IN THE STATEMENT

If you're familiar with prepared statements, the following concept will sound familiar. The Zend_Db component allows you to use placeholders, not only in the INSERT statements but also in the fetch methods. The second parameter available to you in the fetch* methods is just for such occasions.

Using placeholders indicated by a ?, let's update the SQL statement implemented in Listing 5-8. The new statement will be passed into the fetchAll() method along with a second parameter containing the string value 'active':

SELECT id, username, created_date FROM Accounts WHERE status = ?

When the fetchAll() method is invoked by Zend Framework, it places the 'active' string into the first ? marker it finds in the SELECT statement and then executes. You can have many ? placeholders in the SELECT statement as long as you pass in the same number of replacement values into the second parameter.

## Using fetchOne()

The fetchOne() method returns a string value and is great to use when you want to capture a single return value, such as the total number of records in the table.

The fetchOne() method accepts two parameters:

- The initial parameter accepts either a string SELECT statement or a Zend_Db_Select object.

- The second parameter is a mixed type representing the binding values for the ? placeholders (if present).

Let's use this method to take a count of the number of records in the accounts table. You will then update the view-all.phtml file to display the total active accounts.

The code shown in Listing 5-12 is almost identical to Listing 5-10, with the exception of the new statement and code shown in bold. Listing 5-12 uses the fetchOne() method to fetch the first column the supplied SQL statement specified. In the example shown, the aggregate function COUNT() is used to count the total number of active accounts in the database table accounts. You save the data returned into the $totalMembers view variable for use in the view.

*Listing 5-12. AccountController.php: viewAllAction()*

```
/**
 * View All Accounts.
 *
 */
public function viewAllAction()
{

  //Create Db Object
  require_once "Db/Db_Db.php";
  $db = Db_Db::conn();

  try{

    //Create the SQL statement to select the data.
    $statement = "SELECT id, username, created_date
          FROM accounts
          WHERE status = 'active'";
```

```
        //Fetch the data
        $results = $db->fetchAll($statement);

//Create the SQL statement to
//fetch the COUNT of all active members.
$statement = "SELECT COUNT(id) as total_members
        FROM accounts
         WHERE status = 'active'";

//Fetch ONLY the count of active members.
$count = $db->fetchOne($statement);

        //Set the view variable.
        $this->view->members     = $results;
$this->view->totalMembers = $count;

    }catch(Zend_Db_Exception $e){

      echo $e->getMessage();

    }

}
```

Open the viewall.phtml file located in the views/scripts/account/ directory and make the changes shown in Listing 5-13. This change will display the total active members to the user, along with the list.

***Listing 5-13.*** *Updated Account viewall.phtml*

```php
<?php echo $this->doctype('XHTML1_STRICT'); ?>
<html xmlns="http://www.w3.org/1999/xhtml" xml:lang="en" lang="en">
<head>
  <?php echo $this->headTitle('LoudBite.com – View All Accounts'); ?>
</head>
<body>

<?php echo $this->render("includes/header.phtml"); ?>
<h2>Active User List</h2>

<table width="300" border="1">

<?php if($this->members){ ?>
```

```
Total active members: <?php echo $this->totalMembers; ?>
     <tr align="center">
       <td><b>Member Name</b></td>
       <td><b>Date Joined</b></td>
     </tr>

     <?php
     foreach($this->members as $member){
     ?>

       <tr>
         <td><a href='/<?php echo urlencode($member['username'])?>'>
           <?php echo $member['username']?>
           </a></td>
         <td><?php echo $member['created_date']?></td>
       </tr>
     <?php
     }

     }else{
     ?>
       <tr>
         <td>There are no active members in the system.</td>
       </tr>

     <?php
     }
     ?>

     </table>
     </body>
     </html>
```

Load the http://localhost/account/view-all page to see the total number of active members displayed on top of the list.

# LoudBite Login Page

Putting what you've learned to use, now create the login system of the application, which requires two sections: a form that users can use to enter username, e-mail, and password; and the code to authenticate the submitted data.

You create a login form, which contains two form fields: the e-mail of the user and the password for the account. To do so, create a pair of new methods, getLoginForm() and loginAction(), in the AccountController.php file.

getLoginForm() creates the login form using the Zend_Form object, and the loginAction() initializes the form and sets the view variable to display the form in the view.

The action will be called when the user loads the URL http://localhost/account/login.

Listing 5-14 shows getLoginForm(), and Listing 5-15 shows the code for loginAction().

*Listing 5-14. AccountController.php: getLoginForm()*

```
/**
 * Get Login Form
 *
 * @return Zend_Form
 */
private function getLoginForm()
{

  //Create the form
  $form = new Zend_Form();
  $form->setAction("authenticate");
  $form->setMethod("post");
  $form->setName("loginform");

  //Create text elements
  $emailElement = new Zend_Form_Element_Text("email");
  $emailElement->setLabel("Email: ");
  $emailElement->setRequired(true);

  //Create password element
  $passwordElement = new
        Zend_Form_Element_Password("password");
  $passwordElement->setLabel("Password: ");
  $passwordElement->setRequired(true);

  //Create the submit button
  $submitButtonElement = new
        Zend_Form_Element_Submit("submit");
  $submitButtonElement->setLabel("Log In");

  //Add Elements to form
  $form->addElement($emailElement);
  $form->addElement($passwordElement);
```

```
$form->addElement($submitButtonElement);

return $form;

}
```

The form created in Listing 5-14 uses the Zend_Form object to create not only the form but also the supporting password element, e-mail element, and submit button. After the elements are created, you add each element to the form and return the form object for other methods to use. (For additional information, refer to Chapter 4.)

Listing 5-15 is the action called when the user arrives at the URL http://localhost/account/login. The action instantiates the login form you created in the getLoginForm() method and saves an instance of the form for use in the view.

***Listing 5-15.*** *AccountController.php: loginAction()*

```
/**
 * Load the Login Form.
 *
 */
public function loginAction(){

  //Initialize the form for the view.
  $this->view->form = $this->getLoginForm();

}
```

Let's now take a look at the view. The login.phtml view should be created in the views/scripts/account directory. Copy the code shown in Listing 5-16 and visit the URL http://localhost/account/login to view the login page.

***Listing 5-16.*** *View Login Page*

```
<?php echo $this->doctype('XHTML1_STRICT'); ?>
<html xmlns="http://www.w3.org/1999/xhtml" xml:lang="en" lang="en">
<head>
  <?php echo $this->headTitle('LoudBite.com – Login'); ?>
</head>
<body>

  <?php
  echo $this->render("includes/header.phtml");
  echo $this->form;
  ?>
```

```
</body>
</html>
```

With the view created, you now need to create the authentication section of the login page. The authentication will retrieve the values that the user submits using the form and determine whether the combination is found in the database. You will use the data along with the fetchOne() method to determine whether the login data is valid. If the e-mail/password combination is valid, you redirect the user to the account management page; otherwise, redisplay the form so the user can try again.

You create a new action, authenticateAction(), in the AccountController.php file, as shown in Listing 5-17.

**Listing 5-17.** *Account Login Authentication*

```
/**
 * Authenticate login information.
 *
 */
public function authenticateAction(){

  $form = $this->getLoginForm();

  if($form->isValid($_POST)){

    //Initialize the variables
    $email    = $form->getValue("email");
    $password = $form->getValue("password");

    //Create a db object
    require_once "Db/Db_Db.php";
    $db = Db_Db::conn();

    //Quote values
    $email    = $db->quote($email);
    $password = $db->quote($password);

    //Check if the user is in the system and active
    $statement = "SELECT COUNT(id) AS total From accounts
            WHERE email = ".$email."
            AND password = ".$password."
            AND status = 'active'";

    $results  = $db->fetchOne($statement);
```

```
//If we have at least one row then the users
//email and password is valid.
if($results == 1){

    //Fetch the user's data
    $statement = "SELECT id, username, created_date FROM accounts
            WHERE email = ".$email."
            AND password = ".$password;

    $results = $db->fetchRow($statement);

    //Set the user's session
    $_SESSION['id']        = $results['id'];
    $_SESSION['username']   = $results['username'];
    $_SESSION['dateJoined'] = $results['created_date'];

    //Forward the user to the profile page
    $this->_forward("accountmanager");

}else{

    //Set the error message and re-display the login page.
    $this->view->message = "Username or password incorrect.";
    $this->view->form  = $form;
    $this->render("login");
}

}else{
    $this->view->form  = $form;
    $this->render("login");
}
}
```

The controller contains a new action: authenticateAction(). The action uses the built-in form validation to determine whether the user has successfully entered the required data. In this case, e-mail and password text fields are required fields. If the data was valid, continue by initializing the data followed by initializing a database object.

You then create an instance of the database connection and create the SELECT statement, which simply takes a count of the number of records returned that meet the combination. You call the fetchOne() method passing in the SELECT statement to fetch the count. If the return value is 1, you know that the combination is valid and you can continue to set the user session information. If the return value is not 1, issue an error and store it into the $message variable to display on the login page.

After you determine whether the user is valid, move down the code and create another SELECT statement. This time, the SELECT statement will retrieve the ID of the user along with the user's username. To do so, use the fetchRow() method.

When you execute this statement, you retrieve only the values for the first row regardless of whether there are any additional rows. You store the user ID and username into a session and allow the remaining action logic to continue.

Because the code forwards the user to an account manager page if the login was a success, you need to create both the action and the view for the page. In the same AccountController.php file, create a new empty action, accountmanagerAction(), and copy the code shown in Listing 5-18.

**Listing 5-18.** *accountmanagerAction()*

```
/**
 * Account Manager.
 *
 */
public function accountmanagerAction()
{
}
```

Also create an accountmanager.phtml file in the views/scripts/account directory.

When the user logs in, the reference to Zend_Session added to the public/index.php file will start the session and keep the session information through the lifetime of the user's visit.

Pull up the login page by visiting the URL http://localhost/account/login and try it out. You should be able to successfully log into the system.

# LoudBite User Profile Page

Now that the user can successfully log in, you wouldn't want the user to visit an empty profile page, so let's use the fetchAll() method to display all the user's favorite artists along with profile data. You have already created the empty accountmanager.phtml file, so you now need to create three sections: the user profile section containing the user's username and date joined information, a section containing a list of the user's artists, and the means to check whether the user is logged in.

To start, open the accountmanager.phtml file and update the file, as shown in Listing 5-19.

**Listing 5-19.** *Account Manager View*

```
<?php echo $this->doctype('XHTML1_STRICT'); ?>
<html>
<head>
 <?php echo $this->headTitle('LoudBite.com – Account Manager'); ?>
</head>
<body>
<?php echo $this->render("includes/header.phtml"); ?>
<h2>LoudBite My Page - <?php echo $this->escape($this->username); ?></h2>
```

```
<!--- MAIN CONTAINER -->
<table>
<tr><td valign="top">

  <!--PROFILE DATA-->
  <table width="300" border="1">
  <tr><td>Username: <?php echo $this->escape($this->username); ?></td></tr>
  <tr><td>Date Joined: <?php echo $this->dateJoined?></td></tr>
  </table>

</td>
<td valign="top">

  <!--FAVORITE BAND LIST-->
  <table width="300" border="1">
  <?php if($this->artists){?>

    <tr align="center">
    <td><b>Artist Name</b></td>
    <td><b>Date Became A Fan</b></td>
    </tr>

  <?php foreach($this->artists as $artist){?>
    <tr>
      <td><a href='artist/<?php echo
        urlencode($artist['artist_name'])?>'>
        <?php echo $this->escape($artist['artist_name']); ?></a></td>
      <td><?php echo $this->escape($artist['date_became_fan']); ?></td></tr>

  <?php }

  }else{
  ?>

<tr><td>You currently have no favorite artists.</td></tr>

<?php }?>
  </table>

</td>
</tr>
```

```
</table>
</body>
</html>
```

To populate the sections, you need to update the accountmanagerAction(), as shown in Listing 5-20.

**Listing 5-20.** *AccountController: accountmanagerAction()*

```
/**
 * Account Manager.
 *
 */
public function accountmanagerAction()
{

  //Check if the user is logged in
  if(!isset($_SESSION['id'])){
    $this->_forward("login");
  }

  try{

    //Create a db object
    require_once "Db/Db_Db.php";
    $db = Db_Db::conn();

    //Initialize data.
    $userId    = $_SESSION['id'];
    $userName   = $_SESSION['username'];
    $dateJoined = $_SESSION['dateJoined'];


    //Fetch all the users favorite artists.
    $statement = "SELECT b.artist_name, b.id,
           aa.created_date as date_became_fan
           FROM artists AS b
           INNER JOIN accounts_artists aa ON aa.artist_id = b.id
           WHERE aa.account_id = ?
           AND aa.is_fav = 1";

    $favArtists = $db->fetchAll($statement, $userId);
```

```
//Set the view variables
$this->view->artists   = $favArtists;
$this->view->username  = $userName;
$this->view->dateJoined = $dateJoined;


}catch(Zend_Db_Exception $e){
  echo $e->getMessage();
}


}
```

If you're already logged into the application, load the URL http://localhost/account/accountmanager. You should see a page shown in Figure 5-4.

Listing 5-20 uses the fetchAll() and fetchRow(). Start the action by checking whether the user has logged in. This is done by determining whether the user contains the session information set on login. If the session information is not set, the user is redirected to the login action. If the user is logged in, you create a Db_Db object and set the user ID using the data stored in the session. The first SQL statement contained in $favArtists retrieves all the artists the user has marked as a favorite. It uses an INNER JOIN to merge both the artist and accounts_artists tables. You pass in the variable into the fetchAll() method and use the second parameter to pass in the user ID to indicate the binding value. You then set the $username, $artists, and $dateJoined view variables.

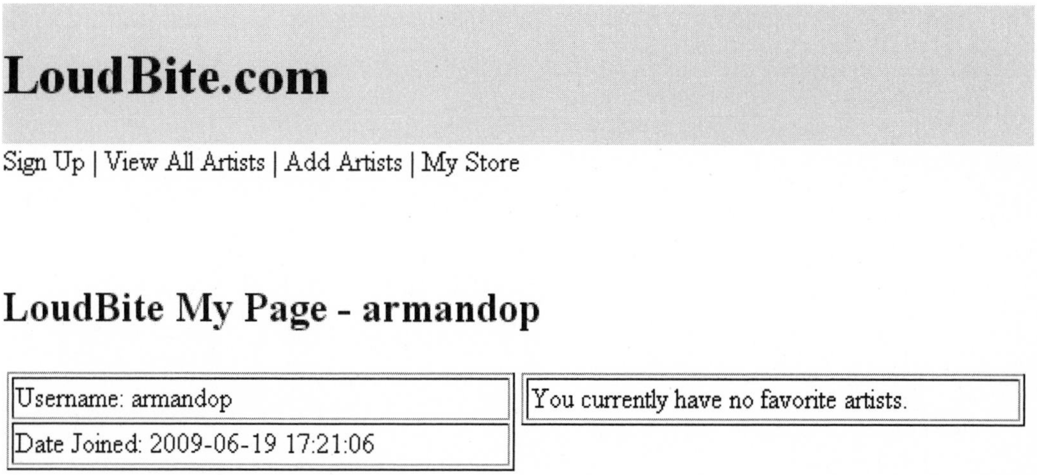

# LoudBite.com

Sign Up | View All Artists | Add Artists | My Store

## LoudBite My Page - armandop

| Username: armandop | | You currently have no favorite artists. |
| --- | --- | --- |
| Date Joined: 2009-06-19 17:21:06 | | |

*Figure 5-4. User profile page*

# Deleting Records

You've learned how to save data to the database, and you've taken additional steps to fetch and display the data using the Zend Framework database modules, but fetching and saving is only half the battle when it comes to web data. You need a way to delete data from the database.

Deleting records from a table using SQL is a three-step process:

1. Create a connection to the database.

2. Prepare the DELETE statement.

3. Execute the DELETE statement.

Zend Framework allows you to do this by using the query() method—as when you composed the INSERT statement and then executed the code using the query() method. Keeping to the theme of limiting the amount of SQL you need to write, let's delete records without SQL.

The delete() method accepts two parameters.

- The initial parameter is a string and contains the name of the table on which you want to run the DELETE statement.

- The second optional parameter is a mixed type—it can be either a string or an array. The string must contain a complete conditional statement that the record you plan to delete must meet; for example, username='test_1'. If you need more than a single conditional statement, use an array in which each element in the array represents a condition.

If you omit the second parameter, you allow the delete() method to remove all the records from the table. When executing, the method returns the total number of records that were affected. Listing 5-21 demonstrates the deletion process.

**Listing 5-21.** *Deleting Records*

```
/**
 * Example- Delete Specific Account.
 *
 */
public function testDeleteAction()
{

  require_once "Db/Db_Db.php";
  $db = Db_Db::conn();

  try{

    //Delete the record with
    //username = 'testinguser9' AND status = 'active'
    $conditions[] = "username = 'testinguser9'";
    $conditions[] = "status = 'active'";
```

```
//Execute the query.
$results = $db->delete('accounts', $conditions);

//If the execution deleted 1 account then show success.
if($results == 1){

  echo "Successfully Deleted Single Record.";

}else{

  echo "Could not find record.";

}

}catch(Zend_Db_Exception $e){

  echo $e->getMessage();

}

//Supress the View.
$this->_helper->viewRenderer->setNoRender();

}
```

Listing 5-21 creates a new action in the AccountController.php file: testDeleteAction(). The action demonstrates the delete() functionality by removing one of the test users previously inserted into the accounts table.

You begin the script by creating a connection to the database using the database model. You then set the conditions that will determine the records to delete. In this example, the record must have two conditions it must meet:

• The record must have the username equal to 'testinguser9'.

• The status must be equal to 'active'.

You now get to delete the records. To do so, call the delete() method and pass in accounts as the first parameter and $conditions as the second parameter. The following line checks whether the deletion removed only a single user because there is currently only a single user that meets the conditions in the database. Load the URL http://localhost/account/test-delete to remove the user.

# Updating Records

Let's now take a look at updating records using the Zend_Db component. The Zend_Db_Abstract object contains an update() method. Like all other create, read, update, delete (CRUD) functionality, you can use a standard SQL statement along with the query() method to execute an update, but you can also do it without SQL by using the update() method.

The update() method accepts three parameters:

- The first parameter is a string and is the name of the table on which you want to run the update.

- The second parameter accepts a mixed type. It can be either a string representing the update to commit; for example, status='active'. Or you can pass an array in which each element in the array is the update you want to commit.

- The third parameter is optional and is a mixed type. It places conditions on which records should be updated. You can pass in a string for a single condition or you can pass in an array in which each element in the array is a condition much like the delete() method. When the conditions are resolved, they are joined together via an AND statement. If you leave out the third parameter, apply the changes to all records in the tables.

Let's take an example in which you update a user's data in the accounts table (see Listing 5-22).

**Listing 5-22.** *AccountController.php: Updating Records*

```
/**
* Example - Update Account
*
*/
public function testUpdateAction(){

  require_once "Db/Db_Db.php";
  $db = Db_Db::conn();

  try{

    //Update the account 'test_1'
    //Set the email to exampleupdate@loudbite.com
    $conditions[] = "username = 'test_1'";
    $conditions[] = "status = 'active'";

    //Updates to commit
    $updates = array("email" =>
            'exampleupdate@loudbite.com');
```

```
$results = $db->update('accounts',
                $updates,
                $conditions);

if($results == 1){

    echo "Successfully Updated Record.";

}else{

    echo "Could not update record.";

}

}catch(Zend_Db_Exception $e){

    echo $e->getMessage();

}

//Supress the View.
$this->_helper->viewRenderer->setNoRender();

}
```

Listing 5-22 outlines the steps you take when updating a record. The code starts by creating an instance of a database object; then you initialize the $conditions variable, which contains the conditions the record must meet for the update. In this example, the record must have the username equal to test 1 and the status equal to active. Finally, create the array that contains the data you want to update. You'll update the e-mail address of the user from test1@loudbite.com to exampleupdate@loudbite.com. You then call the update() method to commit the changes. If the update was successful, the returned value will be 1 because the table currently contains only 1 record that matches the conditions. That's all there is to it for updating.

# Transaction Control

When you deal with databases and actions you want to perform on data such as inserting, deleting, or updating, you might have problems executing these statements. This is common and will happen regardless of what you try to do in the code. A database might go offline in the middle of the transaction, for example, which becomes a bigger problem when you deal with a set of actions on the data that relies on each action executing and completing successfully.

One of the most common examples of a complex set of actions is withdrawing money from a bank account. The process goes like this: a bank has bank accounts, and users can open accounts and make withdrawals and deposits to their account. The use case (transaction) is shown as follows:

1. User has $100 in a bank account.

2. User goes to an ATM and withdraws $45.

3. User's account is updated to $55.

4. User is given cash.

Each step from 2–4 can realistically fail. If the use case failed at step 4, steps 2–3 would continue to execute, and you would have a very angry customer. The user asked for $45, the account was deducted $45, but it was not received because of a fatal error in the database side.

To control transactions, Zend Framework provides the following transaction-control methods:

- beginTransaction(): Identifies when the transaction will start. The method is called before any of the database actions you want to take. Without this method call, Zend Framework will not know that the following actions are controllable.

- commit(): Called when there are no errors in the transaction. All the changes made in the transaction are then made permanent.

- rollback(): Called if the PHP script has encountered an error while executing database commands. It will undo any actions in the database made in the transaction.

Transaction control is dependent on the database engine you use. For example, the MySQL engine MyISAM does not support transaction control, so you might want to refer to your database's documentation before implementing this feature.

The three methods enable you to try a complete transaction in the database. If one of the actions in the database fails, you can undo any changes made to the database during that transaction. In the previous example, if step 4 failed, steps 2–3 would be rolled back, and the customer would continue to have $100 in the account. Let's see this in action using a modified example with the table setup (see Listing 5-23).

**Listing 5-23.** *Transaction Example*

```
/**
* Save Artist to Db
*
*/
public function saveArtistAction(){

  //Create instance of artist form.
  $form = $this->getAddArtistForm();

  //Check for logged in status
  if(!isset($_SESSION['id'])){

    $this->_forward("login");
```

```
}

//Check if there were no errors
if($form->isValid($_POST)){

    //Initialize the variables
    $artistName = $form->getValue('artistName');
    $genre     = $form->getValue('genre');
    $rating     = $form->getValue('rating');
    $isFav     = $form->getValue('isFavorite');

    //Set the temporary account id to use.
    $userId = $_SESSION['id'];

    //Create a db object
    require_once "Db/Db_Db.php";
    $db = Db_Db::conn();

    $db->beginTransaction();

    try{

        //Initialize data to save into DB
        $artistData = array("artist_name"  => $artistName,
                    "genre"     => $genre,
                    "created_date" =>
                    new Zend_Db_Expr("NOW()"));

        //Insert the artist into the Db
        $db->insert('artists', $artistData);

        //Fetch the artist id
        $artistId = $db->lastInsertId();

        //Initialize data for the account artists table
        $accountArtistData = array("account_id"  => $userId,
                    "artist_id"     => $artistId,
                    "rating"     => $rating,
                    "is_fav"     => $isFav,
                    "created_date" =>
                    new Zend_Db_Expr("NOW()"));
```

```
        //Insert the data.
        $db->insert('accounts_artists', $accountArtistData);

        $db->commit();

    }catch(Zend_Db_Exception $e){

        //If there were errors roll everything back.
        $db->rollBack();
        echo $e->getMessage();

    }

  }else{

    $this->view->errors = $form->getMessages();
    $this->view->form = $form;

  }

}
```

Listing 5-23 is an update to ArtistController.php's saveAction(). The initial code did not contain a transaction call when you saved an artist into the artists table. There could have been a failure while saving the artist to the table, but the user's association to the artist was saved in the accounts_artists table. With transaction calls, if there are any failures of any kind, the database removes any changes it made.

The goal to separate the PHP developer from writing SQL should be apparent by this point. If it's not, hold on; I'll now introduce new tools that will allow you to create SQL statements of any complexity using an object-oriented concept. Yes, SQL queries can be created using objected-oriented methods.

# Object-Oriented SELECT Statements

The Zend_Db_Select class allows developers to create SELECT statements using the standard clauses ranging from a simple SELECT clause to a GROUPING clause; it automatically escapes the user-entered input and removes the overhead of filtering any possible SQL injection attack. You can then use the SELECT statement to query the database.

Let's go through each clause, working with a couple of examples that range from simple statements to the more complex JOIN statements you typically see.

You need a SQL statement to reference before you start an object-oriented statement. You start by creating a simple SELECT statement:

SELECT * FROM `artists`

The statement queries the artists table in the database and retrieves all columns and records stored in the table (it is indicated by the * wildcard symbol in the columns list). Translating the statement into an object-oriented call using the Zend_Db_Select class, you create the initial SELECT portion of the script, as shown in Listing 5-24. Yes, simply calling the Zend_Db_Select class creates a statement, but this statement is not that smart; it won't do anything at this point.

***Listing 5-24.*** *Simple Object-Oriented Statement: testoostatementAction*

```
/**
* Test - Object Oriented Select Statement
*
*/
public function testoostatementAction() {

  //Create DB object
  require_once "Db/Db_Db.php";
  $db = Db_Db::conn();

  echo $select = new Zend_Db_Select($db);

  //Supress the View
  $this->_helper->viewRenderer->setNoRender();

}
```

At this point, if you wrote out the POSQL created in Listing 5-24, the result would be a string such as the following:

```
"SELECT"
```

Copy the code shown in Listing 5-24 to the ArtistController.php file.

# Querying Records from Tables Using from()

You need to give the SQL statement you're using a bit more power and intelligence. The statement needs to know from which table you will fetch data. Using the same Zend_Db_Select object, you'll use the from() method to identify a table and the __toString() method to convert the SELECT statement you're currently building to a POSQL string. Doing this enables you to compare the object-oriented statement with the intended POSQL.

Listing 5-25 builds on Listing 5-24 by using the from() method to distinguish which table the SQL statement should retrieve data from.

The from() method accepts three parameters:

- The initial parameter is the name of the table you want to reference as a string.

- The second parameter is a list of columns. To retrieve all the columns, use the * wildcard symbol; if you want to specify specific columns, use an array. The default value is *.

- The third parameter (optional) is the schema name you want to reference.

***Listing 5-25.*** *Using Object-Oriented from(): Updated testoostatementAction()*

```
/**
* Test - Object Oriented Select Statement
*/
public function testoostatementAction() {

  //Create DB object
  require_once "Db/Db.php";
  $db = Db_Db::conn();

  //Create the statement
  //Select * FROM `artists`;
  $select = new Zend_Db_Select($db);
  $statement = $select->from('artists');

  //Compare Statement
  echo $statement->__toString();

  //Supress the View
  $this->_helper->viewRenderer->setNoRender();


}
```

The table is identified by using the from() method and passing in the artists string value. At this point, the full POSQL is the following:

```
SELECT `artists`.* FROM `artists`
```

You can use the __toString() method to view the generated statement. Load the URL http://localhost/artist/testoostatement and view the statement.

# Querying Specific Columns

Sometimes you don't need all the table columns, so the POSQL must change from using the wildcard symbol to identifying which columns you want to fetch. Updating the example statement previously mentioned, you'll pull three columns for each record, the ID of the artist, the name of artist, and the genre the artist belongs to. The new statement looks like this:

SELECT `artists`.`id`, `artists`.`artist_name`, `artists`.`genre` FROM `artists`

Using the from() method's second parameter, pass in an array. You can create an array containing string elements representing the individual column names (see Listing 5-26).

***Listing 5-26.*** *Identifying Specific Columns to Fetch*

```
/**
* Test - Object Oriented Select Statement
*
*/
public function testoostatementAction() {

  //Create DB object
  require_once "Db/Db_Db.php";
  $db = Db_Db::conn();

  //Create the statement
  //SELECT `artists`.`id`, `artists`.`artist_name`, `artists`.`genre`
  //FROM `artists`
  $select = new Zend_Db_Select($db);

  //Determine which columns to retrieve.
  $columns = array('id', 'artist_name', 'genre');
  $statement = $select->from('artists', $columns);

  //Compare Statement
  echo $statement->__toString();

  //Supress the View
  $this->_helper->viewRenderer->setNoRender();

}
```

For ease of use, create a $columns array variable that contains a list of all the columns you want to fetch from the table and pass it into the from() method's second parameter. Each element in the array represents a column name in the table you are fetching records from. Load the URL http://localhost/artist/testoostatement and look at the created statement. It contains the columns specified now. So how do you execute the statements?

# Executing Object-Oriented Statements

The statement now contains enough intelligence to determine which columns to pull from the table. It's time to execute the statement and fetch data.

There are two ways to execute the query you've built. One way is to use the database method query(), which accepts a string or Zend_Db_Select object, as shown in Listing 5-27. The other way is by calling query() directly from the Zend_Db_Select object. Both methods are followed by a call to the desired fetch method shown in Table 5-3. You can then use an iteration function to iterate through the result set.

***Listing 5-27.*** *Executing Object-Oriented Statement*

```
/**
 * Test - Object Oriented Select Statement
 *
 */
public function testoostatementAction() {

   //Create DB object
   require_once "Db/Db_Db.php";
   $db = Db_Db::conn();

   //Create the statement
   //SELECT `artists`.`id`, `artists`.`artist_name`, `artists`.`genre`
   //FROM `artists`
   $select = new Zend_Db_Select($db);

   //Determine which columns to retrieve.
   $columns = array('id', 'artist_name', 'genre');
   $statement = $select->from('artists', $columns);

   //Query the Database
   $results = $db->query($statement);
   $rows    = $results->fetchAll();

   //Compare Statement
   echo $statement->__toString();

   //Supress the View
   $this->_helper->viewRenderer->setNoRender();
}
```

## Creating Column and Table Aliases

Continuing with the from() method, I'll now touch on aliases. You use aliases on tables and columns when you want to name a column differently from the way it's presented in the table or when you want to assign a different name to the table you are querying. You would use an alias when you have a statement that calls two or more tables that contain columns of the same name such as id. In such cases, you need to distinguish which id column you want to pull data from.

The Zend_Db_Select object allows you to create table aliases and column aliases by using the first and second parameters in the from() method call. Let's start by creating an alias on the artists table, as shown in Listing 5-28. You'll give the table the alias a in the next example and update the columns to use aliases as well. The final statement is the following:

SELECT `a`.`id` AS `artist id`, `a`.`artist_name` AS `name`, `a`.`genre`
FROM `artists` AS `a`

**Listing 5-28.** *Implementing Table and Column Aliases*

```
/**
 * Test - Object Oriented Select Statement
 *
 */
public function testoostatementAction() {

    //Create DB object
    require_once "Db/Db_Db.php";
    $db = Db_Db::conn();

    //Create the statement
    //SELECT `a`.`id` AS `artist id`, `a`.`artist_name` AS `name`,
    //`a`.`genre` FROM `artists` AS `a`
    $select = new Zend_Db_Select($db);

    //Determine which columns to retrieve.
    //Determine which table to retrieve data from.
    $columns   = array("artist id" => 'id',
                "name"    => 'artist_name',
                "genre"   => 'genre');

    $tableInfo = array("a" => "artists");
    $statement = $select->from($tableInfo, $columns);

    //Query the Database
    $results = $db->query($statement);
    $rows    = $results->fetchAll();

    //Compare Statement
    echo $statement->__toString();

    //Supress the View
```

```
$this->_helper->viewRenderer->setNoRender();
```

```
}
```

       Start by making the changes to the $columns array variable. Instead of using a standard array, you create a key-value array where the key is the alias for the column and the value is the column to retrieve. The next change you make is to the first parameter in the from() method. You update the parameter from a string to a variable: $tableInfo. The variable contains a key-value array where the key represents the alias you plan on using, a, and the value is the name of the table.

       If you now execute the object-oriented statement by loading the URL http://localhost/artist/testoostatement, it will retrieve the same number of records that the query in Listing 5-27 returned, and the desired statement will display on the screen.

## Narrowing Down the Search with a WHERE Clause

You can narrow down your searches with a WHERE clause just like any standard POSQL statement. A WHERE clause allows you to fetch all the records from a table with a given condition. In some cases, you want to retrieve all the records in a table that match a given string, are higher than a specified value, or do not meet a condition.

       Continuing with the statement previously created, let's expand it and return only the artist information for the artist Groove Armada. The new statement looks like this:

SELECT `a`.`id`, `a`.`artist_name` AS `name`, `a`.`genre` FROM `artists`

AS `a` WHERE (artist_name='Groove Armada')

       Translating the preceding statement into an object-oriented call requires you to use the where() method in the Zend_Db_Select object. The where() method accepts two parameters:

- The initial string parameter represents the complete condition the record must match for it to be included into the result set. Placeholders can also be used in the condition.

- The second optional parameter is a string representing the binding value.

       Listing 5-29 adds the new method where() to the code shown in Listing 5-30. Because you want the result set to contain only the artist named Groove Armada, you pass in the value artist_name=?. The artist_name is the column you are identifying to match records to, and? is the placeholder that will be replaced by the escaped value used in the second parameter (in this case, Groove Armada).

***Listing 5-29.*** *Using the Where Clause*

```
/**
 * Test - Object Oriented Select Statement
 *
 */
public function testoostatementAction() {

  //Create DB object
  require_once "Db/Db_Db.php";
```

```
$db = Db_Db::conn();

//Create the statement
//SELECT `a`.`id`, `a`.`artist_name` AS `name`, `a`.`genre`
//FROM `artists` AS `a` WHERE (artist_name='Groove Armada')
$select = new Zend_Db_Select($db);

//Determine which columns to retrieve.
//Determine which table to retrieve data from.
$columns   = array("id"    => 'id',
           "name"   => 'artist_name',
           "genre"  => 'genre');

$tableInfo = array("a" => 'artists');

$statement = $select->from($tableInfo, $columns)
           ->where("artist_name=?", 'Groove Armada');

//Query the Database
$results = $db->query($statement);
$rows    = $results->fetchAll();

//Compare Statement
echo $statement->__toString();

//Supress the View
$this->_helper->viewRenderer->setNoRender();


}
```

Load the URL http://localhost/artist/testoostatement to see the resulting query statement.

Now let's update the POSQL statement and search for all records with the artist name Groove Armada that belongs to the electronic genre. You'll add a new condition to the SELECT statement. You want to be absolutely sure that you are retrieving the artist Groove Armada because there might be other Groove Armadas in different genres.

Adding the new condition to the POSQL statement requires the AND clause. The new POSQL statement looks like this:

```
SELECT `a`.`id`, `a`.`artist_name` AS `name`, `a`.`genre` FROM `artists`
AS `a` WHERE (artist_name='Groove Armada') AND (genre='electronic')
```

Using the object-oriented approach, you create the new statement using another where() method call. Using another where() method call is the same as appending an AND clause to the statement. You create the new WHERE clause the same way as in the previous example. You pass in the condition as a string in the first parameter, as shown in Listing 5-30.

***Listing 5-30.*** *Using an Additional where()*

```
/**
 * Test - Object Oriented Select Statement
 *
 */
public function testoostatementAction() {

  //Create DB object
  require_once "Db/Db_Db.php";
  $db = Db_Db::conn();

  //Create the statement
  //SELECT `a`.`id`, `a`.`artist_name` AS `name`, `a`.`genre`
  //FROM `artists` AS `a`
  //WHERE (artist_name='Groove Armada') AND (genre='electronic')
  $select = new Zend_Db_Select($db);

  //Determine which columns to retrieve.
  //Determine which table to retrieve data from.
  $column  = array("id"    => 'id',
            "name"   => 'artist_name',
            "genre"  => 'genre');

  $tableInfo = array("a" => 'artists');

  $statement = $select->from($tableInfo, $column)
            ->where("artist_name=?", 'Groove Armada')
            ->where('genre=?', 'electronic');

  //Query the Database
  $results = $db->query($statement);
  $rows   = $results->fetchAll();

  //Compare Statement
  echo $statement->__toString();

  //Supress the View
  $this->_helper->viewRenderer->setNoRender();
```

}

Of course, if you're a fan of electronic music you might be telling yourself that an electronic genre is much too broad, and Groove Armada might be placed under the house genre instead. To satisfy this requirement, you need a way to translate this new condition onto a statement. You can't use the AND clause because an artist can belong to only one genre at a time. You use the OR search clause in the statement to check both the electronic and house genres. The new POSQL statement is the following:

SELECT `a`.`id`, `a`.`artist_name` AS `name`, `a`.`genre` FROM `artists` AS `a`

WHERE (artist_name='Groove Armada') AND (genre='electronic')

OR (genre='house')

Instead of using another where() method, you use the orWhere() method, which accepts the same number and type of parameters as the standard where() method. The final testoostaetmentAction() looks like Listing 5-31.

***Listing 5-31.*** *Using orWhere()*

```
/**
 * Test - Object Oriented Select Statement
 *
 */
public function testoostatementAction() {

  //Create DB object
  require_once "Db/Db_Db.php";
  $db = Db_Db::conn();

  //Create the statement
  //SELECT `a`.`id`, `a`.`artist_name` AS `name`, `a`.`genre`
  //FROM `artists` AS `a`
  //WHERE (artist_name='Groove Armada')
  //AND (genre='electronic') OR (genre='house')
  $select = new Zend_Db_Select($db);

  //Determine which columns to retrieve.
  //Determine which table to retrieve data from.
  $columns   = array("id"     => 'id',
                "name"   => 'artist_name',
                "genre"  => 'genre');


  $tableInfo = array("a" => 'artists');
```

207

```
$statement = $select->from($tableInfo, $columns)
              ->where("artist_name=?", 'Groove Armada')
->where('genre=?', 'electronic')
              ->orWhere('genre=?', 'house');

//Query the Database
$results = $db->query($statement);
$rows    = $results->fetchAll();

//Compare Statement
echo $statement->__toString();

//Supress the View
$this->_helper->viewRenderer->setNoRender();


}
```

## Querying Two or More Tables using JOIN

Demonstrating the benefits of using the Zend_Db_Select statement requires you to expand on simply retrieving a specific artist. You now want to retrieve all the fans for a specific artist. In the application, users have lists of artists they listen to; if users contain an artist, they are considered to be a fan of that artist.

Constructing the POSQL statement requires two tables: artists and accounts_artists. The new POSQL statement is the following:

SELECT `a`.`id` AS `artist id`, `a`.`artist_name` AS `name`, `a`.`genre`,

`aa`.`account_id` AS `user_id`, `aa`.`created_date` AS `date_became_fan` FROM

`artists` AS `a` INNER JOIN `accounts_artists` AS `aa` ON aa.artist_id = a.id

The Zend_Db_Select object contains six types of JOIN statements that can be executed successfully if the RDBMS supports it. Zend_Db_Select supports inner joins, left joins, right joins, full joins, natural joins, and cross joins. The statement uses the INNER JOIN SQL call, so you use the join() method. A full list of available join() methods can be seen in Table 5-5.

**Table 5-5.** *Join Methods*

| Method | Description | Parameters |
|---|---|---|
| join() OR joinInner() | INNER JOIN SQL call | join(table name, join condition, columns to retrieve) Example: join(array("tableAlias" => "tableName"), "table1.id = table2.id", array("column_alias" => "column")); |

*(Continued)*

| | | |
|---|---|---|
| joinLeft() | LEFT JOIN SQL call | joinLeft(table name, join condition, columns to retrieve)<br>Example:<br>join(array("tableAlias" => "tableName"), "table1.id = table2.id", array("column_alias" => "column")); |
| joinRight() | RIGHT JOIN SQL call | joinRight(table name, join condition, columns to retrieve)<br>Example:<br>joinRight(array("tableAlias" => "tableName"), "table1.id = table2.id", array("column_alias" => "column")); |
| joinFull() | FULL JOIN SQL call | joinFull(table name, join condition, columns to retrieve)<br>Example:<br>joinFull(array("tableAlias" => "tableName"), "table1.id = table2.id", array("column_alias" => "column")); |
| joinCross() | CROSS JOIN SQL call | joinCross(table name, columns to retrieve)<br>Example:<br>joinCross(array("tableAlias" => "tableName"), array("column_alias" => "column")); |
| joinNatural() | NATURAL JOIN SQL call | joinNatural(table name, columns to retrieve)<br>Example:<br>joinNatural(array("tableAlias" => "tableName"), array("column_alias" => "column")); |

Taking the inner join used in the preceding statement, use the join() method call:

- The first parameter accepts a mixed type. It can be a key-value array where the key is the alias you want to use for the table, and the value is the name of the table you want to use.

- The second parameter is the condition on which you want to join the tables.

- The third parameter contains the columns you want to fetch from the table. This parameter also accepts a key-value array where the key is the alias to the column and the value is the column name.

Let's now implement a join() method and transform the query to an object-oriented statement. Open the ArtistController.php file and create a new action: testoofansAction.

The new action created in the ArtistController.php file is shown in Listing 5-32 and uses much of the code created in the previous examples. Again, you create a $columns variable that contains the column you want to retrieve as well as specify the $tableInfo variable that contains the alias and the table you want to fetch data from.

**Listing 5-32.** *testoofansAction using join()*

```php
/**
 * Test - Get All Fans
 *
 */
public function testoofansAction(){

  //Create DB object
  require_once "Db/Db_Db.php";
  $db = Db_Db::conn();

  //Create the statement
  //SELECT `a`.`id` AS `artist id`, `a`.`artist_name` AS `name`,
  //`a`.`genre`,aa`.`account_id` AS `user_id`,
  //`aa`.`created_date` AS `date_became_fan`
  //FROM `artists` AS `a`
  //INNER JOIN `accounts_artists` AS `aa` ON aa.artist_id = a.id
  $select = new Zend_Db_Select($db);

  //Determine which columns to retrieve.
  //Determine which table to retrieve data from.
  $columns  = array("artist id" => 'a.id',
             "name"    => 'a.artist_name',
             "genre"   => 'a.genre');

  $tableInfo = array("a" => 'artists');

  $statement = $select->from($tableInfo, $columns)
            ->join(array("aa" => 'accounts_artists'),
                'aa.artist_id = a.id',
                array("user_id" => 'aa.account_id',
                   "date_became_fan" =>
                   'aa.created_date'));

  $results = $db->query($statement);
  $rows    = $results->fetchAll();

  //Compare Statement
  echo $statement->__toString();
```

```
//Supress the View
$this->_helper->viewRenderer->setNoRender();


}
```

After the columns and the table are set, you can use the join() method. You supply it with an array containing the alias you want to give the accounts_artists table: aa. You also supply the join condition, which specifies the column that will associate the records to each other in the artists and accounts_artists tables. In this case, you are using the artists.id and the accounts_artists.artist_id columns. Finally, you supply the third parameter with an array containing the columns and its aliases you want to use.

Load the URL http://localhost/artist/testoofans to see the resulting POSQL that is created.

# Limiting and Ordering the Result Set

You returned all artists along with their fans, but it didn't return many rows because the system is not full of user data at the moment. What would happen if there were millions of accounts and associated artists? You need a way to limit the number of results returned.

Many RDBMSs contain the LIMIT clause, which allows you to pass two parameters: a starting index and the number of rows to retrieve. The Zend_Db_Select object also contains a way to limit the amount of rows returned from the database.

You'll now transform the object-oriented statement into the following statement, which only appends a LIMIT to the number of rows you return:

```
SELECT `a`.`id` AS `artist id`, `a`.`artist_name` AS `name`, `a`.`genre`,

`aa`.`account_id` AS `user_id`, `aa`.`created_date` AS `date_became_fan` FROM

`artists` AS `a` INNER JOIN `accounts_artists` AS `aa` ON aa.artist_id = a.id

LIMIT 10
```

The preceding statement returns only ten records from the list. By using the limit() method along with a parameter of 10, you can achieve the same results. Listing 5-33 contains the updated $statement, which uses a limit() method.

# Ordering Result Sets

You now want to return the freshest information displayed for the users. What you now want is the ability to display all the fans (based on the date when they became fans).

To accomplish this, you need to use the ordering functionality available in the RDBMS. The ORDER BY clause allows you to order the records based on a column. You can sort the data by descending or ascending order. If the column type is an integer, descending order sorts the column from greatest to least; if the column is noninteger, the information will be returned alphabetically reversed.

Using this concept you now use the order() method call as well as demonstrate the use of limit() (see Listing 5-33).

***Listing 5-33.*** *testoofansAction Using order()*

```php
/**
 * Test - Get All Fans
 *
 */
public function testoofansAction(){

  //Create DB object
  require_once "Db/Db_Db.php";
  $db = Db_Db::conn();

  //Create the statement
  //SELECT `a`.`id` AS `artist id`, `a`.`artist_name` AS `name`,
  //`a`.`genre`, `aa`.`account_id` AS `user_id`,
  //`aa`.`created_date` AS `date_became_fan`
  //FROM `artists` AS `a`
  //INNER JOIN `accounts_artists` AS `aa` ON aa.artist_id = a.id
  //ORDER BY `date_became_fan` DESC LIMIT 10
  $select = new Zend_Db_Select($db);

  //Determine which columns to retrieve.
  //Determine which table to retrieve data from.
  $columns  = array("artist id" => 'a.id',
                "name"    => 'a.artist_name',
                "genre"   => 'a.genre');

  $tableInfo = array("a" => 'artists');

  $statement = $select->from($tableInfo, $columns)
              ->join(array("aa" => 'accounts_artists'),
                  'aa.artist_id = a.id',
                  array("user_id" => 'aa.account_id',
                      "date_became_fan" =>
                      'aa.created_date'))
              ->order("date_became_fan DESC")
              ->limit(10);;

  $results = $db->query($statement);
  $rows    = $results->fetchAll();
```

```
//Compare Statement
echo $statement->__toString();

//Supress the View
$this->_helper->viewRenderer->setNoRender();

}
```

The order() method accepts a mixed type parameter. It will accept a single string value containing the columns you want to order, immediately followed by the way in which you want to order the content: DESC or ASC. You can also use an array that provides each element within the array in the same format. If you do not present the type of ordering, the Zend_Db_Select object uses DESC by default.

## Database Expressions

The Zend_Db_Select object also allows you to use database expressions such as NOW(), SUB(), ADD(), and DATE_FORMAT(), among others. Using database expressions is easy and can be done within the from() method call.

Create a testoocountAction() action within the ArtistController.php file and copy the code shown in Listing 5-34. This POSQL query is generated:

SELECT COUNT(id) AS `total_fans` FROM `accounts_artists` AS `aa`

***Listing 5-34.*** *Implementing the count() Method*

```
/**
 * Test – Database expression.
 *
 */
public function testoocountAction(){

  //Create Db object
  require_once "Db/Db_Db.php";
  $db = Db_Db::conn();

  //Create the statement
  // SELECT COUNT(id) AS `total_fans` FROM `accounts_artists` AS `aa`
  $select = new Zend_Db_Select($db);

  //Determine which columns to retrieve.
  //Determine which table to retrieve data from.
  $columns  = array("total_fans" =>'COUNT(id)');
  $tableInfo = array("aa" => 'accounts_artists');
```

```
$statement = $select->from($tableInfo, $columns);

$results = $db->query($statement);
$rows    = $results->fetchAll();

//Compare Statement
echo $statement->__toString();

//Supress the View
$this->_helper->viewRenderer->setNoRender();


}
```

The example uses the $columns parameters in the from() method to simply pass in a database expression directly into the array. In this case, you're taking the count of all results returned with the given condition.

Another popular query statement is to fetch all distinct records in a table. The DISTINCT() call allows you to fetch all unique records. For example, if you want to query the Artists table and fetch all distinct genres currently in the system, you can create the following SQL statement and execute it:

```
SELECT DISTINCT `a`.`genre` FROM `artists` AS `a`
```

Let's go ahead and create the object-oriented equivalent of this statement (see Listing 5-35).

**Listing 5-35.** *Implementing the distinct() Method*

```
/**
 * Test - Return distinct genres
 *
 */
public function testoogenrelistAction(){

  //Create Db object
  require_once "Db/Db_Db.php";
  $db = Db_Db::conn();

  //Create the statement
  //SELECT DISTINCT `a`.`genre` FROM `artists` AS `a`
  $select = new Zend_Db_Select($db);

  //Determine which columns to retrieve.
  //Determine which table to retrieve data from.
```

```
$columns   = array("genre" =>'a.genre');
$tableInfo = array("a" => 'artists');

$statement = $select->from($tableInfo, $columns)
                    ->distinct();

$results = $db->query($statement);
$rows    = $results->fetchAll();

//Compare Statement
echo $statement->__toString();

//Supress the View
$this->_helper->viewRenderer->setNoRender();

}
```

# Paginating Records

Applications can contain hundreds and even millions of records. Members of a site, artist information, a list of images—all these items can be displayed. If the application contained hundreds of records and displayed the content to the user all at once, the user would be overwhelmed with too much data at a single time. The user also might become frustrated by the time it takes for the content to load because the query would fetch all the records at once.

You can solve the dilemma by using pagination, which allows applications to fetch smaller result sets there by displaying content in manageable and faster loading portions. The result sets are usually broken up into numbered pages. For example, if you have 1,000 records and applied pagination, you can display the content in a set 10 pages, each page containing 100 records. As the user continues to click on the next page, the application retrieves the next set of data.

To add pagination to any application, you can use the Zend_Paginator library, which has the capability to paginate any collection of data in an array as well as result sets from a database using the Zend_Db_Select object. It also allows you to apply any type of view to render the content.

## Using the Zend_Paginator

The Zend_Paginator can be used by loading the Zend_Paginator class into a PHP file.

After the class is loaded, you can instantiate a Zend_Paginator object using its constructor and supply it with a Zend_Paginator_Adaptor object. The supported adaptors are the following:

- Zend_Paginator_Adaptor_Array

- Zend_Db_Select

- Zend_Db_Table_Select

- Iterator

Depending on the type of data you want to paginate, use the required adaptor. If you want to paginate data for an array, use the Zend_Paginator_Adaptor_Array class. To use database result sets, you can create either a Zend_Db_Select object or a Zend_Db_Table_Select object. You can also allow Zend_Paginator to automatically create the adaptor for you by using the Zend_Paginator::factory() method and pass in an array or the object you want to use.

The Zend_Paginator provides additional functionality to manipulate the data presented to the user. These methods are shown in Table 5-6.

**Table 5-6.** *Zend_Paginator Setters*

| Method | Description |
| --- | --- |
| setCurrentPageNumber() | Sets the current page number; the default is 1. |
| setItemCountPerPage() | Sets the number of records to display per page; the default is 10. |
| setPageRange() | Sets the total number of pages to display in the pagination control; the default is 10. |
| setView() | Sets the view that you want to associate with this pagination. |

Aside from providing helpful methods, Zend_Paginator requires interaction by the user. The user must click a given page number to inform the Zend_Paginator what set of records it needs to fetch. Depending on the current page the user is on, a different set of records will be displayed. To determine which page the user is requesting, you need to use a query to pass in the data. Retrieving the page number is then something the PHP file must capture using the Request object.

Using the table, let's work on a small example that will use the methods and the factory() method. What you'll need is an action and a view. Open the ArtistController.php file and create listAction(). The action will contain the pagination example shown in Listing 5-36.

**Listing 5-36.** *ArtistController.php: listAction()*

```
/**
 * Display all the Artists in the system.
 */
public function listAction(){

  //Create a sample array of artist
  $artist = array("Underworld", "Groove Armada", "Daft Punk",
          "Paul Oakenfold", "MC Chris", "Ramones",
          "The Beatles", "The Mamas and the Papas",
          "Jimi Hendrix");

  //Initialize the Zend_Paginator
  $paginator = Zend_Paginator::factory($artist);

  $currentPage = 1;
  //Check if the user is not on page 1
```

```php
    $i = $this->_request->getQuery('i');
    if(!empty($i)){ //Where i is the current page

        $currentPage = $this->_request->getQuery('i');

    }

    //Set the properties for the pagination
    $paginator->setItemCountPerPage(2);
    $paginator->setPageRange(3);
    $paginator->setCurrentPageNumber($currentPage);

    $this->view->paginator = $paginator;

}
```

Listing 5-36 demonstrates the new listAction(). The method begins by initializing the data you'll paginate through. It's a set of nine electronic music artists, all contained in an $artist array. Once initialized, you create a Zend_Paginator object and use its factory method to pass in the data to paginate. Because you're using an array, this will become a Zend_Paginator_Adaptor_Array object behind the scenes.

You now need to determine what page the user is on. To do this, pass a query value using the URL. The query value is represented by the variable i, and the URL will look like this: http://localhost/artist/list?i=<pagenumber>. If the variable i is not set, you know that the user is in the initial page, and you can use the default value you set as 1. Finally, set the total number of artists to display in a single page, 2; set the number of pages to display in the paginator control, 3; and set the page the user is currently loading for this request.

Create a new file in the views/scripts/artist directory and call it list.phtml. The view will render the records. Copy the code shown in Listing 5-37 into the list.phtml file.

***Listing 5-37.*** *list.phtml*

```php
<?php echo $this->doctype('XHTML1_STRICT'); ?>
<html xmlns="http://www.w3.org/1999/xhtml" xml:lang="en" lang="en">
<head>
   <?php echo $this->headTitle('LoudBite.com - Artist Listing'); ?>
</head>
<body>
<?php echo $this->render("includes/header.phtml")?>

<table border='0' width='600'>

<?php
if ($this->paginator){
```

```php
foreach($this->paginator as $item){

    echo "<tr><td>".$item."</td></tr>";

}

}else{?>

    <tr><td>There were no artists present in the system.
        Add one now!</td></tr>

<?php
}
?>


</table>
</body>
</html>
```

Listing 5-37 demonstrates how to display the content to the user using a view. Because the collection to paginate is stored into Zend_Paginator, which uses the Iterator class, you can use a loop function such as foreach to iterate through the record set. Go ahead and try it out. Load the URL http://localhost/artist/list to return the first two records and then try http://localhost/artist/list?i=3 to return records 5 and 6 from the artist variable.

Now you need a way to allow the user to move through a set of records by clicking either next or previous links or buttons; you need a paginator control.

## Adding Control to the Paginator

The paginator control allows you to display not only a next or previous button the user can use to move through the result set, but also provides functionality that allows you to display the total number of pages. This can be accomplished by using the paginationControl() method of Zend_Paginator.

The function accepts three parameters:

- The initial parameter accepts a Zend_Paginator object.

- The second parameter accepts a string value representing the type of style to implement. Acceptable values are shown in Table 5-7.

- The third parameter accepts a string value representing the location of the view to use for the pagination control.

**Table 5-7.** *Pagination Controller Styles*

| Scrolling Style | Description |
| --- | --- |
| All | Displays all the pages available to the user regardless of whether you use setPageRange(). |
| Elastic | Displays an initial set of pages. As the user moves from page to page, the number of pages displayed on the paginator control will expand. |
| Jumping | Displays a given range; moves on to the next range when the user gets to the end of the first range. |
| Sliding | Displays the page range set using setPageRange(). Places the current page number as close to the center as possible. |

Each style displays the content and interacts in different ways with the user. Try out the different combinations to see which one you like.

**Table 5-8.** *Zend_Paginator Properties*

| Property | Description | Return Type |
| --- | --- | --- |
| first | Returns the initial page number in the set of pages. | String |
| firstItemNumber | Returns the index of the first record in the result set on the current page. | String |
| firstPageInRange | Returns the first page in the scrolling range for the current page. | String |
| current | Returns the current page number in the scrolling page range. | String |
| currentItemCount | Returns the current number of records displayed in the current page. | String |
| itemCountPerPage | Returns the total number of records that can be displayed per page. | String |
| last | Returns the last page number in the total set of pages. | String |
| lastItemNumber | Returns the index of the last record on the current page. | String |
| lastPageInRange | Returns the last page number in the current scrolling page range. | String |

*(Continued)*

| | | |
|---|---|---|
| next | Returns the next page number to be fetched. | String |
| pageCount | Returns the total number of pages. | String |
| pagesInRange | Returns all the page numbers to display in the current scrolling page range. Key-value array: Value represents the page number. | Array |
| previous | Returns the previous page number. | String |
| totalItemCount | Returns the total number of records to paginate. | String |

Using both tables, let's add a paginator control to the list.phtml view. You now need to create the view that the pagination control will implement. The view contains the look and feel for the pagination control and is the file that you need to modify to make the control look the way you want. Create a new file, paginationcontrol.phtml, in the directory includes/ and copy the code shown in Listing 5-38. The file is not required to live here; you are just saving it to this location to easily reuse the view for other paginator instances.

**Listing 5-38.** *Pagination Control View*

```
<?php
if($this->pageCount){
?>

<table>
<tr>

<!-- ADD PREVIOUS BUTTON -->
<?php
if(isset($this->previous)){
?>

  <td><a href="list?i=<?php echo $this->previous?>"> &lt;-
    Previous</a> |
  </td>

<?php } ?>

<!-- SHOW THE AVAILABLE PAGES -->
<?php
foreach($this->pagesInRange as $page){
```

```
    if($page != $this->current){

?>

  <td>
    <a href="list?i=<?php echo $page?>"><?php echo $page; ?></a> |
  </td>

<?
  }else{

?>

    <td><?php echo $this->current; ?> |</td>

<?
  }
}
?>


<!-- ADD NEXT BUTTON -->
<?php
if(isset($this->next)){
?>
<td><a href="list?i=<?php echo $this->next?>">Next -&gt;</a></td>
<?}?>

</tr>
</table>
<?php
}
?>
```

The pagination control shown in Listing 5-38 checks whether there are pages to paginate. If so, create the controls that contain a previous button and a next button. To display the number of pages the user can view at a single time, use the foreach() iteration function and iterate through each page. (Of course, you are not tied down to this layout and can design the pagination any way you want as long as you use the properties in Table 5-8 to control and display pages.)

Integrating the pagination control requires a single line to add anywhere you want to display the controls. Open the views/scripts/artist/list.phtml file and update the file as shown in Listing 5-39.

***Listing 5-39.*** *list.phtml Update: Using paginationControl*

```php
<?php echo $this->doctype('XHTML1_STRICT'); ?>
<html xmlns="http://www.w3.org/1999/xhtml" xml:lang="en" lang="en">
<head>
  <?php echo $this->headTitle('LoudBite.com – Artist List'); ?>
</head>
<body>

<?php echo $this->render("includes/header.phtml")?>

<table border='0' width='600'>

<?php
if ($this->paginator){

  echo " <tr><td><b>Total Artists:</b> ".
      $this->paginator->getTotalItemCount()."</td></tr>";

  foreach($this->paginator as $item){

    echo "<tr><td>".$item."</td></tr>";

  }

  echo "<tr><td>";
  echo $this->paginationControl($this->paginator,
                 'Sliding',
                 'includes/paginationcontrol.phtml');
  echo "</td></tr>";

}else{?>

  <tr>
    <td>There were no artists present in the system.
      Add one now!</td>
  </tr>

<?php

}
```

```
?>

</table>
</body>
</html>
```

Listing 5-39 builds on the example shown in Listing 5-38. Unlike the previous example, you append the call to render the paginator's control. You use the paginationControl() method to do so and pass in three parameters. The initial parameter is the object you created in the listAction: $paginator. The second parameter is the scrolling style from Table 5-7. The third parameter is the location of the pagination control view; in the example, it's in the includes folder. Load the URL http://localhost/artist/list to

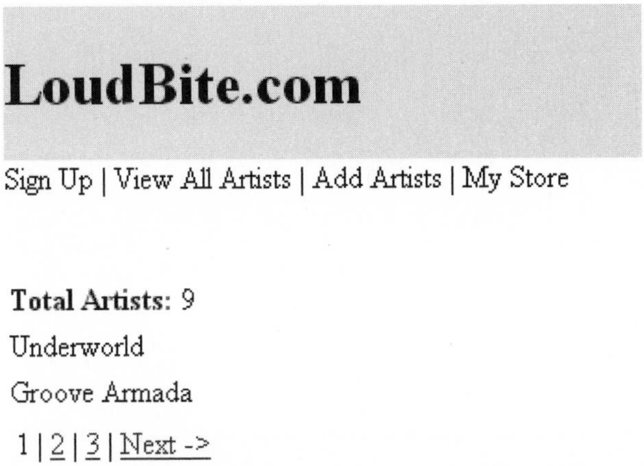

# LoudBite.com

Sign Up | View All Artists | Add Artists | My Store

**Total Artists:** 9

Underworld

Groove Armada

1 | 2 | 3 | Next ->

see the resulting pagination controller and the list of artists, as shown in Figure 5-5.

***Figure 5-5.*** *Artist list with paginator controller*

Let's look at the paginationControl() function in a bit more detail. It accepts three parameters:

- The initial parameter is a Zend_Paginator object.

- The second parameter, a string, is the type of style you want to use in the paginator controller (all possible values are shown in Table 5-7).

- The third parameter accepts a string that is the location of the view that will be used. By default, paginationControl() searches in the views/scripts/ directory for the file.

You created a completely supported pagination page using all the components involved in the pagination of data. Now let's see how to paginate database results.

## Paginating Database Records

The Zend_Paginator does not only support arrays. As shown in the beginning of this section, you can also paginate through database result sets. You can accomplish this by supplying a Zend_Db_Select object.

By supplying a Zend_Db_Select object to the Zend_Paginator, you enable it to query only the number of records you need to display in a single page. This reduces the amount of time it takes to load a page.

Let's update the previous example to query the database to fetch the artist from the database instead of using an array. Open the ArtistController.php file and update the code, as shown in Listing 5-40.

**Listing 5-40.** *Using Zend_Db_Select with Zend_Paginator*

```
/**
 * Display all the Artists in the system.
 */
public function listAction(){

  $currentPage = 1;
  //Check if the user is not on page 1
  $i = $this->_request->getQuery('i');

  if(!empty($i)){ //Where i is the current page

    $currentPage = $this->_request->getQuery('i');

  }

  //Create Db object
  require_once "Db/Db_Db.php";
  $db = Db_Db::conn();

  //Create a Zend_Db_Select object
  $sql = new Zend_Db_Select($db);

  //Define columns to retrieve as well as the table.
  $columns  = array("id", "artist_name");
  $table    = array("artists");

  //SELECT `artists`.`id`, `artists`.`artist_name` FROM `artists`
  $statement = $sql->from($table, $columns);

  //Initialize the Zend_Paginator
  $paginator = Zend_Paginator::factory($statement);
```

```
//Set the properties for the pagination
$paginator->setItemCountPerPage(10);
$paginator->setPageRange(3);
$paginator->setCurrentPageNumber($currentPage);

$this->view->paginator = $paginator;

}
```

The updated listAction() shown in Listing 5-40 demonstrates how you can implement the Zend_Db_Select object previously covered in this chapter in conjunction with Zend_Paginator to fetch and paginate the result set.

Start by setting the default $currentPage value. If the user does not supply a value for the variable i in the URL, use this default value. After setting the $currentPage value, load the database model and create a Zend_Db_Adaptor_Pdo_Mysql object. With the adaptor created, create the SELECT statement using the Zend_Db_Select object. The SELECT statement will fetch the ID, artist_name, and genre for each artist in the artists table. You instantiate the Zend_Paginator object and pass in the object into its constructor, set the properties you want, and finally create the $paginator view variable.

To get the artist's name in list.phtml, you need to access the array containing it. Therefore, change the foreach() loop to the following:

```
foreach($this->paginator as $item){
echo "<tr><td>".$item["artist_name"]."</td></tr>";
}
```

Load the URL http://localhost/artist/list to view the paginated result set of the query. If you do not have any artists in the table, add a few for testing.

## Summary

This chapter covered the implementations of CRUD using Zend Framework. The INSERT statements insert records into a database, fetch statements return records, DELETE statements remove records in the tables, and UPDATE statements update records. All these functions were covered using little or no SQL.

The chapter also covered transaction controls that allow you to roll back any changes that are made to the database if the code encounters any errors along the way. You also learned how to construct an object-oriented statement using the Zend_Db_Select object and why it's beneficial to do so. The chapter ended with the Zend_Paginator component (creating examples using a simple array and a database result set).

■ ■ ■

# CHAPTER 6

# Sending and Receiving E-mail

Any cool web site contains an e-mail process that interacts with the user in one form or another: a sign-up welcome e-mail, a newsletter, or a barrage of junk mail. I'm sure you've seen them all. No matter which flavor of e-mail you prefer, it has come a long way since the early days of the Web, when text e-mail was the only type you could receive.

This chapter will cover how Zend Framework not only sends the standard text based e-mail but also how it implements MIME types to send HTML messages. Almost every modern web site uses them to communicate effectively with each user in the system—with newsletters or personalized e-mail concerning what the user likes. You will also learn how to determine whether a host accepts e-mail, which is useful when validating an e-mail address; focus on exception handling for times when something unforeseen occurs; and see how to attach files to your e-mail using Zend Framework.

This chapter also builds on the main application: the LoudBite application. You'll expand on the AccountController class by creating a welcome e-mail and then an activation e-mail. You'll then create an HTML newsletter to send to users. For personalizing e-mail, you'll create a newsletter using HTML that is geared to target each user's taste.

The plan is to have you quickly create e-mail messages and then create a small scripts to send the e-mail off to your users using Zend_Mail. This will prepare you for any quick projects you're working on where Zend_Mail can lend a hand. So let's get to it.

## Setting Up Mail

A brief word before you dive into the guts of the chapter. Like all the chapters so far, you'll create many examples. To fully see the complete process from creating your e-mail script to receiving the e-mail, you need access to a mail server or an account with any e-mail service such as (but not limited to) Yahoo, GMail, AOL, Hotmail. Not having access to a mail server is like going to a music concert and staying outside to listen to the band while your friends are inside having a great time. You don't get the full experience.

If you have an account with a web hosting company, you're in luck because most web hosting companies have a mail server you can use. Set up a Zend Framework project in your hosted environment and then continue on to the next section. If you have an e-mail address, you'll need your e-mail service SMTP, POP3 or IMAP information along with your account authentication information. Lucky for you, the SMTP, POP3, and IMAP information for the most popular services is covered later in this chapter. Everyone else should continue creating the examples or contact one of the e-mail services mentioned for a free e-mail account. It's not a requirement to have an e-mail or a mail server while reading this chapter, but it is recommended.

## What Is Zend_Mail?

With the "heads up" out of way let's talk a bit about Zend_Mail, the e-mail component of Zend Framework.

Zend_Mail contains easy-to-use features that otherwise would take an expert PHP developer to create and implement. A quick look at what you can do shows how powerful this component is:

- Send e-mail using Sendmail, SMTP

- Receive e-mail using POP3, IMAP

- Send text-based e-mail

- Send HTML–based e-mail

- Use all e-mail functionality (Set Subject, Set BCC, Set CC)

- Attach files to e-mail messages

By default, Zend_Mail uses Sendmail because Zend_Mail is a wrapper for the PHP mail function. Let's get to the first example on how to use different transport protocols to send an e-mail.

# Sending Your First E-mail

Sending your first Zend_Mail e-mail is a fun task because it's a very simple task. In this example, you'll create a very basic e-mail containing the message, "Hey, this is an e-mail message created by Zend_Mail!", and send it off to a personal e-mail box (whether it's a Yahoo!, GMail, or Hotmail e-mail account). You'll initially use Sendmail and then Simple Mail Transfer Protocol (SMTP), a protocol to send e-mail.

Because these examples are not part of the larger application you're creating, you need a new controller. Create the controller EmailController.php by either executing the Zend_Tool command zf create controller email within your project to create the controller or by manually creating the file inside your application/controllers directory and then copying the PHP code shown in Listing 6-1.

**Listing 6-1.** *EmailController.php*

```php
<?php
/**
 * Email Controller.  Contains all Chapter 6 examples.
 *
 * @author <Your Name Here>, <Your Email Address>
 * @package Beginning_Zend_Framework
 */
class EmailController extends Zend_Controller_Action
{

  public function init()
  {
    /* Initialize action controller here */
  }

  public function indexAction()
  {
    // action body
  }
```

```
}
```

The controller shown is simply a shell that will eventually contain all of the chapter's examples. Now add the action sendMailAction, as shown in Listing 6.2, to the controller EmailController.

***Listing 6-2.*** *EmailController.php with sendmailAction()*

```php
<?php
/**
 * Email Controller.  Contains all Chapter 6 examples.
 *
 * @author <Your Name Here>, <Your Email Address>
 * @package Beginning_Zend_Framework
 */
class EmailController extends Zend_Controller_Action
{

  public function init()
  {
    /* Initialize action controller here */
  }

  public function indexAction()
  {
    // action body
  }



  /**
   * Basic example using default settings.
   *
   */
  public function sendMailAction()
  {

    //Send out the welcome message
    $MailObj     = new Zend_Mail();
    $emailMessage = "Hey, this is a Zend_Mail–created e-mail!";
    $fromEmail    = "<FROM_EMAIL_ADDRESS>";
    $fromFullName = "<FROM_FULL_NAME>";
```

```
$to        = "<YOUR_EMAIL_HERE>";
$subject     = "This is an example";

$MailObj->setBodyText($emailMessage);
$MailObj->setFrom($fromEmail, $fromFullName);
$MailObj->addTo($to);
$MailObj->setSubject($subject);

try{

    $MailObj->send();
    echo "E-mail sent successfully";

}catch(Zend_Mail_Exception $e){
    //Your Error message here.
}

//Suppress the view.
$this->_helper->viewRenderer->setNoRender();

    }


}
```

Listing 6-2 demonstrates setting and sending an e-mail using Zend_Mail and handling exceptions. This example begins by instantiating a Zend_Mail object and storing it in the $MailObj variable. . If you aren't using Zend_Loader, you'll need to include the Zend/Mail.php file. You then use the $MailObj setters to set the from address, name of the person/company sending the e-mail, to address, subject, and message body (as text instead of HTML, which I'll cover later in this chapter). Finally, encase the send() method in a try-catch that will catch any Zend_Mail–specific errors using Zend_Mail_Exception. Zend_Mail_Exception provides the standard exception methods getMessage(), getTrace(), and so on.

If you are on a web host or have a mail server on your computer, pull up the URL http://localhost/email/send-mail. The sendMail action will execute, send out the e-mail, and then display the success message "E-mail sent successfully." Let's now see how to expand this example to use SMTP.

## Sending E-mail Using SMTP

Zend_Mail comes with the option to send e-mail using SMTP. It wraps SMTP functionality using the Zend_Mail_Transport_Smtp class, which allows you to set the SMTP host as well as set the authentication information required to connect to the SMTP host.

Using Listing 6-2, let's expand the code to use an SMTP host of your choosing. (The most popular e-mail service settings are shown in Table 6-1.)

**Table 6-1.** *Popular E-mail Host Information*

| Service | SMTP | POP3 | IMAP |
|---------|------|------|------|
| Yahoo | smtp.mail.yahoo.com (port 465, use SSL, use authentication) | pop.mail.yahoo.com (port 995) | N/A |
| GMail | smtp.gmail.com (SSL-enabled, port 465 or 587) | pop.gmail.com (SSL-enabled, port 995) | N/A |
| AOL | smtp.aol.com | N/A | imap.aol.com (port 143) |

You'll create a new action called smtpSendMailAction() in your EmailController file. The action will set the SMTP information, set the e-mail values, inform Zend_Mail to use the SMTP mail server, and finally send the e-mail. The updated code is shown in Listing 6-3.

**Listing 6-3.** *EmailController.php with smtpSendMailAction()*

```php
<?php
/**
 * Email Controller.  Contains all Chapter 6 examples.
 *
 * @author <Your Name Here>, <Your Email Address>
 * @package Beginning_Zend_Framework
 */
class EmailController extends Zend_Controller_Action
{

  public function init()
  {
    /* Initialize action controller here */
  }

  public function indexAction()
  {
    // action body
  }


  /**
   * Basic example using default settings.
   *
```

```php
    */
    public function sendMailAction()
    {

        //Send out the welcome message
        $MailObj     = new Zend_Mail();
        $emailMessage = "Hey, this is a Zend_Mail–created e-mail!";
        $fromEmail    = "FROM_EMAIL_ADDRESS";
        $fromFullName = "FROM_FULL_NAME";
        $to           = "YOUR_EMAIL_HERE";
        $subject      = "This is an example";

        $MailObj->setBodyText($emailMessage);
        $MailObj->setFrom($fromEmail, $fromFullName);
        $MailObj->addTo($to);
        $MailObj->setSubject($subject);

        try{

            $MailObj->send();
            echo "Email sent successfully";

        }catch(Zend_Mail_Exception $e){
            //Your Error message here.
        }

        //Suppress the view.
        $this->_helper->viewRenderer->setNoRender();

    }

    /**
     * Send email using SMTP Host.
     *
     */
    public function smtpSendMailAction()
    {

        //Create SMTP connection Object
        $configInfo = array('auth'    => 'login',
                    'ssl'    => 'tls',
```

```
                   'username' => '<YOUR ACCOUNT USERNAME>',
                   'password' => '<YOUR SMTP ACCOUNT PASSWORD>',
                   'port'    => '<SMTP PORT NUMBER>');
 $smtpHost  = new Zend_Mail_Transport_Smtp('<SMTP HOST>',
                         $configInfo);


    //Create Zend_Mail object.
    $MailObj = new Zend_Mail();

    //Initialize parameters.
    $emailMessage = "Hey, this is a Zend_Mail–created e-mail!";
    $fromEmail   = "FROM_EMAIL_ADDRESS";
    $fromFullName = "FROM_FULL_NAME";
    $to        = "YOUR_EMAIL_HERE";
    $subject    = "This is an example";

    $MailObj->setBodyText($emailMessage);
    $MailObj->setFrom($fromEmail, $fromFullName);
    $MailObj->addTo($to);
    $MailObj->setSubject($subject);



    //Send Email using transport protocol.
    try{

      $MailObj->send($smtpHost);
       echo "Email sent successfully";

    }catch(Zend_Mail_Exception $e){
      //Your error message here.
       echo $e->getMessage();
    }

    //Suppress the view.
    $this->_helper->viewRenderer->setNoRender();

  }
}
```

Let's go over the important sections in the code shown in Listing 6-3. The action starts with initializing SMTP authentication information by creating a key-value array: $configInfo. The array sets the authentication type, the type of SSL to use, username, password, and port number to use. If your ISP does not support SSL authentication or a port number, you can remove the ssl and port key-value from $configInfo.

The values used in the code can be found on your e-mail service provider's web site. Once the configuration values are set, you can create the Zend_Mail_Transport_Smtp object by passing in the SMTP hostname as the initial value and the configuration information as the second value.

---

■ **Note** The e-mail settings can also be set as instance properties of the controller and reused throughout the code. They are defined in the action method for your reference and to demonstrate that they do not necessarily have to be class-level settings.

---

Now for the important question. How do you inform Zend_Mail to use the SMTP information you set? Easy! Pass in the Zend_Mail_Transport_Smtp object into the send() method.

---

■ **Note** If you are not using autoload, you must include Zend/Mail/Transport/Smtp.php for the example to work.

---

Load the URL http://localhost/email/smtp-send-mail. Once the URL completely loads, you will see the e-mail message, "E-mail sent successfully" and will receive an e-mail with the message "Hey, this is a Zend_Mail-created e-mail."

# Setting More than One Recipient: Cc: and Bcc:

There are projects that require you to send an e-mail to a recipient and a copy of the e-mail to another recipient. The addCc() and addBcc() methods allow you to do just that. Let's continue building on the previous examples in this chapter by expanding smtpSendMailAction() and creating a new action named sendEmailWithCopyAction().

## Adding a Cc:

The addCc() method allows you to copy anyone by passing in two parameters: the e-mail address of the user you want to send a copy of the e-mail to and a string representing the name of the person.

Open the file EmailController.php, add the sendEmailWithCopyAction() action, and add the code shown in Listing 6-4. The new action will send an e-mail to two e-mail accounts using SMTP and the addCc() Zend_Mail method. For the sake of not being redundant, I'm displaying only the action along with the modified items from the code copied from the action smtpSendMailAction().

**Listing 6-4.** *Adding a Cc*

```
/**
 * Send email using SMTP Host and CC.
 *
```

```
*/
public function sendEmailWithCopyAction()
{

    ...

    $MailObj->setBodyText($emailMessage);
    $MailObj->setFrom($fromEmail, $fromFullName);
    $MailObj->addTo($to);
    $MailObj->addCc('<SECONDARY EMAIL>', '<SECONDARY NAME>');
    $MailObj->setSubject($subject);

    ...

}
```

The new action contains only one modification: the new line $MailObj->addCC().Use addCc() when the original recipient knows that a secondary user will also receive the e-mail. Using Cc, all recipients of the e-mail will see each others' e-mail address in the header.

## Adding More than One Cc

To add multiple recipients, continue invoking the addCC() method for each e-mail address you want to Cc, as shown in Listing 6-5.

*Listing 6-5. Adding Multiple CC E-mail*

```
/**
 * Send email using SMTP Host and CC.
 *
 */
public function sendEmailWithCopyAction()
{

    ...

    $MailObj->setBodyText($emailMessage);
    $MailObj->setFrom($fromEmail, $fromFullName);
    $MailObj->addTo($to);
    $MailObj->addCc('<SECONDARY EMAIL>', '<SECONDARY NAME>');
    $MailObj->addCc('<THIRD EMAIL>', '<THIRD NAME>');
```

```
$MailObj->setSubject($subject);

    …

}
```

# Adding a Bcc:

Hiding the additional recipient from the e-mail header can be done by using the addBcc() method. The addBcc() method acts in the same way as entering an e-mail address into the Bcc: field of the e-mail client. It will send a copy of the e-mail, but not display the additional e-mail addresses that were blind copied to everyone.

Unlike addCc(), addBcc()accepts only a single string parameter representing the e-mail address. Let's update the code in Listing 6-5 and replace all addCc() method calls with addBcc(), as shown in Listing 6-6.

***Listing 6-6.** Adding Bcc E-mail*

```
/**
 * Send email using SMTP Host and BCC.
 *
 */
public function sendEmailWithCopyAction(){

    …

    $MailObj->setBodyText($emailMessage);
    $MailObj->setFrom($fromEmail, $fromFullName);
    $MailObj->addTo($to);
    $MailObj->addBcc('<SECONDARY EMAIL>');
    $MailObj->addBcc('<THIRD EMAIL>');

    $MailObj->setSubject($subject);

    …

}
```

Save the file, replace the markers with valid e-mail addresses you have access to, and run the action by loading the URL http://localhost/email/send-email-with-copy. Once the e-mail arrives to the e-mail address specified in the addTo() method, take a look at the headers. You should not see any additional e-mail addresses used in the addBcc() methods. Now that you understand the basics, you're now ready to send HTML e-mail and attach files to them.

# Additional E-mail Getters and Setters

You might have other needs for your e-mail functionality, so Table 6-2 shows a few extra setter and getter methods that allow you to set information for the Zend_Mail object.

**Table 6-2.** *Zend_Mail Getters and Setters*

| Method Name | Description |
| --- | --- |
| setBodyHtml() | Allows you to set the body of the e-mail. It will send out the e-mail as a HTML-based mail. |
| setDate() | Sets the date for the e-mail message. |
| setFrom() | Sets the from address and name. |
| setMimeBoundary() | Sets the MIME boundary to use in the e-mail message. |
| setReturnPath() | Sets the Return-Path header for the e-mail message. |
| setSubject() | Sets the subject of the e-mail. The parameter is a string. |
| setType() | Sets the MIME type of the message. It can be used when sending attachments. |
| getBodyHtml() | Returns the HTML used by the e-mail. |
| getBodyText() | Returns the string used by the e-mail. |
| getCharset() | Returns the character set of the e-mail. |
| getDate() | Returns the date of the e-mail. |
| getFrom() | Returns the e-mail address used in the setFrom() function. |
| getHeaders() | Returns the mail headers. |
| getMimeBoundary() | Returns any information that was present in the setMimeBoundary(). |
| getPartCount() | Returns the number of message parts. |
| getRecipients() | Returns an array of e-mail addresses which will be used to send the e-mail to. |
| getReturnPath() | Returns the value of the Return-Path header. |

*(Continued)*

| | |
|---|---|
| getSubject() | Returns the subject of the e-mail. |
| getType() | Returns the content type of the e-mail message. |

# HTML E-mail

Sometimes you'll want to send out HTML-based e-mail (I've had numerous requests for this feature). Sometimes clients want to create a full-blown ad campaign; other times they just want to have an e-mail look a certain way in terms of bold text, highlighted information, blinking neon signs, and so on. You get the idea. When such a request comes in, I look into my bag of tricks, see old code I already wrote, and then implement the solution. The problem with this solution is that the code often might be out-of-date in terms of security, efficiency, and being bug-free. So you can use Zend_Mail.

With Zend Framework, sending HTML-based e-mail is an easy process that should not take you more than a few seconds to create and implement using the method setBodyHtml().

Open the EmailController and create a new action sendHtmlEmailAction(), as shown in Listing 6-7.

**Listing 6-7.** *Sending HTML-based E-mail*

```
/**
 * Send HTML based email.
 *
 */
public function sendHtmlEmailAction(){

    //Create SMTP connection
    $configInfo = array('auth'     => 'login',
                'ssl'     => 'tls',
                'username' => '<YOUR ACCOUNT USERNAME>',
                'password' => '<YOUR SMTP ACCOUNT PASSWORD>',
                'port'    => '<SMTP PORT NUMBER>');
    $smtpHost  = new Zend_Mail_Transport_Smtp('<SMTP HOST>',
                        $configInfo);

    //Create Zend_Mail object.
    $MailObj = new Zend_Mail();

    $message     = "<h1>Welcome to the example</h1><br>" .
            "<p>An example email.</p>";

    //Initialize parameters.
```

```
$fromEmail   = "FROM_EMAIL_ADDRESS";
$fromFullName = "FROM_FULL_NAME";
$to       = "YOUR_EMAIL_HERE";
$subject    = "This is an example";

$MailObj->setBodyHtml($message);
$MailObj->setFrom($fromEmail, $fromFullName);
$MailObj->addTo($to);
$MailObj->setSubject($subject);

//Send Email using transport protocol.
try{

   $MailObj->send($smtpHost);
   echo "Email sent successfully";

}catch(Zend_Mail_Exception $e){
   //Your Error message here.
}

//Suppress the view.
$this->_helper->viewRenderer->setNoRender();

}
```

At this point, the code looks fairly familiar. It should: it's almost the exact same code that was used in the last few examples. You have to initialize a variable, $MailObj, to create an instance of the Zend_Mail class, which enables you to set up e-mail information such as the recipient, sender, and body of the e-mail. Right before you send out the e-mail, however, there is something you might see that is out of place. Instead of the setBodyText() method you have grown to love, use setBodyHtml(). This method allows you to send HTML messages to the user very easily. There's none of the hassle of changing the MIME type for the display—Zend Framework does it all on its own. That's it! You can now send out HTML-based e-mail.

# E-mail Attachments

The next step should logically be a closer look at the power of Zend Framework, let's take a look at creating an e-mail with attachments. You'll create an e-mail that attaches an image. The techniques discussed in this section can also be applied to other types of files.

## Image File Attachment

Zend_Mail allows you to attach most types of files to e-mail by invoking the createAttachment() method, which accepts four parameters:

createAttachment($fileContent, $mimeType, $disposition, $encoding)

The initial required parameter is the content of the file that is read using PHP's built-in fread() function. The remaining three parameters are optional. The second parameter accepts a string representing the file MIME type. Typical string values are image/gif or application/msword. By specifying the third parameter, the disposition type, you can inform the e-mail client if the attached file content should appear in the e-mail body when the e-mail is opened (Zend_Mime:DISPOSITION_INLINE) or as an icon/link that allows the user to download the file (Zend_Mime::DISPOSITION_ATTACHMENT). The final parameter is the encoding type. Acceptable values are shown in Table 6-3; by default the encoding type is set to base 64.

---

■ **Note** A good online resource containing a list of MIME types is available at http://www.webmaster-toolkit.com/mime-types.shtml.

---

*Table 6-3.* *Encoding Values*

| Zend Constant | Description |
| --- | --- |
| Zend_Mime::ENCODING_7BIT | 7 bit encoding |
| Zend_Mime::ENCODING_8BIT | 8 bit encoding |
| Zend_Mime::ENCODING_QUOTEDPRINTABLE | Quoted Printable |
| Zend_Mime::ENCODING_BASE64 | Base 64 encoding |

In the following example, you'll create an e-mail and attach an image using three parameters, as shown in Listing 6-8. This example will read a binary file such as an image and attach it to the e-mail before sending it to the recipient.

Open the EmailController once more and add the new action sendEmailWithAttachmentAction().

*Listing 6-8.* *Sending an E-mail with an Attachment*

```
/**
 * Send out email with attachment
 *
 */
public function sendEmailWithAttachmentAction()
{

    //Create SMTP connection
    $configInfo = array('auth'    => 'login',
```

```
                   'ssl'     => 'tls',
                   'username' => '<YOUR ACCOUNT USERNAME>',
                   'password' => '<YOUR SMTP ACCOUNT PASSWORD>',
                   'port'    => '<SMTP PORT NUMBER>');

$smtpHost  = new Zend_Mail_Transport_Smtp('<SMTP HOST>',
                            $configInfo);


//Create Zend_Mail object.
$MailObj = new Zend_Mail();

$message = "<h1>Welcome to the example</h1>".
     "<br><p>An example email.</p>";

//Read image data.
$fileLocation = '<PATH TO YOUR FILE>';

   //Check if the file exists and is readable
if(!$fileHandler = fopen($fileLocation, 'rb')){

   throw new Exception("The file could not be
         found or is not readable.");

}

$fileContent = fread($fileHandler, filesize($fileLocation));
fflush($fileHandler);
fclose($fileHandler);

//Initialize parameters.
$fromEmail   = "<FROM_EMAIL_ADDRESS>";
$fromFullName = "<FROM_FULL_NAME>";
$to        = "<YOUR_EMAIL_HERE>";
$subject     = "This is an example";


$MailObj->setBodyHtml($message);
$MailObj->setFrom($fromEmail, $fromFullName);
$MailObj->addTo($to);
$MailObj->setSubject($subject);
```

```
$MailObj->createAttachment($fileContent,
            '<MIME TYPE OF FILE>',
            Zend_Mime::DISPOSITION_ATTACHMENT);



//Send Email using transport protocol.
try{

  $MailObj->send($smtpHost);
  echo "Email sent successfully";

}catch(Zend_Mail_Exception $e){

  //Your Error message here.
  echo $e->getMessage();

}

//Suppress the view.
$this->_helper->viewRenderer->setNoRender();


}
```

The example shown in Listing 6-8 begins like all the other examples in this chapter. You create an instance of Zend_Mail_Transport_Smtp, create an instance of Zend_Mail, and initialize and set all recipient information. But then you use PHP's fread() function to read a file. You should specifically use fread() because it reads binary data. This binary data is the content that will be used in the createAttachment() method. For portability issues, set both r and b values. Once you read the content from the binary file, save the content into the $fileContent variable, flush the output buffer, and close the file handler because you no longer need the file functionality. After setting the recipient information, make a call to createAttachment(). Using the content read from the file, pass in the $fileContent variable as the initial value and specify the second parameter with the MIME type of the file. The third parameter is set to Zend_Mime::DISPOSITION_ATTACHMENT, allowing the browser to know how the attachment should be shown. If you did not specify a MIME type by default, Zend_Mail assumes that the attachment is a binary with a MIME type of application/octet-stream.

Try sending yourself an e-mail with a photo of your favorite band or your dog by updating the placeholders in the code shown in Listing 6-8 and loading the URL http://localhost/email/send-email-with-attachment.

## Validating E-mail Addresses

So far, you've seen how to send e-mail, use SMTP, and attach files to the e-mail. Now focus your attention on validating the format of the e-mail and verifying whether the host actually accepts e-mail. This is useful when you want to limit the amount of bounced-back e-mail or want to stop users dead in their tracks if they supply a false e-mail.

To look at this feature, you have to step away from Zend_Mail and reference the Zend_Validate component of Zend Framework (covered in Chapter 4). I thought it would be best to discuss it here because it deals with e-mail.

Although Zend_Validate contains many validation classes, the important one for this chapter is Zend_Validate_EmailAddress. Using Zend_Validate_EmailAddress you can not only validate the format of the e-mail but also determine whether the host accepts e-mail by checking the DNS entry for the host and verifying whether the Mail Exchange (MX) entry is present. If the MX entry is not present, the host does not accept e-mail.

What does this mean? Using a simple example, if you send an e-mail to dummyaccount101@yahoo.com, Zend_Validate_EmailAddress , you can validate the format of the e-mail and also verify that the host yahoo.com actually accepts e-mail. What you can't do is verify that the specific e-mail exists at yahoo.com.

To use the validation, Zend_Validate_EmailAddress can turn on MX verification by either using its setValidateMx() method or by setting the second parameter in its constructor to either true or false. Windows users were left out in the cold again; this feature works only for Unix systems. Let's see this in action now.

Open the EmailController.php file and update the smtpSendMailAction() action, as shown in Listing 6-9. You'll validate and verify that the e-mail address is valid and that the host can receive e-mail.

**Listing 6-9.** *Verifying E-mail Address Using Zend_Validate_EmailAddress*

```
/**
 * Send email using SMTP Host.
 * Validate e-email address.
 *
 */
public function smtpSendMailAction()
{
  //Create SMTP connection
  $configInfo = array('auth'     => 'login',
             'ssl'      => 'tls',
             'username' => '<YOUR ACCOUNT USERNAME>',
             'password' => '<YOUR SMTP ACCOUNT PASSWORD>',
             'port'     => '<SMTP PORT NUMBER>');

  $smtpHost   = new Zend_Mail_Transport_Smtp('<SMTP HOST>',
                          $configInfo);

  //Create Zend_Mail object.
  $MailObj = new Zend_Mail();


  //Initialize parameters.
  $emailMessage = "Hey, this is a Zend_Mail–created e-mail!";
```

```php
$fromEmail    = "<FROM_EMAIL_ADDRESS>";
$fromFullName = "<FROM_FULL_NAME>";
$to           = "<YOUR_EMAIL_HERE>";
$subject      = "This is an example";

//Check if email is valid.
$validator = new Zend_Validate_EmailAddress(
        Zend_Validate_Hostname::ALLOW_DNS,
        true);

if($validator->isValid($to)){

    $MailObj->setBodyText($emailMessage);
    $MailObj->setFrom($fromEmail, $fromFullName);
    $MailObj->addTo($to);
    $MailObj->setSubject($subject);

    //Send Email using transport protocol.
    try{

        $MailObj->send($smtpHost);
        echo "Email sent successfully";

    }catch(Zend_Mail_Exception $e){

        //Your Error message here.
        echo $e->getMessage();

    }

}else{

    //Messages in array.
    $messages = $validator->getMessages();
    foreach($messages as $message){
        echo $message.'<br/>';
    }
}
```

```
//Suppress the view.
$this->_helper->viewRenderer->setNoRender();
}
```

Listing 6-9 expands on the previous example by validating the e-mail supplied in the to field. You start by instantiating a Zend_Validate_EmailAddress object, $validator, and supplying two parameters: the initial parameter will invoke the validation of the hostname using Zend_Validate_Hostname, and the second parameter will enable MX verification. You then use the validator object's isValid() method to determine whether the e-mail is valid. If it is valid, continue delivering the e-mail; otherwise, print out the error messages.

---

■ **Caution** If you are not using autoload, you must include Zend/Mail.php, Zend/Mail/Transport/Smtp.php, and Zend/Validate/EmailAddress.php to run the example.

---

Try it for yourself. Use a few combinations of the e-mail address to check for both the format as well as verify whether the hostname accepts e-mail by loading the URL http://localhost/email/smtp-send-mail.

Congratulations! You can now call yourself an expert at sending e-mail using Zend_Mail. If you've been following along with the application, you can either continue or head to the next chapter.

# Sending LoudBite E-mail

You'll continue expanding the music application. You'll create a few simple e-mail messages and keep implementing e-mail on the site in an object-oriented fashion. You'll create the welcome e-mail that users receive when they activate their account and the activation e-mail that is sent out to validate that the address entered during sign-up indeed works.

## Welcome E-mail

In a previous chapter, you had the user sign up for an account, and the system saved the user's account information. Not much fun and not that interactive with the user. You probably thought of a few questions after running through this process, such as "How do users know they really signed up?" or "Can't I use a form of activation to make sure that I have a legitimate e-mail address?" Both these questions are valid, which is why I'll answer them now.

It's now standard practice for users who sign up on web sites to receive an e-mail telling them how wonderful they are for joining the new application. To keep up with the times, this application will do the same. Users will sign up, and a welcome e-mail will be sent. But before users can continue, they have to activate their account.

For starters, open the AccountController.php file you created in Chapter 3. You'll focus on the successAction() method for this example and make the changes highlighted in Listing 6-10.

**Listing 6-10.** *The successAction() of the AccountController Sends the E-mail*

```
/**
 * Process Sign up Form.
 *
 */
public function successAction()
{

    //Get the signup form
    $form = $this->getSignupForm();

    //Check if the submitted data is POST type
    if($form->isValid($_POST)){

      $email    = $form->getValue("email");
      $username = $form->getValue("username");
      $password = $form->getValue("password");

      //Set the database parameters as described in Chapter 5

      try{

          //Save the user to the database as described in Chapter 5

//Send out the welcome email.
$config = array('ssl' => 'tls', 'auth' => 'login',
           'username' => '<your SMTP username>',
           'password' => '<your SMTP password>');

$transport = new Zend_Mail_Transport_Smtp
(
 '<your SMTP host>',
  $config
);

$MailObj = new Zend_Mail();
$emailMessage = " Welcome to LoudBite.com.";
$fromEmail    = "welcomeparty@loudbite.com";
$fromFullName = "LoudBite.com";
```

```
$to       = "$email";
$subject  = "Welcome to LoudBite.com";

$MailObj->setBodyText($emailMessage);
$MailObj->setFrom($fromEmail, $fromFullName);
$MailObj->addTo($to);
$MailObj->setSubject($subject);
$MailObj->send($transport);

      }catch(Zend_Db_Exception $e){
        echo $e->getMessage();
      }
    }else{
      $this->view->errors = $form->getMessages();
      $this->view->form = $form;
    }
  }
```

Take a minute to look over the code. It's not that different from the basic e-mail you set up in the opening of this chapter. It has the from address and the e-mail you're sending it to, but no text yet. You then set all the information you'll use in the Zend_Mail class here.

Save the file and try to sign up with a valid e-mail address that you can access and has not been added to the database, or simply remove the account from your database accounts table. If all went well and your e-mail server isn't buggy, you should receive the e-mail.

## Activation E-mail

Next is the activation e-mail, which contains information on how users can activate their account. It's essentially an evolution of the welcome e-mail.

The activation e-mail allows you to keep the pool of active users as real as possible. Without the e-mail activation, anyone could sign up with a nonworking e-mail address, and the user base would contain only junk and filler accounts. To implement the activation feature, create the activation e-mail to contain a URL that a user can click. When users click or copy the link into their browser and load it, they automatically activate their account.

Let's see what the code looks like and put it into practice. You'll focus again on the AccountController.php file using the activateAction() method (see Listing 6-11).

**Listing 6-11.** *activateAction() Sends the Activation E-mail*

```
/**
 * Process Sign up Form.
 *
 */
public function successAction()
{
```

```
$form = $this->getSignupForm();

//Check if the submitted data is POST type
if($form->isValid($_POST)){

    $email    = $form->getValue("email");
    $username = $form->getValue("username");
    $password = $form->getValue("password");

    //Set the database parameters

    try{
        //Insert the user into the database

//Send out thank you email.
$config = array('ssl' => 'tls', 'auth' => 'login',
            'username' => '<your SMTP username>',
            'password' => '<your SMTP password>');

$transport = new Zend_Mail_Transport_Smtp
('<your SMTP host>', $config);

//Set the user's email address
$to = $email;

//Prepare the welcome email
$MailObj = new Zend_Mail();
$subject     = "Welcome to LoudBite.com";
$emailMessage = "Welcome to LoudBite.com. " .
        "We've sent you a separate
         activation email.";
$fromEmail    = "welcomeparty@loudbite.com";
$fromFullName = "LoudBite.com";

//Prepare the activation email
$subjectActivation = "Activate your LoudBite.com account";
$emailActivationMessage =
  "Thanks for taking the time to join LoudBite.com.
  What you do now is up to you.
  You can ignore this email and you won't have
```

access to the best music mashup site in town
or you can click on the link below to
activate your account...
The choice is up to you.

```
http://localhost/account/activate?email=".$email;

$fromActivationEmail    = "activation@loudbite.com";
$fromActivationFullName = "LoudBite.com Activation";

//Send the welcome email
$MailObj->setBodyText($emailMessage);
$MailObj->setFrom($fromEmail, $fromFullName);
$MailObj->addTo($to);
$MailObj->setSubject($subject);
$MailObj->send($transport);

//Send the activation email
$MailObj = new Zend_Mail();
$MailObj->setBodyText($emailActivationMessage);
$MailObj->setFrom(
        $fromActivationEmail,
        $fromActivationFullName);
$MailObj->addTo($to);
$MailObj->setSubject($subjectActivation);
$MailObj->send($transport);
        }catch(Zend_Db_Exception $e){

          echo $e->getMessage();

        }
    }else{

      $this->view->errors = $form->getMessages();
      $this->view->form = $form;

    }
}


/**
```

```
 * Activate account.
 *
 */
public function activateAction()
{

    //Fetch the email to update from the query param 'email'
    $emailToActivate = $this->_request->getQuery("email");

    //Create a db object
    require_once "Db/Db.php";
    $db = Db_Db::conn();

    try{

        //Check if the user is in the system
        $statement = "SELECT COUNT(id) AS total From Accounts
                WHERE email = '".$emailToActivate."'
                AND status = 'pending'";

        $results = $db->fetchOne($statement);

        //If we have at least one row then the user's
        //email is valid.
        if($results == 1){

            //Activate the account.
            $conditions[] = "email = '".$emailToActivate."'";

            //Updates to commit
            $updates = array("status" => 'active');
            $results = $db->update('Accounts',
                            $updates,
                            $conditions);

            //Set activate flag to true
            $this->view->activated = true;

        }else{

            //Set activate flag to false
```

```
$this->view->activated = false;

    }

  }catch(Zend_Db_Exception $e){

    throw new Exception($e);

  }

}
```

In the updated successAction() method, the system sends the user two e-mail messages. Note that a single SMTP connection was used in this example, but you have to use a new Zend_Mail object for each e-mail message. In the activation e-mail, the user will click on the link, and the system will call activateAction() in the AccountController.

In the updated action, you set all the variables you want to use; the only thing that changes in this case is the e-mail message you want to display to the user. Now let's create the view for the activateAction() method.

Create a new file, activate.phtml, inside the views/scripts/account directory and copy the code shown in Listing 6-12.

**Listing 6-12.** *View for activateAction() Method*

```php
<?php echo $this->doctype('XHTML1_STRICT'); ?>
<html xmlns="http://www.w3.org/1999/xhtml" xml:lang="en" lang="en">
<head>
  <?php echo $this->headTitle('LoudBite.com – Account Activation'); ?>
</head>
<body>

  <?php echo $this->render("includes/header.phtml"); ?>
  <h3>Account Activation</h3>
  <?php
  if($this->activated){

    echo "Thank you. Your account has now been activated.";

  }else{

    echo "We're sorry, please sign up for an account.
      <a href='/account/new'>Click here to sign up</a>";
```

```
    }
    ?>
```

```
</body>
</html>
```

Once the activate.phtml file is created, try to sign up yet again and go through the entire process of creating and activating an account.

---

■ **Note** This is one approach to the activation e-mail. Another is to send only the activation e-mail from successAction() and send a confirmation that activation was successful from activateAction(). One is not necessarily better than the other, but I chose this approach to show you how to reuse an SMTP connection.

---

## Summary

This chapter discussed e-mail and how Zend Framework provides support for it using Zend_Mail. In this chapter you learned how to do the following:

- Send e-mail using SMTP

- Use Zend_Mail_Exception to catch any errors

- Add Cc and Bcc e-mail addresses

- Send HTML–based e-mail

- Attach files to an e-mail

- Validate the format of an e-mail

- Verify that a host can actually receive e-mail

- Use exception handling with Zend_Mail.

You also updated the LoudBite application by adding both the welcome e-mail and the activation e-mail.

■ ■ ■

# CHAPTER 7

# Web Services and Feeds

Web services and feeds have become a widely used form of adding depth to online applications. Both technologies provide additional content and functionality that can increase what any application can offer to users. Technology has even reached a point where you can create an application without dealing with any of the heavy lifting that is accompanied with business logic and understanding the domain of the application you intend to create.

Picture walking into a music store with the idea of starting your own rock band. Instead of making your own drums, guitars, and mics, you grab that nice guitar in the corner that everyone had their eyes on, the drum set upstairs, and a few mics because you know that the service providers that produced those products can create far better equipment than you could ever do. Web services and feeds provide the same functionality. They allow you to walk into a figurative music store, pick and choose services and content located around the world and produced by third-party companies that know far more about their domain than you have time for, and mash them all up to create a new product.

This chapter will cover two web service messaging techniques—REST and SOAP—as well as Zend_Rest and Zend_Soap. You will use Zend Framework to create the server and the clients to use the services. You will then cross into the realm of services. You'll look at what web services are, what services Zend Framework contains, and how you can use these services. The chapter closes with feeds and the Zend_Feed component, showing you how to create a feed, how to consume a feed, and how to use the feed content in a view.

## Introducing Web Services

Web services were initially developed at Userland and Microsoft as the XML-Remote Procedure Call (XML-RPC) technology. As the technology evolved, it became what you now know as Simple Object Access Protocol (SOAP), although there are now other approaches to web services that did not evolve from XML-RPC, such as representational state tranfer (REST).

Web services allow developers to easily write applications that are interoperable with external services located anywhere in the world. A PHP application developed in Los Angeles, for example, can easily call and receive a return string from a Java application located in China, making web services platform-independent and location-independent.

Web services are based on the client-server model and contain three primary layers, as shown in Figure 7-1.

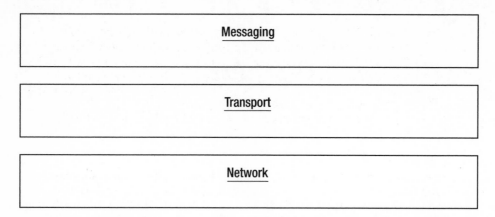

**Figure 7-1.** *Web service stack*

Each of the layers play an important role. The network layer represents the Internet—the layer that the protocols such as HTTP, FTP, and SMTP work in. These protocols represent the transport layer. Using the transport layer you send messages to a web service by calling messaging types such as XML-RPC, SOAP, or REST.

## Web Service Messaging

The messaging layer in the web service stack handles the different ways you can invoke web services. There are many ways of invoking a web service such as a SOAP call or XML-RPC. Even though Zend Framework supports XML-RPC using the Zend_XmlRpc component, in this chapter I'll cover SOAP and REST, the leading web service technologies.

## Representational State Transfer: REST

The leading technology used today to handle web services is representational state transfer (REST) because of its ease of use and stateless nature. REST is not a messaging technology like SOAP; it is a type of software architecture that uses the HTTP protocol. REST clients send GET, PUT, DELETE, and POST requests to a unique service represented by a URI and receive a plain text XML string as a response.

The different types of HTTP requests have all become synonymous with the basic create, read, update, and delete (CRUD) features in a database, as shown in Table 7-1.

**Table 7-1.** *HTTP Methods and Corresponding CRUD Operations*

| HTTP Method | CRUD Operation |
| --- | --- |
| POST | Create |
| GET | Read |
| PUT | Update |
| DELETE | Delete |

If a developer issues a call to a REST service using a GET HTTP request, the service returns a list of content or a list of data. POST requests handle creating new records or updating existing data, PUT requests update records, and DELETE HTTP requests remove data. Of course, the mappings just specified between a request and the action performed on the server don't always match. You might encounter applications that use each request type differently; for example, a PUT HTTP request could be used to create a new record, or a GET HTTP request could be used to delete a record.

Now let's start to work within Zend Framework to see its capability to work with REST.

# Creating a Server

Two main classses, Zend_Rest_Client and Zend_Rest_Server, make up the Zend_Rest component. These classes provide the option to either create a REST client or a server that accepts REST requests. Before you dive into the client and call web services, you'll create your own server, which you'll later use to test the REST client implementations.

Looking under the hood, the Zend_Rest_Server class allows you to specify either a method or a complete class that contains the code to process requests. The Zend_Rest_Server methods, addFunction() and setClass(), provide such features (see Table 7-2). Let's take an example by creating a simple web service that returns a list of artists.

**Table 7-2.** *Zend_Rest_Server Operations*

| Operation | Description |
| --- | --- |
| __construct() | Object constructor. |
| handle() | Specifies how to handle the request. Key-value arrays accepted in the parameter. |
| addFunction() | Specifies a function to add as a web server. Accepts a string value representing the function. |
| getFunctions() | Returns a list of functions that have been fed into the web service using addFunction(). |
| getHeaders() | Returns any extra headers the server has sent. |
| returnResponse() | Determines whether the web service should return a response. |
| setClass() | Specifies a class containing all web services. Accepts a string value representing the class name. |
| setPersistence() | Sets the persistence mode (sets the way the server saves information between requests). |

The web service you will create can be invoked using the service name getartists and will return a SimpleXml object containing information for only one artist: the metal band Poison. To set up the server, you need to create a controller and a model. Create two files: ServicesController.php and Webservices.php. Place the ServicesController.php file inside your application/controllers directory and the WebServices.php file in the new application/models/services/ directory.

The controller will accept all incoming requests to the service URI /services/getartists, while the model will contain the domain logic.

The controller shown in Listing 7-1 is the primary service controller. Each action in the controller represents a service that can be invoked. The getartistsAction() method loads a single file: the file containing the domain logic the web service needs to process and produce a response for the request.

**Listing 7-1.** *ServicesController.php*

```php
<?php
/**
 * ServiceController.php
 *
 * @author <Your name>, <Your e-email address>
 */
class ServicesController extends Zend_Controller_Action
{

  public function indexAction(){}

  /**
   * Display all the artists in the system.
   */
  public function getartistsAction()
  {
    require_once "Services/WebServices.php";

    $server = new Zend_Rest_Server();
    $server->setClass('WebServices');
    $server->handle(array('method' => 'getArtists'));
  }
}
```

Once you load the required file, you create a Zend_Rest_Server object and identify the class that contains the web services WebServices using setClass(). Finally, you call the Zend_Rest_Server::handle() method, which accepts a single parameter as a key-value array. In this example, you pass in the method key, which identifies the method to call within the WebServices class. Let's take a look at this class now.

The model shown in Listing 7-2 contains only a single service. The getartists service returns a SimpleXML object that contains only a single artist. You create the well-formed XML string and pass the string into the PHP simplexml_load_string() function, which converts the XML string into a SimpleXML object. If you need to expand on this example and connect to a database, this is the appropriate place to put such code.

***Listing 7-2.*** *Webservices.php*

```php
<?php
/**
 * WebServices.php
 * Containst full logic for web services.
 *
 * @author <Your Name>, <Your e-mail>
 */
class WebServices
{

/**
 * Return a single artist.
 *
 * @return SimpleXML
 */
 public function getArtists()
 {

    $xml = '<?xml version="1.0" standalone="yes"?><response>';
    $xml .= '<artists><artist><name>Poison</name>';
    $xml .= '<genre>Rock</genre></artist></artists>';
    $xml .= '</response>';
    return simplexml_load_string($xml);
 }

}
```

---

■ **Note** The name of the function does not have to be the same as the action in the web service controller. This was done for ease of use. To change the name of the class method, simply point the value in the method key to the new method you want to use.

---

You now have a service to test the client functionality. That wasn't hard, right? This wraps up the REST server functionality. Let's look at the client side of things. How do you make GET, POST, PUT, and DELETE calls using Zend Framework?

# REST Clients

By using the Zend_Rest component, you can call a service very easily using the Zend_Rest_Client class. With the Zend_Rest_Client methods found in Table 7-3 you can invoke any type of service request.

**Table 7-3.** *Zend_Rest_Client Operations*

| Operation | Description |
|---|---|
| get(serviceURL, array of parameters to pass) | Issues a GET request to the service. |
| post(serviceURL, array of parameters to pass) | Issues a POST request to the service. |
| delete(serviceURL) | Issues a DELETE request to the service. |
| put(serviceURL, array of parameters to pass) | Issues a PUT request. |
| isSuccess() | Boolean value that checks whether the request was successful. |
| __toString() | Converts returned XML response to a string. |

Let's call the getartist service you created earlier. You'll use a GET request because you are doing a read operation.

The REST client code in Listing 7-3 demonstrates the capability to call a service by using the Zend_Rest_Client object. Save it in a file called TestWSController.php in the application/controller directory. The controller will be used throughout this chapter and will be the primary controller in which you test new web service functionality.

**Listing 7-3.** *REST Client Action*

```
public function clientwsAction()
{

  $Client = new Zend_Rest_Client("http://localhost");

  try{
    $results = $Client->get("services/getartists");

    if($results->isSuccess()){
      echo $results->getBody();
    }

  }catch(Zend_Service_Exception $e){ throw $e; }
  //Suppress the view
```

```
    $this->_helper->viewRenderer->setNoRender();

}
```

The Zend_Rest_Client class contains a number of methods that allow you to send any type of HTTP request (refer to Table 7-3). In this example, you issue a GET request to the getArtists service using the get() method. The get() method accepts two parameters: an initial string representing the service you want to invoke and a second parameter that accepts a key-value array containing any parameters you want to send with the request.

Once you issue the request, check whether the object returned any errors using the isSuccess() Boolean method. If the request was a success, request the body (the content) of the returned message using the getBody() method. This request returns the XML you desire. With the XML now in hand, you can manipulate and display the content as you wish. To see it in action, go to http://localhost/test/clientws.

This closes out the intro to the web service capabilities in Zend Framework. But it doesn't stop here; other open web services application programming interfaces (APIs) have been wrapped for you to easily implement in the application.

The bulk of these services implement the Zend_Rest component, so you have a great foundation on how each of the services work.

# Services Overview

YouTube, Amazon, Google, Twitter, and even Netflix have all opened their data for the world to use with web services. Imagine the possibilities of working with such data; it's like tapping into Jimi Hendrix and The Beatles, and then using their material to create and innovate your own music.

One of the ways you can use open APIs is to connect to web services using PHP. With so many APIs to deal with, it's easy to see how you might become overwhelmed with errors and improper methods of handling REST, SOAP, and XML-RPC. That's why Zend Framework has taken great strides in implementing a collection of services.

What this means for you is less code to write and the ability to concentrate on manipulating the data that you have requested from the web service.

As of this writing, Zend Framework has successfully released the libraries for open APIs shown in Table 7-4.

**Table 7-4.** *Zend Services List*

| Web Service | Zend Library |
| --- | --- |
| Akismet | Zend_Service_Akismet |
| AWS | Zend_Service_Amazon |
| Audioscrobbler | Zend_Servcice_Audioscrobbler |
| del.icio.us | Zend_Service_Delicious |
| Flickr | Zend_Service_Flickr |
| Google and YouTube | Zend_Gdata |

*(Continued)*

| | |
|---|---|
| Nirvanix | Zend_Service_Nirvanix |
| ReCaptcha | Zend_Service_ReCaptcha |
| Simpy | Zend_Service_Simpy |
| SlideShare | Zend_Service_SlideShare |
| StrikeIron | Zend_Service_StrikeIron |
| Technorati | Zend_Service_Technorati |
| Twitter | Zend_Service_Twitter |
| Yahoo | Zend_Service_Yahoo |

Given such long lists of services, I'll cover just a handful to give you a look at the power of what each service offers. You'll specifically focus on Flickr, YouTube, and Amazon services by creating examples and continuing to add onto the LoudBite application.

## YouTube Zend Services

Videos on demand are now available—not only from your local Blockbuster or video rental store but also from your neighbors, friends, and anyone and everyone who wants their 15 minutes of fame. YouTube has become a powerhouse, at first delivering amateur content to the most recent movie studio content in the form of short trailers and movie exclusives.

YouTube also allows users to comment on each submitted video, embed videos onto other web sites, rate videos, join groups, and receive updates when specific users updated their video collection.

Zend Framework contains a service library that neatly bundles into the Zend_Gdata component: Zend_Gdata_YouTube. This component allows you to retrieve content as well as do the following:

- Search for videos and sort by most popular

- Retrieve comments on a video

- Retrieve public access user data

- Retrieve user playlists

- Retrieve user subscriptions

- Retrieve videos uploaded by specific users

- Retrieve favorite videos

- Retrieve playlists for users

- Upload videos

# Getting Started with YouTube Services

For each of the services covered throughout this section, you need to sign up for a developer account or a regular account on the site, so be prepared to sign up for multiple accounts.

To have full access to the YouTube web services, the first account you need to create is a YouTube developer account. To sign up for the account, access the YouTube sign-up form located at http://code.google.com/apis/youtube/dashboard/. Once you sign up for an accou.nt you'll receive a product name, client ID, and developer key. You need both the developer key along with the client ID to send data to YouTube. However, you'll just be fetching data, so you won't actually use them in this chapter.

For starters, you'll use the test controller. After you explore the new functionality, you'll add it to the LoudBite application.

The controller at this point contains only one action: testYoutubeAction(), as shown in Listing 7-4.

***Listing 7-4.*** *TestWSController.php*

```
/**
 * Youtube Web services Example.
 * Using getVideoEntry()
 */
public function testYoutubeAction(){

  Zend_Loader::loadClass("Zend_Gdata_YouTube");

  try{

    $YouTube = new Zend_Gdata_Youtube();

    //Get the specific video
    $video = $YouTube->getVideoEntry("NwrL9MV6jSk");
    $this->view->video = $video;

  }catch(Zend Service_Exception $e){ throw $e; }
}
```

The action will return the lip-sync duo Milli Vanilli's video, "Blame it on the Rain." Behind the scenes, Zend Framework is loading all the necessary files, such as the Zend/Gdata/YouTube.php file. This class contains all the operations that allow you to work with YouTube and its web services.

Because you'll fetch only data, you are not required at this point to use the application ID or secret key. So you can leave the Zend_Gdata_Youtube() constructor empty. The constructor accepts four parameters, however: a Zend_HTTP object, application ID, client ID, and developer key. After the $YouTube object is created, call the getVideoEntry() method, which accepts the video ID and the URI location you want to call. You pass in the video ID, NwrL9MV6jSk, of the video that was located by initially fetching the video directly on Youtube.com and parsing out the ID from the URL:

http://www.youtube.com/watch?v=**NwrL9MV6jSk**&feature=related

The portion that is important to you is the highlighted portion of the URL, which is the video ID. After you have the video ID, you pass it into the getVideoEntry() method and fetch a Zend_Gdata_YouTube_VideoEntry object. The object is then placed into a variable that will be used in the view.

Create the view in the /views/scripts/testws/ directory and enter the code as shown in Listing 7-5; if the path is not there, create it. Now the first view will simply be a display of video titles.

*Listing 7-5. test-youtube.phtml*

```php
<?php echo $this->doctype('XHTML1_STRICT'); ?>
<html xmlns="http://www.w3.org/1999/xhtml" xml:lang="en" lang="en">
<head>
  <?php echo $this->headTitle('Example - YouTube'); ?>
</head>
<body>

<h2>Favorite Video of All Time!</h2><br>
<?php
$title       = $this->video->getVideoTitle();
$uri         = $this->video->getVideoWatchPageUrl();
$description = $this->video->getVideoDescription();
$thumbnails  = $this->video->getVideoThumbnails();
$duration    = $this->video->getVideoDuration();
$thumbnail   = $thumbnails[1]['url'];
?>

<table>
<tr><td><img src='<?php echo $thumbnail ?>' height=50 width=50></td>
  <td valign="top"><a href='<?php echo $uri ?>'><?php echo $title ?></a><br>
  Duration <?php echo $duration ?> sec</td>
</tr>
</table>
</html>
```

Bring up the URL http://localhost/test/test-youtube and take a look at what you just created using only a few pieces of code. You should see a page resembling Figure 7-2.

# Favorite Video of All Time!

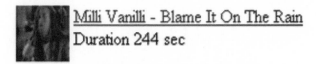

Milli Vanilli - Blame It On The Rain
Duration 244 sec

*Figure 7-2. Fetching single video results screenshot*

You'll now continue seeing how to use the libraries for searching, fetching comments, and rating videos.

## Search Features

Most of the functionality you'll probably do with YouTube is retrieve content to populate your own application, so you want to spend a bit of time fetching, ordering, and sorting videos. Searching through the mass collection of videos can be accomplished through the query operations in the Zend_Gdata object. These query operations allow you to search through categories, keywords, or a combination of both; determine how many results you require, and sort the results by different criteria.

The new action in Listing 7-6 demonstrates keyword searches for a specific video using YouTube's powerful query functionality.

*Listing 7-6. Keyword Search Example*

```
/**
 * Youtube Keyword search example.
 *
 */
public function testYoutubeKeywordAction()
{

  try{

    $YouTube = new Zend_Gdata_Youtube();

    //Create a new query
    $query = $YouTube->newVideoQuery();

    //Set the properties
    $query->videoQuery = 'Marvin Gaye';
```

```
    $query->maxResults = 5;

    //Get a video from a category
    $videos = $YouTube->getVideoFeed($query);

    //Set the view variable
    $this->view->videos = $videos;

  }catch(Zend_Service_Exception $e){ throw $e; }

}
```

Start by loading the Zend_Gdata_YouTube class and creating a new query using the newVideoQuery() method. The query allows you to set any number of properties. In this case, set the keywords Marvin Gaye along with the total number of results you want to return. After you create a query, pass the query into the getVideoFeed() method, which returns a Zend_Gdata_YouTube_VideoFeed object. Add the object to the view variables to use in the view.

Copy the code from Listing 7-6 into your TestWSController.php file; then create a new file in the application/views/scripts/test folder called test-youtube-keyword.phtml and copy the code in Listing 7-7 into that file. The view in Listing 7-7 takes the Zend_Gdata_YouTube_VideoFeed object and loops through each video in the object. Because each video in the object is a Zend_Gdata_YouTube object, you can use the same operations as in Listing 7-5.

***Listing 7-7.*** *Keyword Search View*

```php
<?php echo $this->doctype('XHTML1_STRICT'); ?>
<html xmlns="http://www.w3.org/1999/xhtml" xml:lang="en" lang="en">
<head>
  <?php echo $this->headTitle('Example - YouTube Keyword Search'); ?>
</head>
<body>

<?php
foreach($this->videos as $video){

$title       = $video->getVideoTitle();
$uri         = $video->getVideoWatchPageUrl();
$description = $video->getVideoDescription();
$thumbnails  = $video->getVideoThumbnails();
$duration    = $video->getVideoDuration();
$thumbnail   = $thumbnails[1]['url'];
?>
```

```
<table>
<tr><td><img src='<?php echo $thumbnail ?>' height=50 width=50></td>
    <td valign="top"><a href='<?php echo $uri ?>'><?php echo $title ?></a><br>
    Duration <?php echo $duration ?> sec</td>
</tr>
</table>

<?php
}
?>
</html>
```

Now pull up the URL http://localhost/test/test-youtube-keyword to see the list of Marvin Gaye videos shown in Figure 7-3.

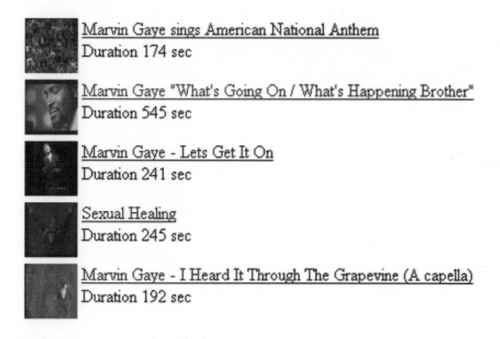

*Figure 7-3. Keyword search results*

## Video Comments and Ratings

Comments and ratings are very important to YouTube because users can determine which videos are worth watching and users can participate in both criticing any video uploads. In the following example, you'll retrieve the video ratings along with comments.

Retrieving a video rating does not require you to call another web service; you can use either the Zend_Gdata_Extension_Rating object, which is returned by the video search method, or the getVideoRating() method. getVideoRating()accepts the video ID and returns a key-value array that contains the average rating and the number of people who rated the video.

Using the code created in Listing 7-7, fetch the video ratings and display them (see Listing 7-8). The only change that you need to make is to the view (the test-youtube.phtml file).

***Listing 7-8.*** *Displaying Ratings*

```php
<?php echo $this->doctype('XHTML1_STRICT'); ?>
<html xmlns="http://www.w3.org/1999/xhtml" xml:lang="en" lang="en">
<head>
  <?php echo $this->headTitle('Example - YouTube'); ?>
</head>
<body>

<h2>Favorite Video of All Time!</h2><br>
<?php
$title       = $this->video->getVideoTitle();
$uri         = $this->video->getVideoWatchPageUrl();
$description = $this->video->getVideoDescription();
$thumbnails  = $this->video->getVideoThumbnails();
$duration    = $this->video->getVideoDuration();
$thumbnail   = $thumbnails[1]['url'];
$ratingInfo  = $this->video->getRating();
?>
<table>
<tr><td valign="top"><img src='<?php echo $thumbnail ?>' height=50 width=50></td>
   <td valign="top"><a href='<?php echo $uri ?>'><?php echo $title ?></a><br>
   Duration <?php echo $duration?> sec<br>
   Avg Rating: <?php echo $ratingInfo->average ?><br>
   Total Rated: <?php echo $ratingInfo->numRaters ?></td>
</tr>
</table>
</html>
```

Because the Zend_Gdata_Video object contains the rating information, you simply need to fetch the rating information by calling the getRating() method. getRating() returns a Zend_Gdata_Extension_Rating object containing the total number of users who rated the video (numRaters), the average rating (average), the highest rating (max), and the lowest rating (min). Refreshing the URL http://localhost/test/test-youtube will load a page that looks like Figure 7-4.

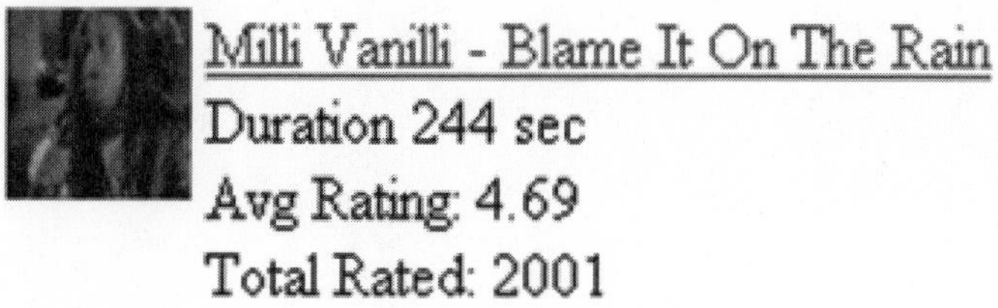

Milli Vanilli - Blame It On The Rain
Duration 244 sec
Avg Rating: 4.69
Total Rated: 2001

*Figure 7-4. Rating information screenshot*

You can fetch the comments for a particular video in two ways. You can either use getVideoCommentFeed(), which accepts the ID of the video you want to fetch the comments for, or the object that accompanies the video object (as you did with ratings).

## Artist Video List Module

The application you've been building now has many more items to it. In this section, you'll add videos to the artist page. You'll apply what you've learned and create a module that allows you to place up to five music videos or related videos of an artist on the artist page.

You need to modify the controller, ArtistController.php, and create a new view, video-list.phtml, in /application/views/scripts/artist. The bulk of the code is already done when it comes to the controller. Load the TestWSController.php file and copy the testYoutubeKeywordAction() method to the ArtistController's videoListAction(). Then update the code, as shown in Listing 7-9.

*Listing 7-9. videoListAction()*

```
/**
 * Fetch videos for a specific artist.
 *
 */
public function videoListAction(){

  $artist = $this->_request->getParam('artist');

  //Check if the artist name is present
  if(empty($artist)){
    throw new Exception('Whoops you need to name an artist');
  }

  try{
    $YouTube = new Zend_Gdata_Youtube();
```

```
//Create a new query
$query = $YouTube->newVideoQuery();

//Set the properies
$query->videoQuery = $artist;
$query->maxResults = 5;

//Get a video from a category
$videos = $YouTube->getVideoFeed($query);

//Set the view variable
$this->view->videos = $videos;


}catch(Zend_Excetion_Service $e){ throw $e; }


}
```

Listing 7-9 contains a small portion of updates. The action now initializes the artist that you want to pull data from and also checks whether the artist parameter is empty. If the user tries to load the page with no artist present, an error will trigger; otherwise, the artist name is used as the keyword to fetch videos from YouTube.

The view has also been created. Copy the code in Listing 7-7, change the title in the headTitle() method to Loudbite.com – Artists Videos, and save the content into the video-list.phtml file. Now load the URL http://localhost/artist/video-list?artist=b52; you should see something similar to Figure 7-5. You can also substitute the keyword b52 for anything you like.

Love Shack - B-52s
Duration 256 sec

B52's - Planet claire
Duration 238 sec

B-52's Private Idaho
Duration 200 sec

B-52's Rock Lobster
Duration 250 sec

B-52Â's Roam
Duration 238 sec

**Figure 7-5.** *videolist screenshot*

# Flickr and Zend_Rest_Flickr

Flickr.com has become one of the leading personal image storage websites. Take a look at it by loading up the web site http://www.flickr.com. You can search for specific snapshots taken by users just like you and me, upload your own photographs, group your photographs, add cool excerpts to the photo, and even purchase a snapshot using one of their third-party applications.

Zend Framework utilizes the Zend_HTTP and Zend_Rest components to provide the easy access to Flickr that the Zend_Service_Flickr gives you.

So what can you do with the Zend_Service_Flickr component?

- Retrieve photos based on specific tags/keywords.

- Retrieve photos for a specific users.

- Retrieve photos for a specific group ID.

- Return image details.

- Move seamlessly through result sets using the SeekableIterator.

## Getting Started with the Flickr Service

To get you started using Zend_Service_Flickr features, you need a developer account, which allows Flickr.com to generate your very own application ID and a secret key. You need only the application ID in the following examples. Open the URL http://www.flickr.com/services and click the link "Apply for a new API key." Once you have successfully created a uique key, you're set.

## Connecting to the Flickr Web Service API

The first test will be to connect to the web service API. You will create a simple connection and return a user's photos based on the e-mail address.

You create a new test action, testFlickrConnAction(), in the TestWSController.php file. The action will use the Zend_Service_Flickr component to connect to the Flickr web services and then search for all photos available for a specific e-mail address. The code in Listing 7-10 automatically loads the required file Zend/Service/Flickr.php. The file contains all the operations that allow you to instantiate and use methods for searching.

*Listing 7-10. Retrieving Photos by E-mail*

```
/**
 * Testing our Flick Connection and retreiving images.
 *
 */
public function testFlickrConnAction()
{

  try{
    $flickr = new Zend_Service_Flickr('API_KEY');

    //get the photos by the user. Find the user by the email.
    $photos = $flickr->userSearch("USER_EMAIL");

    $this->view->photos = $photos;
  }catch(Exception $e){ throw $e; }
}
```

After you load the required file, you create a Zend_Service_Flickr object: $flickr. The constructor requires the application ID Flickr generated for you before you can successfully instantiate the Zend_Service_Flickr object. You use the userSearch() method, which allows you to fetch photos for a specific user by passing in a string e-mail address into it. Finally you store the result set into a class view variable: $photos.

Because the results are stored inside the $photos variable as a Zend_Service_Flickr_ResultSet object, you can then use the view variable in a new view: test-flickr-conn.phtml, as shown in Listing 7-11.

*Listing 7-11. Flickr Test View test-flickr-conn.phtml*

```
<?php echo $this->doctype('XHTML1_STRICT'); ?>
<html xmlns="http://www.w3.org/1999/xhtml" xml:lang="en" lang="en">
<head>
```

```php
<?php echo $this->headTitle('Example - Flickr '); ?>
</head>
<body>
<?php echo $this->render("includes/header.phtml")?>

<?php
foreach($this->photos as $photo){
  $thumbnail = $photo->Thumbnail->uri;
?>
<img src='<?php echo $thumbnail ?>'>
</body>
</html>
<?php } ?>
```

Copy the markup into a new file and place it into the application/views/scripts/testws folder  and then load the http://localhost/test/test-flickr-conn URL.

# Search Using Tags

Searching for user-based content, as Listing 7-10 demonstrates, is one way of locating photos if you know which user has the best pictures for your subject. But what if you don't know which user has the photo you want? You could try to look through each user's profile, but with Flickr containing millions of users, and each user owning up to 100 or more photos, you can spend your whole life searching for the right photo. There's a better way: search for photos using a tag-based approach:

```
tagSearch(string, array)
```

The tagSearch() method accepts two parameters: the initial parameter contains a keyword the photo must contain. The second optional parameter is a key-value array of options.

The code demonstrated in Listing 7-12 starts like Listing 7-10, but instead of the userSearch() method, tagSearch() is used.

***Listing 7-12.*** *tagSearch() Implementation*

```php
/**
 * Test flick Tag based searching.
 *
 */
public function testFlickrTagsAction()
{

  try{

    $flickr = new Zend_Service_Flickr('API_KEY');
```

271

```
    $options = array('per_page' => 20);
    $photos = $flickr->tagSearch("php,zend", $options);

    $this->view->photos = $photos;

  }catch(Exception $e){ throw $e; }
}
```

Pass the php and zend tags into the tagSearch() method. You then store the result set for later use in the view. By default, the result set contains 10 photos; with the second parameter you can overwrite this option and set it to 20 by using one of the options found in Table 7-5.

**Table 7-5.** *Flickr Options*

| Option | Description |
| --- | --- |
| per_page | Number of photos to display per request |
| page | Page to start fetching results from |
| tag_mode | any is an OR combination of tags the photo must have.<br>all is an AND combination of tags the photo must have. |
| min_upload_date | Minimum upload date—fetches photos on or after this date |
| max_upload_date | Maximum upload date—fetches photos on or before this date |
| min_taken_date | Minimum taken date—fetches photos on or after the date taken |
| max_taken_date | Maximum taken date—fetches photos on or before the date taken |

Using the same view markup you used in Listing 7-12, create a new view, test-flickr-tags.phtml, and save into the application/views/scripts/testws directory. Now load the URL http://localhost/test/test-flickr-tags and you should see a similar result set as shown in Figure 7-6.

**Figure 7-6.** *Tag-based search result*

# Search for User

The Zend_Service_Flickr component contains three methods that allow developers to seach for user photos based on an e-mail address and to retrieve the ID of the user using the e-mail address or username.

The userSearch() method accepts two parameters: the initial parameter is the full e-mail address of the user you want to retrieve the photos from; the second optional parameter should contain the options located in Table 7-5.

The remaining two methods allow you to return the ID of the user based on an e-mail address and username. getIdByEmail() and getIdByUsername() both accept a single string parameter and return a string containing the ID of the user, if found. Calling the method can be done like so:

```
$flickr->getIdByEmail('someemail@test.com');
```

The code returns the ID of the user with the specified e-mail address (if it exists).

# Search for Group Photos

Flickr offers a wide variety of photo support and user participation. Users can comment on each other's photos, so it comes as no suprise that Flickr has allowed users to join together into groups that share the same interests. If you're a fan of crazy costumed fans at KISS concerts, you can find others who share their recent Gene Simmons and gang photos on Flickr. Let's see how you can view it by using the Zend_Service_Flickr component.

You need the group ID, which you find by doing a search for a group. Head to the Flickr site and do a quick search for Kiss Army. If nothing comes up, don't worry; click the Groups tab on top of the page. You should now see the KISS ARMY group. Give it a click and watch the photos come up. Great; so now what? The following URLs represent two that you might see for a group: http://flickr.com/groups/**kissarmy**/ and http://flickr.com/groups/**642715@N22**/.

One is the kissarmy URL; the other is the Pedro Infante group, which does not have a resolved group ID; it has a numerical representation of the group ID. You can use either as the group ID. Listing 7-13 shows how to get the group photos.

**Listing 7-13.** *GroupPoolGetPhotos Example*

```
public function testFlickrGroupsAction()
{
```

```
try{
   $flickr = new Zend_Service_Flickr('API_KEY');
   $options = array('per_page' => 20);
   $photos = $flickr->groupPoolGetPhotos("kissarmy");

    $this->view->photos = $photos;

 }catch(Exception $e){ throw $e; }

}
```

## Zend_Service_Flickr_ResultSet

The result set of a call into Flickr returns not only a collection of photos but also provides you with a Zend_Service_Flickr_ResultSet object. The object contains basic functionality—the capability to loop through a collection of photos using a foreach() function and discover the total number of photos returned.

## Zend_Service_Flickr_Result

The Zend_Service_Flickr_ResultSet object contains a collection of Zend_Service_Flickr_Result object(s) if there are photos found. The object contains valuable information that you want and is the meat and potatoes of what you're after.

Table 7-6 contains a full list of information you can retrieve from inside the object.

**Table 7-6.** *Zend_Flickr_Result Attributes*

| Attribute | Description |
|-----------|-------------|
| id | ID of the image. |
| owner | ID of the owner of the image. |
| secret | Secret key used in the URL. |
| server | Server name used in URL reconstruction. |
| title | Title of the image. |
| ispublic | Determines whether the photo is public. |
| isfriend | Checks whether the photo is visible to only friends. |
| isfamily | Checks whether the photo is visible to only family. |

| license | Type of license the photo contains. |
| dateupload | Date the photo was uploaded. |
| datetaken | Date the photo was taken. |
| ownername | Display name of the photo's owner. |
| iconserver | Server used to create icon URLs. |
| Square | 75 x 75 thumbnail image. Image size attribute must start with capital letter. |
| Thumbnail | 100-pixel image of the photo. Image size attribute must start with capital letter. |
| Small | 240-pixel image of the photo. Image size attribute must start with capital letter. |
| Medium | 500-pixel image of the photo. Image size attribute must start with capital letter. |
| Large | 640-pixel image of the photo. Image size attribute must start with capital letter. |
| Original | Original photo size. Image size attribute must start with capital letter. |

# LoudBite: Artist Flickr Photo Stream

You'll continue expanding the application by adding a gallery to each of the artist pages. The beauty of it is that you have to create only one set of PHP files that will add the gallery to the site. The module will need two pieces; the initial piece is the controller that has already been created: ArtistController.php. The second item is the view that contains the markup to render the located photos.

The first piece of the module is the controller. Create a new action, listPhotosAction(), to handle the retrieval of artist photos and will place the photos into the view. It will also check whether the user has supplied the artist name. If not, the user is taken to an error page.

The action shown in Listing 7-14 demonstrates the behavior you need. When the user loads the URL http://localhost/artist/list-photos?artist=yourartist, the action will check whether the artist name has been passed into the action as a parameter using the request object's getParam() method. If the action detects the artist name, continue on to the Flickr call.

***Listing 7-14.*** *listPhotosAction()*

```
public function listPhotosAction()
{

  //check if the artist is present
  $artist = $this->_request->getParam('artist');

  if(empty($artist)){
    throw new Exception("Whoops you did not supply an artist.");
```

```
    }

    try{
      $flickr = new Zend_Service_Flickr('API_KEY');

      //get the photos.
      $options = array('per_page' => 10);
      $photos = $flickr->tagSearch($artist, $options);

      $this->view->photos = $photos;

    }catch(Exception $e){ throw $e; }
    }
```

You create an instance of the Zend_Service_Flickr object, $flickr, pass in the developer key, and call the tagSearch() REST web service method. By using the tagSearch() method, you fetch all the photos that have been tagged with the artist's name and expect a Zend_Service_Flickr_ResultSet object returned. Finally, you pass the object into the view. Listing 7-15 shows the list-photos.phtml file that you should save in application/views/scripts/artist.

***Listing 7-15.*** *list-photos.phtml*

```
<?php echo $this->doctype('XHTML1_STRICT'); ?>
<html xmlns="http://www.w3.org/1999/xhtml" xml:lang="en" lang="en">
<head>
    <?php echo $this->headTitle('Loudbite.com - Flick Photos'); ?>
</head>
<body>
<?php echo $this->render("includes/header.phtml")?>

<body>
<?php
if($this->photos->totalResults() > 0){
    foreach($this->photos as $photo){
        $thumbnail = $photo->Thumbnail->uri;
        $original = $photo->Original->uri;
?>
    <?php
    if(!empty($origin)){?>
    <a href='<?php echo $original ?>'>
    <?php }?>
    <img src='<?php echo $thumbnail ?>'>
```

```
<?php {?>
</a>
<?php }?>
```

```
<?php
  }
}else{ ?>
We're sorry there were no photos available.
<?php } ?>
</body>
</html>
```

The foundation of the view can be taken from any of the other examples. Take a look at Listing 7-12; you can use the same markup as list-photos.phtml. You want it compact enough to fit anywhere but also able to display enough photos so that the module makes sense to have. You start off by seeing whether the result set, $this->photos, contains any photos. This allows you to display a friendly message to the user if there are no photos. If there are photos, go ahead and create the layout. Create a foreach loop that loops though the result set in the middle of the layout to retrieve the Zend_Service_Flickr_Result and then Zend_Service_Flickr_Image objects. You primarily use the Small portions of the result object and the image location for display. You also create a hyperlink that will link the thumbnail in the module to the full image on Flickr.

# Amazon and Zend_Service_Amazon

You know what Amazon.com is and what it does: it sells books, clothing, and electronics (among other things), and it has become the leading online retail store. Amazon.com has recently opened its inventory to developers by creating the Amazon.com Associates Web Service (AWS), which allows developers to search and retrieve information regarding specific products.

The Amazon.com AWS allows developers to do the following:

- Retrieve product descriptions based on keywords or by a specific Amazon Standard Identification Number (ASIN)

- Retrieve product images

- Retrieve customer reviews for specific products

- Retrieve editorial reviews for specific products

- Retrieve a list of similiar products

- Retrieve special offers by Amazon.com

- Retrieve ListMania listings

Having these features available enabled Zend Framework to create the Zend_Service_Amazon component by using both the Zend_HTTP_Client and Zend_Rest components of the framework to handle the web service communication shown in Figure 7-7.

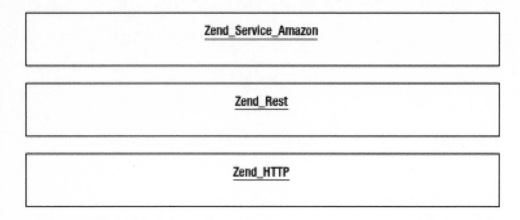

*Figure 7-7. Zend_Service_Amazon object layers*

It also consolidated commonly used features of the Amazon.com API to allow developers to simply pass in specific parameters, such as the ASIN of a product, and return the desired product detail; allowing developers to worry about their application instead of worrying about constructing the proper message for the type of protocol to use and dealing with exceptions that might arise.

## Getting Started with the Amazon Service

Before you continue, you need to sign up for an Amazon.com developer account. Like all other developer accounts, it allows you to use the extensive collection of web services that Amazon.com offers.

To sign up, load the URL http://www.amazon.com/gp/aws/landing.html and click the Sign Up Now button on the page to create an Amazon.com user account. If you already have an Amazon.com account, log in. Once you have successfully signed up or logged in to your account, you will receive an e-mail with a URL. Click the URL to fetch a set of authentication items such as the AWS application ID, secret access key, and certificate file. You'll need only the AWS access key ID.

With the AWS access key, Amazon.com allows the application to use the web services available from Amazon.com and identifies the application to Amazon.com (this access key is unique and should not be shared).

You're now set. Open up the editor and try to search for an Amazon.com product using Zend Framework.

The code shown in Listing 7-16 is a basic skeleton to test the access key as well as a simple example demonstrating how to fetch item information. You create a new test action named amazonTestAction() in the TestWSController.php file. The action will help you understand the different components required to do a simple and complex item search.

*Listing 7-16. amazonTestAction()*

```
public function amazonTestAction()
{

  try{

    $amazon = new Zend_Service_Amazon('API_KEY', 'US');
```

```
  $results = $amazon->itemSearch(array('SearchIndex' => 'Music',
                     'Keywords'    => 'Motley Crue'));

  foreach($results as $result){
    echo $result->Title."<br>";
  }
}catch(Zend_Exception $e){ throw $e; }
//Suppress the view
$this->_helper->viewRenderer->setNoRender();
}
```

Zend Framework automatically loads the file that powers the Zend/Service/Amazon.php service. You then create a new instance of a Zend_Service_Amazon object by passing in two parameters: the access ID created for you by Amazon.com and the country code you are accessing the data from. Once you instantiate the object, query the Amazon.com data set by executing the itemSearch() method on the Zend_Service_Amazon object. The itemSearch() method requires a key-value array with keys representing the different search-and-display criteria and the values for each criterion.

You call the web service and retrieve a Zend_Service_Amazon_ResultSet object. You iterate through the resulting result set using the foreach loop. The result set is a collection of Zend_Service_Amazon_Item objects, so you can access the item's data using object attribute calls.

Pull up http://localhost/test/amazon-test to see the results. If successful, you should see the list of items for sale that match the search, as shown in Figure 7-8.

Saints of Los Angeles
Motley Crue - Greatest Hits
Shout at the Devil
Red, White, & Crue
Girls, Girls, Girls
Decade of Decadence '81-'91
Dr. Feelgood
Too Fast for Love
Motley Crue: Carnival of Sins
Theatre of Pain

**Figure 7-8.** *List of Motley Crue music listings*

## Amazon.com Item Search

Take a look at Listing 7-16 again. When you instantiated a Zend_Service_Amazon object, you intentionally used the second parameter:

Zend_Service_Amazon('API_KEY', 'US');

The first parameter is the access key ID, and the second parameter is your country. Amazon's AWS allows you to use different country codes. You can request a service from France, Japan, Germany, or other locations by replacing the default country code, US, with any of the country codes listed in Table 7-7.

**Table 7-7.** *Country Codes*

| Country | Country Code | Description |
|---|---|---|
| Canada | CA | Results returned in English. Searches in the Canadian inventory. Changes the access point to http://webservices.amazon.ca. |
| Germany | DE | Results returned in German. Searches in the German inventory. Changes access point to http://webservices.amazon.de. |
| France | FR | Results returned in French. Searches in France's inventory. Changes access point to http://webservices.amazon.fr. |
| Japan | JP | Results returned in Japanese. Searches in the Japanese inventory. Changes access point to http://webservices.amazon.co.jp. |
| United Kingdom | UK | Results returned in English. Searches in the UK inventory. Changes access point to http://webservices.amazon.co.uk. |
| United States | US | Results returned in English (default). Access point is http://webservices.amazon.com. |

The beauty of changing the country code is that it enables you to integrate the Amazon.com web services into a localized web application. If the application is targeted to a German audience or a Japanese audience, the web service call accesses products for the given country. After it fetches the data, it returns the result set in the spcific country language. It even changes the currency to the appropriate equivalent based on the country code.

Open the TestWSController.php file once more and create a new action amazonCountryCodeTestAction(). You will fetch items using the country code FR which returns the result set in French (see Listing 7-17).

**Listing 7-17.** *Setting the Country Code to France*

```
public function amazonCountryCodeTestAction(){

  try{

    $amazon = new Zend_Service_Amazon('API_KEY', 'FR');
```

```
    $results = $amazon->itemSearch(array('SearchIndex' => 'Music',
                          'Keywords'   => 'Motley Crue'));


    foreach($results as $result){
       echo $result->Title."<br>";

    }
  }catch(Zend_Exception $e){ throw $e; }
  $this->_helper->viewRenderer->setNoRender();
}
```

If you load the action in the browser http://localhost/test/amazon-country-code-test, you will see the new result set shown in Figure 7-9.

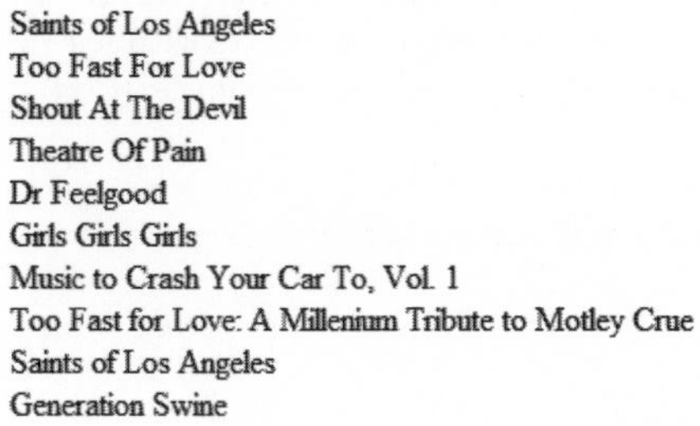

Saints of Los Angeles
Too Fast For Love
Shout At The Devil
Theatre Of Pain
Dr Feelgood
Girls Girls Girls
Music to Crash Your Car To, Vol. 1
Too Fast for Love: A Millenium Tribute to Motley Crue
Saints of Los Angeles
Generation Swine

*Figure 7-9. Result set for Motley Crue results (none in French, but a different selection of music)*

## Searching for Items using ItemSearch

Using the code in Listing 7-17 as a road map, let's continue analyzing the components much more in depth. After you initialize the Zend_Service_Amazon object, you run a query by issuing the call itemSearch(), which calls the ItemSearch web service in Amazon.

The itemSearch() method accepts one parameter as a key-value array. It allows you to search for products in the Amazon.com database and opens up additional operations that narrow down the search into specific categories, brands, and manufacturers.

By default, itemSearch() allows you to sort the result and set the maximum and minimum price of the products . Take a look at Table 7-8 to see all acceptable key values.

**Table 7-8.** *Acceptable itemSearch() Table for U.S. Country Code*

| Request Parameter | Description |
| --- | --- |
| SearchIndex | Determines which category to search in. Available values are as follows: Blended, Books, Classical, DVD, Electronics, ForeignBooks, Kitchen, Music, MusicTracks, Software, SoftwareVideoGames, Toys, VHS, Video, VideoGames, Watches |
| Keywords | Determines the keyword the product must contain to be part of the result. Multiple keywords can be separated by commas. |
| ResponseGroup | Narrows down the fields that are important to developers to use. Acceptable values are as follows: Accessories, BrowseNodes, EditorialReview, ItemAttributes, ItemIds, Large, ListmaniaLists, Medium, MerchantItemAttributes, OfferFull, Offers, OfferSummary, Reviews, RelatedItems, SearchBins, Similarities, Subjects, Tags, TagsSummary, Tracks, VariationMinimum, Variations, VariationSummary |
| Sort | Sorting order done to the results found. Please see specific country code and category search for sorting values. |
| Condition | Condition the product must be in. Default is New. If All is used, three items of each group is returned per page. New, All, Refurbished, Used, Collectible |
| MaximumPrice | Maximum price products must not go over. Example: $20.30 is represented as 2030. |
| MinimumPrice | Minimum price products must not go under. Example: $20.30 is represented as 2030. |
| ItemPage | Sets the page number to pull data from. If the page number is over the total pages returned, totalPages(), a 404 error is returned. |

Each of the parameters outlined in Table 7-8 is supported by the majority of the searches, but other parameters can be used depending on the category in which you are searching. (You'll take a look at these different combinations in the next section.)

The SearchIndex option allows you to determine in which category you want to conduct the search. In the example shown in Listing 7-16, you searched in the category Music, but you could have easily changed it to VideoGames or Toys.

Listing 7-18 changes the search.

**Listing 7-18.** *Fetching Used PHP Book with Price Range from $10.00 to $20.00*

```
public function amazonMultikeysTestAction(){

    try{
```

```
    $amazon = new Zend_Service_Amazon('API_KEY', 'US');

    $results = $amazon->itemSearch(array('SearchIndex' => 'Books',
                        'Keywords'     => 'PHP',
                        'Condition'    => 'Used',
                        'MaximumPrice' => '2000',
                        'MinimumPrice' => '1000'));

    foreach($results as $result){
      echo $result->Title."<br>";
    }


  }catch(Zend_Exception $e){ throw $e; }
  $this->_helper->viewRenderer->setNoRender();
}
```

Using five of the possible parameters outlined in Table 7-8, you use Keywords; SearchIndex; Condition; and both MaximumPrice and MinimumPrice. You change the category you want to search in from Music to Books, add the Condition key to fetch only the used books, and set the price range you prefer.

## Narrowing Down the Search Using Combinations

You don't get a feel for the power of the Amazon.com AWS Web Services API until you begin to narrow down the searches. Depending on the category you're searching, you can open additional options to search. For example, if you want to search in the Books category, the additional options to specify the Publisher and Author would be available, as shown in Listing 7-19.

***Listing 7-19.*** *Using Additional Combination Parameters*

```
public function amazonSearchByPublisherTestAction(){

  try{

    $amazon = new Zend_Service_Amazon('API_KEY', 'US');

    $results = $amazon->itemSearch(array('SearchIndex' => 'Books',
                        'Keywords'   => 'PHP',
                        'Condition'  => 'All',
                        'Publisher'  => 'Apress'));

    foreach($results as $result){
      echo $result->Title."<br>";
    }
```

```
    }catch(Zend_Exception $e){ throw $e; }
    $this->_helper->viewRenderer->setNoRender();
}
```

Listing 7-19 contains a small update, but changes the result set that is returned from Amazon.com. Instead of returning all books with the keyword PHP, you narrow down the search to return the subset published by Apress from the result set containing the keyword PHP. To accomplish this, add the Publisher key with the value of Apress and allow the web service to do the rest. Run it by visiting http://localhost/test/amazonsearchbypublishertest.

A list of the commonly used U.S.-based category combinations is shown in Table 7-9.

*Table 7-9.* *U.S. Category Combinations*

| Category | Parameter |
| --- | --- |
| Books | Author |
| Books | Publisher |
| DVD | Actor |
| DVD | AudienceRating |
| DVD | Director |
| DVD | Publisher |
| Electronics | Manufacturer |
| Music | Artist |
| Music | MusicLabel |
| Software | Manufacturer |
| VideoGames | Author |
| VideoGames | Brand |
| VideoGames | Manufacturer |

To see a complete list of category combinations visit the Amazon.com documentation at: http://docs.amazonwebservices.com/AWSECommerceService/2009-02-01/DG/ USSearchIndexParamForItemsearch.html.

## Sorting the Result Set

You can successfully and effectively return data from Amazon.com. Now let's sort the data. Using the sorting criteria used in the itemSearch() array, you can search the result set by a number of values identified in Table 7-8. Much like the combination searches, sorting also depends on which category you're searching and which country code you use.

Using the category, you can sort using the values relevancerank, salesrank, reviewrank, pricerank, and titlerank, among others. Listing 7-20 uses the titlerank sorting value, which returns the result set alphabetically. Try it out.

***Listing 7-20.*** *Sorting Books Alphabetically*

```
public function amazonSortingBooksTestAction(){

  try{

    $amazon = new Zend_Service_Amazon('API_KEY', 'US');

    $results = $amazon->itemSearch(array('SearchIndex' => 'Books',
                        'Keywords'  => 'PHP',
                        'Condition'  => 'Used',
                        'Publisher'  => 'Apress',
                        'Sort'       => 'titlerank'));

    foreach($results as $result){
      echo $result->Title."<br>";
    }
  }catch(Zend_Exception $e){ throw $e; }
  $this->_helper->viewRenderer->setNoRender();

}
```

Pull up the URL http://localhost/test/amazon-sorting-books-test to see the result set listed alphabetically.

The Zend_Service_Amazon_ResultSet also has additional operations that allow you to return the number of items retrieved and how many pages each result set contains, thereby giving you additional sorting features.

The totalResults() and totalPages() operations return the number of items the web service call found and how many pages of data were returned, respectively. Listing 7-21 shows the total number of books published by Apress that Amazon.com is selling.

***Listing 7-21.*** *Sorting the Result Set*

```
public function amazonSortingBooksTestAction(){

  try{

    $amazon = new Zend_Service_Amazon('API_KEY', 'US');
```

```
$results = $amazon->itemSearch(array('SearchIndex' => 'Books',
                        'Keywords'   => 'PHP',
                        'Condition'  => 'Used',
                        'Publisher'  => 'Apress',
                        'Sort'       => 'titlerank',
                        'ItemPage'   => '3'));


  foreach($results as $result){
    echo $result->Title."<br>";
  }
}catch(Zend_Exception $e){ throw $e; }


echo "<br>";
echo "Total Books: ".$results->totalResults();
echo "<br>";
echo "Total Pages: ".$results->totalPages();
$this->_helper->viewRenderer->setNoRender();
}
```

The example in Listing 7-21 shows a number of new items. For starters, you print out the total number of items and pages using the Zend_Service_Amazon_ResultSet's totalPages() and totalResults() methods. By default, each page contains ten items. If you pull up the URL http://localhost/test/amazon-sorting-books-test, you can see the number of Apress books (new and used) that Amazon.com is selling that contain the PHP keyword. By default, when you present the data, you pull from the initial page. But because there are multiple pages, use the ItemPage key and set the value to 3 to pull from page 3. If you passed in a numerical value that is larger than the total number of pages available, you receive a 404 error.

The Zend_Service_Amazon_ResultSet contains additional operations for iterating through the result set (see Table 7-10).

**Table 7-10.** *Iteration Operations*

| Operation | Description |
| --- | --- |
| Seek | Pulls a specific index in the result set. |
| Next | Increments the current index flag. |
| Key | Returns the current index the interation is in. |
| Rewind | Decrements the current index. |
| Current | Returns the current item set by using the index. |

# Searching for Similar Products

Let's go into more advanced use of Amazon AWS by returning similar products. Refer to Table 7-8 to view which key allows you to fetch similar products. Using the ResponseGroup key and specifying the Similarities value, the result set will return an array of Zend_Service_Amazon_SimilarProduct objects. Each object contains the attributes outlined in Table 7-11.

**Table 7-11.** *Zend_Service_Amazon_SimilarProduct Object Attributes*

| Attribute | Description |
| --- | --- |
| ASIN | Unique Amazon ID for the product |
| Title | Title of the product |

The power of the Zend_Service_Amazon library is that you need only two operations to make a call to fetch product information, and the only thing you have to worry about is which parameter fetches the proper data for you and how you can display the data. Listing 7-22 demonstrates this by calling similar products for you. You use the ResponseGroup key and the Small value, which is the default ResponseGroup value and fetches all the standard data, and Similarities to return the similar titles. With the result set fetched, you now have the Zend_Service_Amazon_ResultSet's SimilarProducts attribute. The attribute contains a collection of Zend_Service_Amanzon_SimilarProducts objects that can be accessed in a loop.

**Listing 7-22.** *Fetching Similar Products*

```
public function amazonSimilarProductsTestAction()
{

  try{

    $amazon = new Zend_Service_Amazon('API_KEY', 'US');

    $results = $amazon->itemSearch(array('SearchIndex' => 'Books',
                    'Keywords'   => 'PHP',
                    'Condition'  => 'Used',
                    'Publisher'  => 'Apress',
                    'Sort'       => 'titlerank',
                    'ItemPage'   => '3',
                    'ResponseGroup' =>
                      'Small,Similarities'));

    //Foreach item return the Similar Products
    foreach($results as $result){
      echo "<b>".$result->Title."</b><br>";
```

```
    $similarProduct = $result->SimilarProducts;

    if(empty($similarProduct)) {
      echo "No recommendations.";
    } else {
      foreach($similarProduct as $similar){
        echo "Recommended Books: ".$similar->Title."<br>";
      }
    }
    echo "<br><br>";
  }

}catch(Zend_Exception $e){ throw $e; }

echo "<br>";
echo "Total Books: ".$results->totalResults();
echo "<br>";
echo "Total Pages: ".$results->totalPages();
$this->_helper->viewRenderer->setNoRender();

}
```

# Returning Product Reviews

Each of the products returned contains reviews, and also provides customer reviews of the product and reviews made by editors. The Zend Amazon service allows you to return each review as a Zend_Service_Amazon_*Review object. If the review is a customer review, the object is a Zend_Service_Amazon_CustomerReview. If the review is an editor's review, the object is a Zend_Service_Amazon_EditorialReview. Listing 7-22 shows how to get the reviews.

*Listing 7-22. Returning Product Reviews from Amazon.com*

```
public function amazonFetchReviewsTestAction()
{

try{
    Zend_Loader::loadClass("Zend_Service_Amazon");
    $amazon = new Zend_Service_Amazon('API_KEY', 'US');

    $results = $amazon->itemSearch(array('SearchIndex'  => 'Books',
                        'Keywords'     => 'PHP',
                        'Condition'    => 'Used',
                        'Publisher'    => 'Apress',
```

```
                         'Sort'        => 'titlerank',
                         'ItemPage'    => '3',
                         'ResponseGroup' =>
                          'Small, Similarities,
                            Reviews, EditorialReview'));

  //Foreach item return the Similar Products
  foreach($results as $result){
    echo "<b>".$result->Title."</b><br>";

    //Fetch the Customer Reviews and display the content.
    $customerReviews = $result->CustomerReviews;

    if(empty($customerReviews)) {
      echo "No customer reviews.<br>";
    } else {
      foreach($result->CustomerReviews as $customerReview){
        echo "Review Summary: ".$customerReview->Summary."...<br>";
      }
    }

    $similarProduct = $result->SimilarProducts;

    if(empty($similarProduct)) {
      echo "No recommendations.";
    } else {
      foreach($similarProduct as $similar){
        echo "Recommended Books: ".$similar->Title."<br>";
      }
    }
    echo "<br><br>";
  }

}catch(Zend_Exception $e){ throw $e; }
echo "<br>";
echo "Total Books: ".$results->totalResults();
echo "<br>";
echo "Total Pages: ".$results->totalPages();
$this->_helper->viewRenderer->setNoRender();

}
```

Let's go over the code in Listing 7-22. Because you know all the basic building blocks to create a call to the web service, let's focus on the changes to fetch the customer reviews. First look at the Reviews string appended to the ResponseGroup value. This returns the product reviews, along with all the data you request. With the result set returned, call the CustomerReviews ResultSet attributes. The return value is a collection of Zend_Service_Amazon_CustomerReview objects.

To display the customer reviews, loop through each element in the $customerReviews array, and display the date and the summary by calling the Zend_Service_Amazon_CustomerReview Summary and Date attributes.

Run the new update to the code by calling the same URL, http://localhost/test/amazon-fetch-reviews-test, and you should now see the title of the book, similar products, and all reviews for the product.

Each of the review objects contains different atributes that you can use to display the content of the review. Table 7-12 shows all the available attributes that the Zend_Service_Amazon_CustomerReview class contains.

***Table 7-12.*** *Zend_Service_Amazon_CustomerReviews*

| Attribute | Description |
| --- | --- |
| Rating | Overall rating given to the review |
| HelpfulVotes | Number of total helpful votes given to the review by Amazon users |
| CustomerId | ID of user who made the comment |
| TotalVotes | Total number of votes |
| Date | Date the comment was created |
| Summary | Brief summary of the review |
| Content | Full content of review |

# Zend_Service_Amazon_EditorialReview

Editorial reviews can be retrieved and displayed like customer reviews. The only difference is that you have to add in EditorialReviews to the ResponseGroup.

The result is a collection of Zend_Service_Amazon_EditorialReview objects that can be accessed by calling the Zend_Service_Amazon_ResultSet attribute EditorialReview. The EditorialReview class has the attributes shown in Table 7-13.

***Table 7-13.*** *Zend_Service_Amazon_EditorialReview Object Attributes*

| Attribute | Description |
| --- | --- |
| Source | Source of the editorial review |
| Content | Full content of review |

# Looking Up Specific Items

So you want to drill down a bit more and just want to return a specific Amazon product? The Zend_Service_Amazon library provides you with such a operation: itemLookup().

itemLookup(String ASIN, array)

The initial parameter is the ASIN, which can be found by doing a search using the itemSearch() method. It returns the ASIN in the result set for each product or it can be located by navigating through the Amazon.com site and locating the product using the portion of the following URL:

http://www.amazon.com/Beginning-Zend-Framework-Armando-Padilla/dp/**1430218258**/ref=
sr_1_1?ie=UTF8&s=books&qid=1228174324&sr=8-1

The second parameter, which is optional, allows you to set sorting and return value information. It is identical to the key-value array in the itemSearch() method.

The itemLookup() example shown in Listing 7-23 changes the way you retrieve data from Amazon.com. This example looks up data for this book with the 1430218258 ASIN number.

***Listing 7-23.*** *itemLookUp() Example*

```
public function amazonLookupTestAction()
{

  try{

    $amazon = new Zend_Service_Amazon('API_KEY', 'US');

    $results = $amazon->itemLookup("1430218258",
                    array('Condition'    => 'Used',
                        'Publisher'    => 'Apress',
                        'ResponseGroup' =>
                          'Small,Similarities,Reviews,EditorialReview'));

    echo "<b>".$results->Title."</b><br>";

  }catch(Zend_Exception $e){ throw $e; }
  $this->_helper->viewRenderer->setNoRender();
}
```

View the item by visiting http://localhost/test/amazon-lookup-test.

---

■ **Note** When using itemLookup(), you still separate search criteria with a comma, but there should be no whitespace in the string as there was in other examples.

---

The result set contains only a single Zend_Service_Amazon_Item object, which has the attributes shown in Table 7-14.

**Table 7-14.** *The Zend_Service_Amazon_Item Object*

| Attribute | Attribute Description |
| --- | --- |
| ASIN | Amazon Standard Identification Number |
| DetailPageURL | URL of the products profile on Amazon.com |
| Title | Title of the product |
| ProductGroup | Category of the product |

Additional functionality and search combinations can be found on the Amazon AWS web site: http://docs.amazonwebservices.com/AWSECommerceService/latest/DG/.

# LoudBite: Adding Amazon Product Information

Now you have more than enough of a foundation to add additional functionality to the application you've created throughout this book. You can now add a product module to the site.

The product module presents users with a set of products they might find interesting depending on the music they enjoy and the groups they have in their favorites list. The module pulls in CD, music, and apparel information from Amazon.com, and displays a small image and summary of the product, orders the products by "coolness," and displays a link where the user can purchase the product on Amazon.com.

First, you need to create the controller and actions for the pages. You will create a new controller called ProductController.php; you don't want to give the impression that it's a store because people will be standoffish if they think you're selling them something. The ProductController will contain two actions: a quickProductDisplayAction() and an indexAction(), as shown in Listing 7-24.

**Listing 7-24.** *ProductController: indexAction()*

```
public function indexAction()
{

    //Get the artist name from the request.
    $artistName = $this->_request->getParam("artistName");
```

```
    //If there is no artist name in the request send the user to an oops page
    if(empty($artistName)){
        throw new Exception("Oh man i think you broke something.  No not really,
you just got here by mistake.");
    }

    try{

        $amazon = new Zend_Service_Amazon('API_KEY', 'US');

        //Get the apparel t-shirts items
        $apparelItems = $amazon->itemSearch(
                        array('SearchIndex' => 'Apparel',
                            'Keywords'   => $artistName.' t-shirt',
                            'ResponseGroup' => 'Small, Images'));

        //Get the music tracks
        $cds = $amazon->itemSearch(array('SearchIndex' => 'Music',
                            'Artist'    => $artistName,
                            'ResponseGroup' => 'Small, Images'));

        //Get the posters
        $posters = $amazon->itemSearch(array(
                            'SearchIndex'  => 'HomeGarden',
                            'Keywords'     => $artistName.' posters',
                            'ResponseGroup' => 'Small, Images'));

        //Set the view variables
        $this->view->products = $apparelItems;
        $this->view->cds    = $cds;
        $this->view->posters = $posters;
    }catch(Zend_Exception $e){ throw $e; }
}
```

The new ProductController contains the indexAction() method, which allows you to fetch three types of items from Amazon.com:

- CDs for an artist

- T-shirts for an artist

- Posters for an artist

Use the itemSearch() operation for all three instances. Before you reach these calls, see whether the artist name was supplied. The artist name is retrieved from inside the request; if it is empty, you redirect the user to a general error page. Once you return the data for each itemSearch() call, you initialize three view variables to use in the view: $cds, $products, and $posters. These steps are shown in Listing 7-25.

***Listing 7-25.*** *ProductController: quickProductDisplayAction()*

```
public function quickProductDisplayAction(){

  //Get the artist name from the request.
  $artistName = $this->_request->getParam("artistName");

  //If there is no artist name in the request send the user to an oops page
  if(empty($artistName)){
    throw new Exception("Oh man i think you broke something.  No not really,
you just got here by mistake.");
  }

  try{

    $amazon = new Zend_Service_Amazon('API_KEY', 'US');

    //Get the Music tracks
    $cds = $amazon->itemSearch(array('SearchIndex' => 'Music',
                  'Artist'   => $artistName,
                  'ResponseGroup' => 'Small, Images'));

    //Set the view variables
    $this->view->products = $cds;
  }catch(Zend_Exception $e){ throw $e; }
}
```

The quickProductDisplayAction() method is not as extensive as indexAction(); you don't have to do any extensive querying for different items because you simply want to fetch the artist's CDs and display them. You use the itemSearch() method again and pass in the Artist key, select the category Music, and ask for both the default data as well as the image data in the returned information. On to the display.

The first files you need to create are the quick-product-display.phtml and index.phtml files within the application/views/scripts/product directory. The files will act as the views to display the data.

The quick-product-display.phtml file is a small module that will display up to ten products on the user's profile page (see Listing 7-26). The index.phtml file is the view that will display a complete collection of CDs, apparel items, and posters the user can purchase. Both pages are linked from a View More Items link in the user's profile page and the artist profile page.

**Listing 7-26.** *quick-product-display.phtml*

```
<?php echo $this->doctype('XHTML1_STRICT'); ?>
<html xmlns="http://www.w3.org/1999/xhtml" xml:lang="en" lang="en">
<head>
  <?php echo $this->headTitle('Loudbite.com - Artist Products'); ?>
</head>
<body>
<?php echo $this->render("includes/header.phtml")?>

<?php if($this->products->totalResults()){ ?>
<table border="1" width="300">

 <tr><td colspan="2">You might be interested in these items</td></tr>

 <?php foreach($this->products as $product){?>
   <tr><td><img src="<?php echo $product->SmallImage->Url ?>" width="50"
        height="50"></td>
   <td>
    <a href="<?php echo $product->DetailPageURL ?>"><?php echo $product->Title ?>
    </a>
   </td></tr>
<?php } ?>

</table>
<?php } ?>
</body>
</html>
```

Once you save the file and load the URL http://localhost/product/quick-product-display?artistName=guns%20n%20roses, you will see a list of CDs for the band Guns n' Roses. The index.phtml page is very similar except you build a table of posters and T-shirts as well as CDs. Create the index.phtml file within the application/views/scripts/product directory by copying the code shown in Listing 7-26, saving it, and then loading the URL http://localhost/product?artistName=guns%20n%20roses. That's all there is to it!

You've learned about the latest web service technology as well as how Zend Framework uses its built-in web service components to talk with external applications such as YouTube to expand on your application. Now let's focus on how to provide additional content on the site using syndicated content with RSS feeds.

# RSS and Zend Framework

Yes, really simple syndication, or RSS for short, is here to stay. RSS allows developers, users of applications, and just about anyone with access to a computer and a connection to the Internet the ability to share their news articles, blog articles, videos, and images to anyone around the world once a user subscribes to the content.

RSS provided the web world with two benefits: a centralized location for the user to read content from their favorite sites and a standardized structure that application developers could agree on when sharing content between applications. Let's go back in time before RSS to see why this was a big deal.

In the beginning there was no RSS. Users of the Web had to visit every site they frequented on a daily basis to gather their news, entertainment gossip articles, favorite blogs, and daily doses of tech information. During the initial surge of web usage, this was not a problem—a user would go to one or two sites and receive the information. As the web world grew with the vast number of web users in the millions and possibly reaching a billion, the number of web sites catering to every possible niche emerged. Likewise, the number of web sites each user now visited has increased. Instead of one or two sites, the user now visits five or even ten sites per day just to fill the empty feeling of "I'm behind the times."

As you can imagine, this daily routine can get tiresome and take up most of your day. It can also become a burden when you reach a site that contains very old or stale content. So the idea to create a centralized location to gather and read your favorite site's articles (much like how your favorite magazines arrive at your doorstep instead of you having to go bookstore to bookstore) was starting to take shape. The centralized location? An RSS reader.

On the technical side, RSS provides a standardized structure based on XML to distribute and syndicate content between sites. Without the standard and structure, developers would not only have to support their own sites but would also have the added task of supporting any changes the owners of the syndicated content decided to make on their end. This isn't a problem if you deal with only one source, but it becomes a big problem if the you have to use syndicated content from multiple sources. Using an example, you can see this take shape.

Let's say the site decided to use syndicated content from three other sites: Site A, Site B, and Site C. Site A decides to send you an XML document containing the format shown in Listing 7-27.

**Listing 7-27.** *Site A Example Feed*

```
<articles>
 <article>
  <title>PHP  = Pretty Hot People</title>
  <description>That's the real meaning. </description>
 </article>
</articles>
```

Site B uses the format shown in Listing 7-28.

**Listing 7-28.** *Site B Example Feed*

```
<feeds>
 <article>
  <heading>PHP  = Parent Helping Parents</heading>
  <excerpt>Popular site where you can get PHP news, tips and info.  No this isn't
the cool most awesome PHP language.</excerpt>
 </article>
</feeds>
```

And Site C uses the format shown in Listing 7-29.

***Listing 7-29.*** *Site C Example Feed*

```
<articles>
 <item>
  <title>My Puppy took my pants.</title>
  <excerpt>Puppies all over the world are turning into crooks.
 Fictitious city
mayor reaches out to create after school programs for "at risk" puppies and their
owners. Citizens blame education system.</excerpt>
 </item>
</articles>
```

All three sites are syndicating their content using different formats. Sites A and C use <articles> as a parent tag; Site B uses <feeds>. Site C uses <item>; Sites A and B use <article>. Sites A and C use <title>; Site B uses <heading>. In such a case, you would need to create three XML parsers, one for each format. If either one of the sites decided to change its format, you must take time off the current project, update the XML reader, perform a test, and then release to production. This process that can take all day. The better option is to use one standard when sharing data using RSS that all three sites can use.

# A Look at RSS

With the talk of a unifying format and structure, you might be wondering what RSS looks like. RSS is an XML document containing specific sets of tags to describe the articles the author has decided to syndicate. Each syndicated article is required to contain <title>, <description>, and <link> tags; but it can also use the additional optional tags listed in Table 7-15, which provide supporting information (metadata) about the article. Listing 7-30 shows an example of an RSS 2.0 document containing two articles to syndicate.

***Listing 7-30.*** *Full RSS Document*

```
<?xml version="1.0" encoding="UTF-8" ?>
<rss version="2.0">
 <channel>
  <title>My Music Web Site Home Page</title>
  <link>http://www.loudbite.com</link>
  <description>Weekly articles diving head first into the gossip, new releases,
concert dates, and anything related to the music industry around the world.
  </description>

  <!-- This is a comment. Start list of articles -->
  <item>
   <title>Criss Cross, now 35, continue wearing pants backward to look cool.
   </title>
   <link>http://www.loudbite.com/full link to your article</link>
   <description>Rap duo, Criss Cross continue to wear pants backward after
```

repeated attemps to inform them,  the 90s are over...let it go...let it go.
```
    </description>
  </item>


  <item>
    <title>New PWG LP released!</title>
    <link>htp://www.loudbite.com/link to this articles page</link>
    <description>The new Puppies Wearing Glasses LP has hit the street.
First slated for October 3rd it's now officially out.
    </description>
  </item>
 </channel>
</rss>
```

Every XML document must be well-formed; an RSS 2.0 document is no different. A well-formed XML document must follow three basic rules:

- Each opening tag must have a closing tag.

- Each element must be properly nested.

- The XML document must contain one root node.

- Referencing Listing 7-30, the RSS 2.0 document expands the initial rules determined by a well-formed XML document:

- <rss> must be the parent node in the XML document.

- Each <item> element must be nested inside the <channel> element.

- Elements <item> and <channel> must contain child elements <title>, <description>, and <link>.

Moving down the example, you begin the RSS 2.0 document by setting the xml directive:

```
<?xml version="1.0" encoding="UTF-8" ?>
```

This allows XML parsers to identify both the encoding and the version number of the document. You then start the RSS data by declaring the RSS specification version number. You're using version 2.0 of the RSS specification, so set the attribute version to 2.0:

```
<rss version="2.0">
```

Use the <channel> element to initiate the description of the feed using the <title>, <description>, and <link> channel elements. The data contained in these elements provides the title of the web page providing the feed, a short description of the site, and a link to the web page. For this example, the web site is called My Music Web Site, has the domain name http://www.loudbite.com, and has a short description ("Weekly articles diving head first"), all set in the appropriate elements.

Using one or more <item> elements nested in the <channel> tag allows you to add as many articles to the feed as you want. In the example, you have two <item> tags, each one representing an article to syndicate. Like the <channel> element, the <item> element has three required elements: <title>, <description>, and <link>, but can also include a collection of optional tags, shown in Table 7-15. The <title> element contains the title of the article, the <description> element contains a short description of the article (usually the first few sentences of the article), and the <link> element contains a direct hyperlink to the full article.

Expanding on the RSS document you created, you now want to include additional information such as the author of each article, the published date of the RSS feed, the published date of individual articles, copyright information, the language of the feed, helpful information for aggregators using the <category> element, a supporting image for each article, and an advanced setting that sets the period of time the content is considered fresh using the <ttl> element. To accomplish this, you'll need the optional tags shown in Table 7-15 and Table 7-16.

**Table 7-15.** *Optional <item> Tags*

| Element | Description |
| --- | --- |
| author | Contains the e-mail address of the author of the article. |
| category | Allows articles to be placed into different groupings. |
| comments | Allows article to link to comments concerning it. This is usually a URL. |
| enclosure | Allows article to contain media elements such as music and photos. The media is not downloaded; it is loaded by refreshing a URL where it is hosted. |
| guid | Unique ID for the article. |
| pubDate | Sets the published date for the article. |
| source | Used to specify the original publisher of the article. Used to specify the third party, if any. |

**Table 7-16.** *Optional <channel> Tags*

| Element | Description |
| --- | --- |
| category | Allows you to group your feed. Primarily used by RSS aggregators when searching for feeds. |
| cloud | Allows author of feed to create process to notify you about updates to the channel. |
| copyright | Copyright information for your feed. |
| docs | URL to the location of information regarding the feed format. |
| generator | Name of the program that generated the feed. |

*(Continued)*

| | |
|---|---|
| image | Supporting image for your feed. |
| language | Sets the language the feed is written in. |
| lastBuildDate | Sets the last time the feed was generated. |
| managingEditor | Sets the e-mail address to the editor of the feed. |
| pubDate | Sets the last published date of the feed. |
| rating | Sets the PICS rating for the feed. Allows reader to determine to type of content. |
| skipDays | Sets the days the feed reader can skip updating the feed. |
| skipHours | Sets the hours the feed reader can skip updating the feed. |
| textInput | Allows you to display a text input field with the feed. |
| ttl | Stands for *time to live*. Sets the length of time, in minutes, the feed can remain in cache. Once the TTL is expired, the feed is fetched from the source and stored again into cache. |
| webMaster | Sets the e-mail address of the webmaster of the feed. |

The complete RSS document can be seen in Listing 7-31.

**Listing 7-31.** *Complete RSS Document*

```
<?xml version="1.0" encoding="UTF-8" ?>
<rss version="2.0">
  <channel>
    <title>My Music Web Site Home Page</title>
    <link>http://www.loudbite.com</link>
    <description>Weekly articles diving head first into the gossip, new releases,
concert dates, and anything related to the music industry around the world.
    </description>

<!-- Cache for 3 hours -->
<ttl>180</ttl>

<!-- Set the copyright info -->
<copyright>Music News 2008</copyright>
```

```
<!-- Set the language info -->
<language>English</language>

<category>Music</category>

<pubDate>October 03, 2008</pubDate>

        <!-- Start list of articles -->
        <item>
 <author>fuglymaggie@example.com</author>
 <enclosure url="" type="" />
        <title>Criss Cross, now 35, continue wearing pants backward to look cool.
        </title>
        <link>http://www.loudbite.com/full link to your article</link>
        <description>Rap duo, Criss Cross continue to wear pants backward after
    repeated attemps to inform them,  the 90s are over...let it go...let it go.
        </description>
        </item>

        <item>
 <author>someeditor@example.com</author>
 <enclosure url="" type="" />
        <title>New PWG LP released!</title>
        <link>htp://www.loudbite.com/link to this articles page</link>
        <description>The new Puppies Wearing Glasses LP has hit the street.  First
    slated for October 3rd its now officially out. </description>
        </item>
    </channel>
 </rss>
```

At this point, the RSS document is ready to be published and consumed by users. How you do this and what tools you need to successfully consume a feed will be covered next.

## Publishing and Reading RSS

Creating an RSS document is the initial step for syndicating the data; now you need a way to allow the users to subscribe to it. Providing access to the RSS feed is done by placing a hyperlink anywhere on the web page. The hyperlink will take the user to the RSS document where the web browser formats the XML and presents it to the user in the browser-specific format.

If the user is using an RSS reader, the same link you created can be used as a point of reference for their feed reader application to load the document.

Because feed readers don't allow you to modify the look of each article and integreate articles as you want, you need a tool that loads, handles, and modifies the content within RSS feeds effortlessly.

# Zend_Feed Component

The Zend_Feed component is like a Swiss Army knife for feeds. You would usually create an XML parser to load the XML document, parse each element, and finally place the information into an array for easy access to the data. The final amount of PHP code you write can be up to 100 lines. The better solution is use the Zend_Feed component.

This component allows you to load RSS documents directly from a web source, from a string, or from a document stored locally. Zend_Feed also allows you to access feed elements and their attributes as an array and create RSS documents on the fly. It also has support for Atom feeds (another type of RSS).

## Loading RSS Documents

The Zend_Feed component provides three different ways to load RSS documents:

- Load from a web source that's provided as a URL location.
- Load a string containing the RSS XML.
- Load an RSS document stored locally.

### Loading from the Web

Many RSS feeds that you might find interesting to use in the application will tend to be feeds that have been created by other developers and published online. You need an easy approach to consume RSS content from online sources. Using the URL to the RSS feed, along with the Zend_Feed component, you can accomplish the task. For the following example you'll use the Apress RSS feed.

This particular RSS feed, which lists all the new books Apress has published, is located at http://www.apress.com/resource/feed/newbook. Using your browser, load the RSS feed. Once loaded, it should look like Figure 7-10.

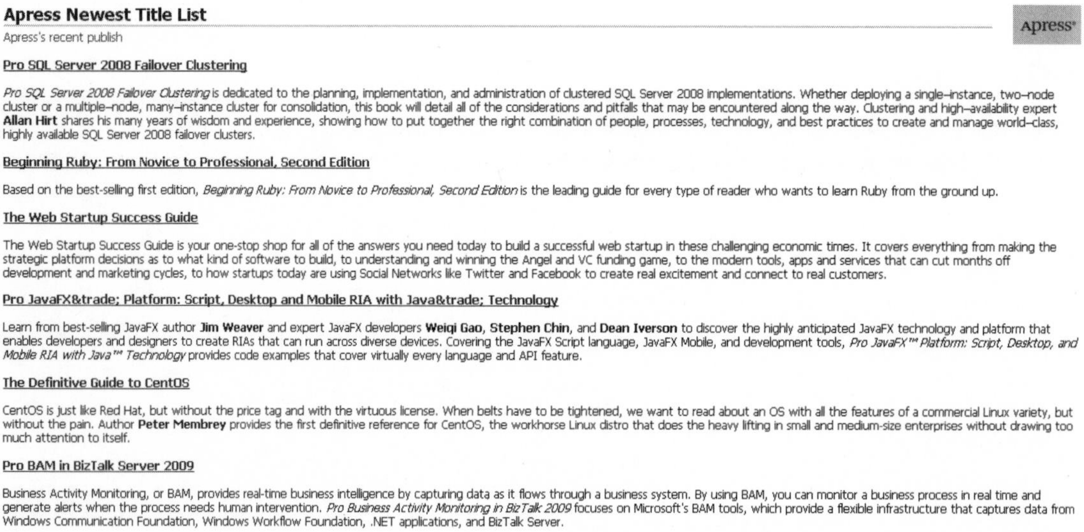

---

**Apress Newest Title List**

Apress's recent publish

*apress*

**Pro SQL Server 2008 Failover Clustering**

*Pro SQL Server 2008 Failover Clustering* is dedicated to the planning, implementation, and administration of clustered SQL Server 2008 implementations. Whether deploying a single-instance, two-node cluster or a multiple-node, many-instance cluster for consolidation, this book will detail all of the considerations and pitfalls that may be encountered along the way. Clustering and high–availability expert **Allan Hirt** shares his many years of wisdom and experience, showing how to put together the right combination of people, processes, technology, and best practices to create and manage world-class, highly available SQL Server 2008 failover clusters.

**Beginning Ruby: From Novice to Professional, Second Edition**

Based on the best-selling first edition, *Beginning Ruby: From Novice to Professional, Second Edition* is the leading guide for every type of reader who wants to learn Ruby from the ground up.

**The Web Startup Success Guide**

The Web Startup Success Guide is your one-stop shop for all of the answers you need today to build a successful web startup in these challenging economic times. It covers everything from making the strategic platform decisions as to what kind of software to build, to understanding and winning the Angel and VC funding game, to the modern tools, apps and services that can cut months off development and marketing cycles, to how startups today are using Social Networks like Twitter and Facebook to create real excitement and connect to real customers.

**Pro JavaFX&trade; Platform: Script, Desktop and Mobile RIA with Java&trade; Technology**

Learn from best-selling JavaFX author **Jim Weaver** and expert JavaFX developers **Weiqi Gao**, **Stephen Chin**, and **Dean Iverson** to discover the highly anticipated JavaFX technology and platform that enables developers and designers to create RIAs that can run across diverse devices. Covering the JavaFX Script language, JavaFX Mobile, and development tools, *Pro JavaFX™ Platform: Script, Desktop, and Mobile RIA with Java™ Technology* provides code examples that cover virtually every language and API feature.

**The Definitive Guide to CentOS**

CentOS is just like Red Hat, but without the price tag and with the virtuous license. When belts have to be tightened, we want to read about an OS with all the features of a commercial Linux variety, but without the pain. Author **Peter Membrey** provides the first definitive reference for CentOS, the workhorse Linux distro that does the heavy lifting in small and medium-size enterprises without drawing too much attention to itself.

**Pro BAM in BizTalk Server 2009**

Business Activity Monitoring, or BAM, provides real-time business intelligence by capturing data as it flows through a business system. By using BAM, you can monitor a business process in real time and generate alerts when the process needs human intervention. *Pro Business Activity Monitoring in BizTalk 2009* focuses on Microsoft's BAM tools, which provide a flexible infrastructure that captures data from Windows Communication Foundation, Windows Workflow Foundation, .NET applications, and BizTalk Server.

*Figure 7-10. Apress RSS feed*

Now let's use Zend Framework to pull in the content from the RSS feed. Add the rssTestAction()action shown in Listing 7-32 into the TestWSController.php file.

**Listing 7-32.** *Loading RSS from Web Source*

```php
<?php
 public function rssTestAction()
{

    //Load the RSS document.
    try{
      $url  = "http://www.apress.com/resource/feed/newbook";
      $feed = Zend_Feed::import($url);

    }catch(Zend_Feed_Exception $e){ throw $e; }
    //Parse and store the RSS data.
  }
}
```

Referring to Listing 7-32, you encase the call to the Apress RSS feed in a try-catch. Zend_Feed has its own exception handling using Zend_Feed_Exception. Like all other exception handlers, it also contains the standard method calls, which you can use in the error handlers. Using the import() method, you pass in the URL location to the feed and save the returned Zend_Feed_RSS object into the $feed variable for later use. Before loading this code in a browser, let's look at all the ways you can load an RSS feed.

## Loading from a String
A web source RSS feed might not be available, or you might need to load your RSS feed after you run it through a filter or a process that requires you to load the RSS feed via a string. In such cases, the Zend_Feed component also allows you to do that by using the importString() method, as shown in Listing 7-33.

**Listing 7-33.** *Loading an RSS String*

```php
<?php
public function rssLoadFromStringTestAction()
{

    //Load the RSS document.
    try{
      $rssFeedAsString = '<?xml version="1.0"?>
        <rss version="2.0">
         <channel>
           <title>My Music Web Site Home Page</title>
           <link>http://www.loudbite.com</link>
```

```
            <description>Weekly articles diving head first into the gossip,
new releases, concert dates, and anything related to the music industry around
the world. </description>

            <!-- Cache for 3 hours -->
            <ttl>180</ttl>

            <!-- Set the copyright info -->
            <copyright>Music News 2008</copyright>

            <!-- Set the language info -->
            <language>English</language>

            <category>Music</category>

            <pubDate>October 03, 2008</pubDate>

            <!-- Start list of articles -->
            <item>
              <author>fuglymaggie@ficticiousexample.com</author>
              <enclosure url="" type="" />
              <title>Criss Cross, now 35, continue wearing pants  backward
to look cool.</title>
              <link>http://www.loudbite.com/full link to your article</link>
              <description>Rap duo, Criss Cross continue to wear pants  backward
after repeated attemps to inform them,  the 90s are over...let it go...let it go.
              </description>
            </item>
            <item>
              <author>someeditor@ficticiousexample.com</author>
              <enclosure url="" type="" />
              <title>New PWG LP released!</title>
              <link>htp://www.loudbite.com/link to this articles page</link>
              <description>The new Puppies Wearing Glasses LP has hit the street.
First slated for October 3rd its now officially out. </description>
            </item>
          </channel>
        </rss>';

    $feed = Zend_Feed::importString($rssFeedAsString);
```

```
}catch(Zend_Feed_Exception $e){ throw $e; }

//Parse and store the RSS data.

}
```

Using the RSS feed XML you created in Listing 7-31 in the previous section, the PHP displays the file that consumes the RSS feed string. Like reading from a web source, you encase the Zend_Feed::importString() call inside a try-catch, which will allow you to catch any errors. You then call the following:

```
$feed = Zend_Feed::importString($rssFeedAsString);
```

The importString()method allows you to pass in a complete RSS feed that abides by both the XML rules as well as the RSS formatting standards. Once the RSS feed has successfully loaded, the method returns a Zend_Feed_RSS object and stores it in the variable $feed. Let's now look at how to load the RSS from a file.

### Loading from a File

The option to load from a locally stored file is also available. The file must contain well-formatted RSS content. The code to create a Zend_Feed_RSS object is the same as in previous examples except for the method you use. To load the file using Zend_Feed, you use the importFile() method, which accepts the absolute location to the XML file stored locally:

```
Zend_Feed::importFile();
```

Successfully loading an RSS feed with Zend Framework is always painless, but what can you do once you load the RSS document? How do you work with the information, and (most importantly) how does Zend Framework store the feed's content? Let's now see how to work with the feed data you loaded.

## Reading and Parsing RSS

If you want to play the guitar, you can't just pick one up and start strumming away. You need to tune the guitar and understand how it works before you start. In the same way, you need to understand how the Zend_Feed_RSS stores the RSS feed information after it parses the document.

As soon as Zend_Feed loads the RSS document using one the methods provided, it parses all relevant information. RSS has many specifications, so Zend Framework has created a list of tags that the Zend_Feed component will parse and support (see Table 7-17 and Table 7-18).

Zend_Feed stores all feed information as object attributes that can later be retrieved using a getter method. For example, if you wanted to retrieve the <title> channel element, you would issue title() to return the string value stored in the channel <title> element.

You can then continue to use the getters contained in the Zend_Feed_RSS object to return the remaining <channel> elements and <item> elements. Let's see how.

## Parsing and Using <channel> Element Data

Breaking the RSS document into two main sections, the channel and item sections, you can focus on how to use the <channel> element data and then look at the <item> element information in the feeds.

The <channel> element data contains information to describe the contents of the feed and describes the publisher of the feed and caching settings for the feed. Once you load the required libraries to use Zend_Feed and then load the RSS document, you can access all the channel's information using the outlined method calls shown in Table 7-17.

*Table 7-17. Zend_Feed_RSS Supported Channel Tags*

| Element | Method Call | Return Type |
| --- | --- | --- |
| title | title() | String |
| link | link() | String |
| lastBuildUpdate | lastBuildUpdate() | String |
| pubDate | pubDate() | String |
| description | description() | String |
| webMaster | webMaster() | String |
| copyright | copyright() | String |
| image | image() | String |
| generator | generator() | String |
| language | language() | String |
| ttl | ttl() | String |
| rating | rating() | String |
| cloud | cloud() | Array; elements: {domain, port, path,registerProcedure, protocol} |
| textInput | textInput() | Array; elements: {title, description, name, link} |
| skipHours | skipHours() | Array; elements: {hours in 24 format} |
| skipDays | skipDays() | Array; elements: {a day to skip} |

If you still have the RSS document you created in Listing 7-31, great; if not, refer to the listing and create a copy of it. You'll need it for the next example on how to load, parse, store, and display channel information from a feed.

First you need to create a view for the rssTestAction(), as shown in Listing 7-34.

**Listing 7-34.** *rss-test.phtml*

```
<?php echo $this->doctype('XHTML1_STRICT'); ?>
<html xmlns="http://www.w3.org/1999/xhtml" xml:lang="en" lang="en">
<head>
  <?php echo $this->headTitle('LoudBite.com – Artist List'); ?>
</head>
<body>

<?php echo $this->render("includes/header.phtml")?>
  <h3>Channel Information</h3>
  Title: <a href="<?php echo $this->link ?>"><?php echo $this->title ?></a>
   - <i><?php echo $this->copyright ?></i><br/>
  Description: <?php echo $this->description ?><br/>
  Category: <?php echo $this->category ?><br/>
  Published Date: <?php echo $this->pubDate ?><br/>


</body>
</html>
```

The view file rss-test.phtml should be stored inside the directory views/scripts/testws. The file contains PHP to display the channel title, description, a link to the web site of the RSS provider, the category the RSS belongs to, and a publish date. You now have to update the rssTestAction() (see Listing 7-35) as well as create an rssexample.xml file on your local file system. The content of the file must contain the XML string found in the previous listing.

**Listing 7-35.** *Channel Element Parsing Example*

```
public function rssTestAction()
{
    //Load the RSS document.
    try{

$rssFeedAsFile = '<PATH TO rssexample.html FILE>';
        $feed = Zend_Feed::importFile($rssFeedAsFile);

    //Parse and store the RSS data.
    $this->view->title       = $feed->title();
    $this->view->link        = $feed->link();
    $this->view->description = $feed->description();
    $this->view->ttl         = $feed->ttl();
```

307

```
    $this->view->copyright  = $feed->copyright();
    $this->view->language   = $feed->language();
    $this->view->category   = $feed->category();
    $this->view->pubDate     = $feed->pubDate();
}catch(Zend_Feed_Exception $e){ throw $e; }


}
```

    The code displayed in Listing 7-35 updates the code used from the previous example in this section. Load the XML file within a try-catch, and if there are no errors the Zend_Feed component will parse the feed information for you to use. You then use the parsed data by calling the getter methods of each channel element.

    Load the page on your browser by calling the URL http://localhost/test/rss-test. You will see a page that looks like Figure 7-11.

# Channel Information

Title: My Music Web Site Home Page - *Music News 2008*

Description: Weekly articles diving head first into the gossip, new releases, concert dates,

Category: Music

Published Date: October 03, 2008

***Figure 7-11.*** *Channel information RSS data*

## Using Item Elements

Channel element information is only half of what Zend_Feed can parse. The second main section of an RSS document are the items (syndicated articles) contained in the document.

    Table 7-18 shows the full list of tags the Zend_Feed component supports when parsing the document's data. Using the table, you'll expand on the section's example and parse the two articles contained in the rssexample.xml RSS feed.

***Table 7-18.*** *Zend_Feed_RSS Supported Item Tags*

| Element | Method Call | Return Type |
| --- | --- | --- |
| author | author() | String |
| title | title() | String |
| link | link() | String |
| description | description() | String |

| guid | guid() | String |
|------|--------|--------|
| comments | comments() | String |
| pubDate | pubDate() | String |
| source | source() | Array; elements: {title, url} |
| category | category() | M-Array; elements: {term, scheme} |
| enclosure | enclosure() | M-Array; elements: {url, type, length} |

Updating the rssTestAction(), you create the code shown in Listing 7-36.

**Listing 7-36.** *Working with Item Information*

```php
<?php
public function rsstestAction()
{

    //Load the RSS document.
    try{
        $rssFeedAsFile = '<PATH TO rssexample.xml FILE>';
        $feed = Zend_Feed::importFile($rssFeedAsFile);

        //Parse and store the RSS data.
        $this->view->title       = $feed->title();
        $this->view->link        = $feed->link();
        $this->view->description = $feed->description();
        $this->view->ttl         = $feed->ttl();
        $this->view->copyright   = $feed->copyright();
        $this->view->language    = $feed->language();
        $this->view->category    = $feed->category();
        $this->view->pubDate     = $feed->pubDate();

        //Get the articles
        $articles = array();
        foreach($feed as $article){
            $articles[] = array(
            "title"       => $article->title(),
            "description" => $article->description(),
            "link"        => $article->link(),
```

```
        "author"    => $article->author(),
        "enclosure"  =>
         array("url" => $article->enclosure['url'],
            "type" => $article->enclosure['type']));
    }


    $this->view->articles = $articles;
    }catch(Zend_Feed_Exception $e){ throw $e; }
}
```

Before moving on to the updated view of the action, let's look at how you fetch the article information stored in the RSS feed and the Zend_Feed_RSS object.

After loading the RSS feed using the importFile() method, you don't have to do additional coding to parse the data. Zend_Feed automatically parses the channel information and the item information. The feed data is stored in a Zend_Feed_RSS object and is returned upon a successful load of the RSS.

The Zend_Feed_RSS object is a type of Zend_Feed_Abstract object. Why is this important? Because the Zend_Feed_Abstract object implements an iterator and it allows you to use the returned object, Zend_Feed_RSS, inside an iteration loop such as foreach to access the items set for syndication. When using the iterator functionality of the Zend_Feed_RSS object, you loop through the items contained in the feed. By looping through the items, you access each article individually. In the example, you loop through the $feed object and call the getter methods for the title, link, description, and author to fetch the String values stored inside these elements. When you reach an element that contains attributes, the getter method returns an array. The array contains key-value pairs, and the value can be returned by using the following format:

$object-><elementName>['attributeName']

In the example, you accessed the value stored inside the url attribute by directly calling the url key contained in the enclosure element:

$article->enclosure['url'];

Finally, you place all the items into an array you can later use in the view shown in Listing 7-37.

### Listing 7-37. *rss-test.phtml*

```php
<?php echo $this->doctype('XHTML1_STRICT'); ?>
<html xmlns="http://www.w3.org/1999/xhtml" xml:lang="en" lang="en">
<head>
  <?php echo $this->headTitle('LoudBite.com – Artist List'); ?>
</head>
<body>

<?php echo $this->render("includes/header.phtml")?>

<h3>Channel Information</h3>
```

```
Title: <a href="<?php echo $this->link ?>"><?php echo $this->title ?></a>
- <i><?php echo $this->copyright ?></i><br>
Description: <?php echo $this->description ?><br>
Category: <?php echo $this->category ?><br>
Published Date: <?php echo $this->pubDate ?><br>

<h3>Articles</h3>
<p>
<?php foreach($this->articles as $article){ ?>

  <a href="<?php echo $article['link'] ?>"><?php echo $article['title'] ?></a>
 </b><br>
 <?php echo $article['description'] ?><br/>
<?php } ?>
</p>


</body>
</html>
```

Now focus your attention on creating an RSS feed of the site using Zend.

## Creating RSS Documents

In the beginning of this section, you reviewed the specifications of an RSS feed and created a simple RSS example using your favorite text editor. Creating RSS feeds manually can be tiresome, and you need a better solution that is quick to implement and easy to learn. Aside from easily parsing RSS data, the Zend_Feed component also easily creates RSS feeds.

The Zend_Feed component is bundled with the Zend_Feed_Builder. The class allows you to use a simple PHP array containing key-value pairs that you pass into either of the importArray() or importBuilder() methods.

The importArray() method accepts two parameters: an initial parameter of a key-value array and a second parameter, either "rss" or "atom", indicating what type of feed you want to generate. Listing 7-38 demonstrates a simple example of how to use the importArray() method to create the RSS document based on an array.

***Listing 7-38.*** *Creating RSS Using importArray()*

```
public function createRssAction()
{


  //PHP Array
  $rssContainer = array("title"       => "Channel Title",
              "link"       => "Channel Link",
              "description" => "Channel Description",
```

```
                      "charset"     => "utf8");

    try{

       //Create Builder Object
       $feedObject = Zend_Feed::importArray($rssContainer, "rss");
       header('Content-type: text/xml');
       echo $feedObject->saveXml();

    }catch(Zend_Feed_Exception $e){ throw $e; }
    $this->_helper->viewRenderer->setNoRender();


}
```

The new action created in the TestWSController.php file, createRssAction(), starts by creating a new array: $rssContainer. The array contains the required keys to generate the RSS. Without title, link, or charset keys, Zend_Feed will throw an exception. The array is then passed into the importArray() method as the initial parameter. Because you want to generate an RSS feed, you pass the "rss" string that allows the builder to know that you want an RSS, not an Atom feed format. If there are no exceptions thrown, the returned value of the importArray() method is a Zend_Feed_RSS object.

Using the returned Zend_Feed_RSS object, you can then generate the XML for the array. To do this, call the saveXML() method, which generates and returns a well-formatted RSS document, shown in Listing 7-39, containing only channel information.

**Listing 7-39.** *Generated RSS Document*

```xml
<?xml version="1.0" encoding="utf8"?>
<rss xmlns:content="http://purl.org/rss/1.0/modules/content/" version="2.0">
  <channel>
    <title><![CDATA[Channel Title]]></title>
    <link>Channel Link</link>
    <description><![CDATA[Channel Description]]></description>
    <pubDate>Wed, 21 Jan 2009 13:22:57 +0000</pubDate>
    <generator>Zend_Feed</generator>
    <docs>http://blogs.law.harvard.edu/tech/rss</docs>
  </channel>
</rss>
```

The RSS at this point is complete; what's missing now are a couple of articles to syndicate. Using the code already developed, go ahead and expand on it.

Listing 7-40 adds two articles that the feed will allow users to read. You add the articles by expanding the $rssContainer array and adding a new key: entries. The entries key accepts an array containing arrays, each array represents individual articles.

**Listing 7-40.** *Creating RSS with Two Articles*

```php
public function createRssAction()
{

    //PHP Array
    $rssContainer = array("title"       => "Channel Title",
                "link"        => "Channel Link",
                "description" => "Channel Description",
                "author"      => "author@book.com",
                "charset"     => "utf8",
                //Articles to syndicate
                "entries" => array(
                  array("title"       => "My Article 1",
                      "link"        => "Link to my full article 1",
                      "description" => "Description of my article 1",
                      "guid"        => "1A"
                  ),
                  array("title"       => "My Article 2",
                      "link"        => "Link to my full article 2",
                      "description" => "Description of my article ",
                      "guid"        => "2A")
                )
            );

    try{

        //Create Builder Object
        $feedObject =
            Zend_Feed::importBuilder(new Zend_Feed_Builder($rssContainer), "rss");

        //Return the generated XML
        $xml = $feedObject->saveXML();

        //Print out the generated XML
        header('Content-type: text/xml');
        echo $xml;

    }catch(Zend_Feed_Exception $e){ throw $e; }
```

```
        $this->_helper->viewRenderer->setNoRender();
}
```

Using Table 7-15, you can then add keys into each article's array, describing the syndicated content. You pass this same array into the importArray() method and allow Zend_Feed to do the rest for you. The resulting XML you receive once you call saveXML() using the example array will look like Listing 7-41.

*Listing 7-41.* *Zend_Feed–generated RSS*

```
<?xml version="1.0" encoding="utf8"?>
<rss xmlns:content="http://purl.org/rss/1.0/modules/content/" version="2.0">
 <channel>
  <title><![CDATA[Channel Title]]></title>
  <link>Channel Link</link>
  <description><![CDATA[Channel Description]]></description>
  <pubDate>Wed, 21 Jan 2009 13:22:57 +0000</pubDate>
  <generator>Zend_Feed</generator>
  <docs>http://blogs.law.harvard.edu/tech/rss</docs>
  <item>
   <title><![CDATA[My Article 1]]></title>
   <link>Link to my full article 1</link>
   <guid>1A</guid>
   <description><![CDATA[Description of my article 1]]></description>
   <pubDate>Wed, 21 Jan 2009 13:22:57 +0000</pubDate>
  </item>
  <item>
   <title><![CDATA[My Article 2]]></title>
   <link>Link to my full article 2</link>
   <guid>2A</guid>
   <description><![CDATA[Description of my article ]]></description>
   <pubDate>Wed, 21 Jan 2009 13:22:57 +0000</pubDate>
  </item>
 </channel>
</rss>
```

That's all there is to loading, parsing, and creating RSS documents using Zend Framework.

# Summary

This chapter introduced the concepts of web services and feeds, and how Zend Framework nicely integrates with such technologies. I touched on web services technologies such as REST and created simple examples that demonstrated the Zend_Rest functionality by creating both a server and client for each technology.

You learned about the numerous services Zend Framework has successfully integrated into, such as Amazon's AWS and Google's YouTube API. You also discovered what a feed is; the types of feeds available to consume; and how Zend Framework uses Zend_Feed to create, parse, and consume syndicated content.

# CHAPTER 8

■■■

# Creating a Search Engine Using Zend_Search_Lucene

You bring up your favorite web browser and start your online journey by visiting Google or Yahoo!. You type a keyword into the search field, press Submit, and wait for references to documents published online to appear. The result might contain a brief summary of what the content contains, and might even have the search term highlighted for you. With a search engine, you find relevant data in a matter of seconds instead of trying to determine the domain name of the web page and locate the interesting content within the site yourself.

In this chapter, you'll create your own search engine. I'll cover each of the layers that a search engine is required to have to properly function. From the index to the fields, you'll look at each of these pieces through the eyes of Zend Framework.

You'll look at the Zend_Search_Lucene component, a set of search class based off the Apache Search Engine library, Lucene. You'll learn about the Zend_Search_Lucene_Document, going over how to create documents, what are documents, how to retrieve specific fields within documents, and add content to the documents. With the index and the document covered, you'll learn how to add fields to the document using the Zend_Search_Lucene_Field object, learn what fields are, retrieve values of a field, set encoding types for individual fields, go over the available field types, and when you should use one field type over another.

With the search engine foundation created, you'll see how to retrieve matching content by constructing a query. You'll learn about the query structure: using Boolean operators, wildcard functionality, narrowing down results by using a range, and handling special characters. Finally, you'll see how to display the data that has been matched, display each document and its individual fields, and highlight the words that match the query.

---

■ **Note** For additional information regarding the Apache Search Engine library Lucene take a look at the online resource: http://lucene.apache.org/java/docs/

---

## Search Engine Components

A search engine is a complex application that requires many different parts to function properly. One layer is built on top of the other, and each layer adds additional functionality to the next.

There are four components to the search engine, as shown in Figure 8-1.

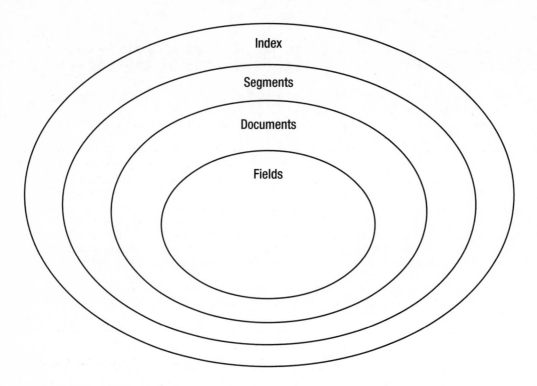

**Figure 8-1.** *Search engine components*

The search engine is composed of an index, segments, documents, and fields. The *index* is the main file that contains a collection of documents. It contains the data the user can search through and is represented as a physical file stored in the local file system. Indexes contain segments that are created each time a document is added into the index.

*Segments* are sub-indexes that can be searched independently. The more segments in an index, the slower the performance of the index and ultimately your searches.

*Documents* contain the actual data the user can search through. Documents contain content such as HTML content from a page, the title of a book, or any other value that is deemed important for the user.

Each document is further broken down into *fields*. Each field in the document contains itemized content. For example, the document containing book information could contain three fields: title field, date field, and description field. Each field is open for the user to search through.

In the world of Zend Framework, each layer shown in Figure 8-1 is represented as objects, except for the segment, which is handled behind the scenes. The index is represented as a Zend_Search_Lucene object and is stored in a directory of your choosing. Documents that are stored in the index are represented as Zend_Search_Lucene_Document objects and contain Zend_Search_Lucene_Field objects.

Let's start creating each of the pieces that the search engine needs .

# Creating the Foundation

The next sections cover how to build the foundations of each of the layers of the search engine, from the index to the fields.

# Creating the Index

Zend Framework represents an index as a Zend_Search_Lucene object. The Zend_Search_Lucene class allows you to create, update, delete, optimize, and add documents. Additional functionality is shown in Table 8-1.

***Table 8-1.*** *Zend_Search_Lucene Methods*

| Method | Parameter | Description |
|---|---|---|
| __construct() | Zend_Search_Lucene ⌐ (String directory, Boolean) | Creates/opens the index located at the directory supplied in the first parameter. If second parameter is false, opens index for updating. If second parameter is true, creates or overwrites index. |
| create() | create(String directory) | Creates a new index at the specified directory. |
| open() | open(String directory) | Opens the index at the directory specified for reading or updating. |
| getDirectory() | getDirectory() | Returns the directory path as a Zend_Search_Lucene_Storage_Directory object. |
| count() | count() | Returns the total number of documents within the index, including deleted documents. |
| maxDoc() | maxDoc() | Returns the total number of documents. |
| numDocs() | numDocs() | Returns the total number of non-deleted documents. |
| isDeleted() | isDeleted(int document_id) | Returns a Boolean value. If the document is deleted, it returns true; if not deleted, it returns false. |
| hasDeletions() | hasDeletions() | Returns a Boolean value. If the index has had documents deleted, it returns true, false otherwise. |

*(Continued)*

| | | |
|---|---|---|
| setDefaultSearch⤸Field() | setDefaultSearchField⤸ (String fieldname) | Sets the field name that will be searched by default.<br>An empty string marks a search to be done on all fields by default. |
| getDefaultSearch⤸Field() | getDefaultSearchField() | Returns a string representing the default search field. |
| setResultSetLimit() | setResultSetLimit(int) | Sets the total number of results to fetch when searching.<br>Default is 0, which returns all. |
| getMaxBufferedDocs() | getMaxBufferedDocs() | Returns the total number of documents in memory that must be met to write the documents into new segment in the file system. |
| setMaxBufferedDocs() | setMaxBufferedDocs(int) | Sets the total number of documents in memory that must be met to write the documents into the file system. Default is 10. |
| find() | find(String query\|Zend_⤸ Search_Lucene_Search_Query) | Queries the search engine.<br>Accepts either a String query or a Zend_Search_Lucene_Search_Query object. |
| getFieldNames() | getFieldNames(Boolean) | Returns an array of unique fields contained in the index. If true, it returns only indexed fields; if false, it returns all field names. |
| getDocument() | getDocument(int) | Returns a Zend_Search_Lucene_Document object of the document ID specified. |
| hasTerm() | hasTerm(Zend_Search_⤸ Lucene_Index_Term) | Returns a Boolean value.<br>If the index contains the term specified, it returns true; otherwise false. |
| terms() | terms() | Returns an array containing all the terms in the index. |
| optimize() | optimize() | Merges all the segments into one segment to increases index quality. |
| commit() | commit() | Commits any changes made when deleting documents. |
| addDocument() | addDocument(Zend_Search_⤸ Lucene_Document) | Adds a document to the index. |

| delete() | delete(int) | Removes a document from the index. |
| docFreq() | docFreq(Zend_Search_⤸ Lucene_Index_Term) | Returns the total number of documents that contain the term. |

The index is created using the Zend_Search_Lucene class by using its constructor or by using the create() factory method. When you use either one of these methods, you create the physical files required for the index. The index file can grow up to 2GB on a 32-bit system, but can reach larger sizes in a 64-bit system.

After the index files are created, the files will be used to store documents that the user can search through. You'll look into adding searchable documents later in this chapter.

---

■ **Note** Index files are compatible with the Java version of the Lucene search engine located at http://lucene.apache.org/.

---

Create a new controller, SearchController.php, and save it in the application/controllers directory. The controller will be used throughout this chapter, so keep it handy. The first action, createIndexAction, contains the functionality to create the index (see Listing 8-1).

**Listing 8-1.** *SearchController::createIndexAction*

```php
<?php
/**
 * Search Controller
 *
 */
class SearchController extends Zend_Controller_Action
{

    /**
     * Create Index.
     *
     */
    public function createIndexAction ()
    {

        //Create an index.
        $Index = Zend_Search_Lucene::create('../application/searchindex');

        echo 'Index created';
```

```
    //Suppress the view.
    $this->_helper->viewRenderer->setNoRender();
  }
}
```

The new controller action shown in Listing 8-1 automatically loads the Zend/Search/Lucene.php file behind the scenes using Zend_Loader covered in chapter 1 which allows us to instantiate a Zend_Search_Lucene object . You create the index by implementing the Zend_Search_Lucene factory method create(), which creates index files in the specified path you set as its first parameter. In the example, you create the index files inside the application/searchindex directory, and finish off the action by suppressing view rendering.

Open your browser and load the URL http://localhost/search/create-index. You will see the Index created text printed out on your page, which indicates that the index was properly created. To verify that everything was created successfully, open the application directory. You should see the new directory, searchindex, as well as a number of new files within that directory (see Figure 8-2).

**Figure 8-2.** *Newly created index*

The newly created files will be used to add documents that the user can later search through.

# Updating the Index

Updating the index can be done by initializing the Zend_Search_Lucene object and either calling its open() factory method or setting the second parameter to the constructor as false. Use the open() methods to add new documents into the index instead of overwriting the content currently stored in it. The open() method can also be used when reading the index for searching as well.

Let's update the index. Open the SearchController.php file and create a new action, updateIndexAction, as shown in Listing 8-2.

**Listing 8-2.** *SearchController::updateindexAction*

```
/**
 * Update Our Index.
 *
 */
public function updateIndexAction()
{
```

```
try{

  //Update an index.
  $Index = Zend_Search_Lucene::open('../application/searchindex');

}catch(Zend_Search_Exception $e){

  echo $e->getMessage();

}

echo 'Index Opened for Reading/Updating';

//Suppress the view.
$this->_helper->viewRenderer->setNoRender();

}
```

Listing 8-2 demonstrates the open() factory method that updates the index located at application/searchindex. In this example we use the open() factory method to open the index file that informs Zend_Search_Lucene that you will update (not create) the index file. Now update the index by loading the URL http://localhost/search/update-index.

Now that you understand the index—how it's created, how it's updated, and where it's saved—you're now ready to add documents to the index for searching.

# Adding Documents

With the index created and stored, the next step is to start the process of adding records to the index. Each record is represented as a document containing fields the search engine can use to narrow down submitted search queries by your users.

With the Zend_Search_Lucene_Document class you can create an instance of a document to save in the index. Once a Zend_Search_Lucene_Document object is instantiated, use any of the methods shown in Table 8-2 to add new data or retrieve field content.

*Table 8-2.* *Zend_Search_Lucene_Document Methods*

| Method | Parameter | Description |
| --- | --- | --- |
| addField() | addField(Zend_Search_Lucene_Field) | Adds a field to the document. |
| getFieldNames() | getFieldNames() | Returns an array containing all the fields in the document. |

*(Continued)*

| | | |
|---|---|---|
| getField() | getField(String) | Returns a Zend_Search_Lucene_Field object. |
| getFieldValue() | getFieldValue(String) | Returns the string value for the specified field name. |
| getFieldUtf8Value() | getFieldUtf8Value(String) | Returns the value for the specified field name as a UTF-8 string. |

Expanding the SearchController.php file, update the createIndexAction() by creating a set of documents to add into the index. Open the file once more and update the action, as shown in Listing 8-3.

**Listing 8-3.** *Creating and Adding Documents to the Index*

```
/**
 * Create Index.
 *
 */
public function createIndexAction ()
{

  try{

    //Create an index.
    $Index = Zend_Search_Lucene::create('../application/searchindex');

    //Create a Document
    $Artist1 = new Zend_Search_Lucene_Document();
    $Artist2 = new Zend_Search_Lucene_Document();
    $Artist3 = new Zend_Search_Lucene_Document();
    $Artist4 = new Zend_Search_Lucene_Document();
    $Artist5 = new Zend_Search_Lucene_Document();

    //Add the documents to the Index
    $Index->addDocument($Artist1);
    $Index->addDocument($Artist2);
    $Index->addDocument($Artist3);
    $Index->addDocument($Artist4);
    $Index->addDocument($Artist5);
```

```
    echo 'Index Opened for Reading/Updating<br/>';
    echo 'Total documents: '.$Index->maxDoc();

  }catch(Zend_Search_Exception $e){

    echo $e->getMessage();

  }

  //Suppress the view
  $this->_helper->viewRenderer->setNoRender();

}
```

Like Listing 8-2, the code in Listing 8-3 begins by instantiating a Zend_Search_Lucene object but then differs in that the updated code creates five Zend_Search_Lucene_Document objects: $Artist[1-5]. These document objects are then placed into the index using the Zend_Search_Lucene addDocument() method. You call the method five times, once for every document that needs to be placed into the index. Finally, the success message and the total number of documents within the index are printed onto the screen using the Zend_Search_Lucene maxDoc() method.

The maxDoc() method returns the total number of documents within the index, including the documents that are marked for deletion.

Reload the URL http://localhost/search/create-index to add the documents into the index. You should see the total number of documents equal to 5.

That's it; you created an index, created five documents, and added the five documents to the index. Unfortunately, if you attempted to search at this point, nothing will return because you need data as well as a few fields for each of the documents the user can search through.

## Updating Documents

A quick word on updating documents. Currently Zend Framework does not allow you to update a document within the index, but you can work around this by removing the document(s) using the Zend_Search_Lucene delete() method, and then re-creating the document(s) within the index. To do so, you need to learn how use the the delete() method.

## Deleting Documents

Deleting documents must be done by issuing the call to the Zend_Search_Lucene delete() method, which accepts a single value, the id of the document to remove.

Retrieve the ID of the document by performing a search for the documents that match a specific search query. If documents are located, a Zend_Search_Lucene_QueryHit object is returned which contains all the matching documents. You can then loop through each of the documents, fetch its id, and pass it into the delete() method, as shown in Listing 8-4.

***Listing 8-4.*** *Deleting Documents*

```
/**
* Delete the Documents
*
*/
public function deleteDocumentAction()
{

  try{

    //Open the index for reading.
    $Index = Zend_Search_Lucene::open('../application/searchindex');

    //Create the term to delete the documents.
    $hits = $Index->find('genre:electronic');

    foreach($hits as $hit){

      $index->delete($hit->id);

    }

    $Index->commit();

  }catch(Zend_Search_Exception $e){

    echo $e->getMessage();

  }
  echo 'Deletion completed<br/>';
  echo 'Total documents: '.$Index->numDocs();

  //Suppress the view
  $this->_helper->viewRenderer->setNoRender();
}
```

The code shown in Listing 8-4 removes all documents with the field genre containing the word electronic. You remove documents by creating a query which specifies the field name and keyword separated by a colon. (Document fields are discussed in greater detail later in the chapter.)

After you receive the results, you loop through each document and fetch its ID. This is the ID that the delete() method requires in order to remove the document. In this case, because you haven't yet created the genre field for the document objects, no documents will be removed.

If there were no errors, print out the text Deletion completed, along with the total number of documents current in the index with the Zend_Search_Lucene numDocs() method. By using the numDocs() method instead of the maxDoc() method, you request a count of only the documents that have not been flagged for deletion.

Let's remove the documents now. Load the URL http://localhost/search/delete-document. The count remains at 5 because there are no documents that contain the genre field.

# Creating Searchable Fields

A search engine uses an index to store all available data that can be searched. Because the index is required to identify items of data to search, you need to construct fields. A field contains data for a specific item of information such as the artist name, description of the artist, and the genre the artist belongs to. This is similar to the way a database table contains any number of columns.

The Zend_Search_Lucene_Field class handles the creation of fields in a document. By instantiating the Zend_Search_Lucene_Field class and using one of the object's methods, you can create fields in a document:

- Keyword()

- Binary()

- Text()

- UnSorted()

- UnIndexed()

All the Zend_Search_Lucene_Field methods accept three parameters. The initial parameter is a string and represents the name of the field you are creating. The second parameter is also a string and contains the data you are saving into the field. The final parameter is optional and is the type of encoding you want to save the data as. By default, the encoding is set to UTF-8.

Constructing a field begins by determining the field type you want to create. Each of the field types shown in Table 8-3 are used in different situations, and it's recommended that you use the proper one for the best search results.

*Table 8-3. Available Field Types*

| Field Type | Description | When to Use |
|---|---|---|
| Keyword | Indexes, stores, but does not tokenize the data. | Used when indexing full phrases, names, or other data not requiring tokenization. |
| UnIndexed | Not indexed or tokenized; is stored. User cannot search in these fields. | Used when indexing supplemental information regarding the search data. |

*(Continued)*

| | | |
|---|---|---|
| Binary | Stores data, but does not index or tokenize it. | Used when indexing binary data. |
| Text | Indexes, stores, and tokenizes the data. | Used when indexing general text. |
| UnSorted | Indexed and tokenized, but not stored. | Used when indexing large amounts of text that is searchable, but does not need to be redisplayed for the user. |

■ **Note** When Zend Framework *tokenizes* a string that will be within a field, it splits up the words when it encounters a space. It treats each word individually as a searchable entity, so the user can search for either "Elton" or "John" instead of "Elton John."

The second important thing to remember when naming a field is to refrain from naming your field by any of the attributes within the Zend_Search_Lucene_QueryHit class, such as id and score. Because an instance of Zend_Search_Lucene_QueryHit is returned when you issue a search query, naming a field using one of the property names will create a conflict when presenting the results to the user,. The attribute id contains the identification of the document found in the index, and the attribute score contains its search score used to determine how relevant a document is.

Let's create a field for the documents using the Text type. Open the SearchController.php file and update the createIndexAction, as shown in Listing 8-5.

***Listing 8-5.*** *Adding Searchable Fields to SearchController.php*

```
/**
 * Create Index.
 *
 */
public function createIndexAction(){

  try{

    //Create an index.
    $Index = Zend_Search_Lucene::create('../application/searchindex');

    //Create a Document
    $Artist1 = new Zend_Search_Lucene_Document();
    $Artist2 = new Zend_Search_Lucene_Document();
```

```
    $Artist3 = new Zend_Search_Lucene_Document();
    $Artist4 = new Zend_Search_Lucene_Document();
    $Artist5 = new Zend_Search_Lucene_Document();

    //Add the artist data
    $Artist1->addField(Zend_Search_Lucene_Field::
        Text('artist_name', 'Paul Oakenfold', 'utf-8'));

    $Artist2->addField(Zend_Search_Lucene_Field::
        Text('artist_name', 'Christopher Lawrence', 'utf-8'));

    $Artist3->addField(Zend_Search_Lucene_Field::
        Text('artist_name', 'Sting', 'utf-8'));

    $Artist4->addField(Zend_Search_Lucene_Field::
        Text('artist_name', 'Elton John', 'utf-8'));

    $Artist5->addField(Zend_Search_Lucene_Field::
        Text('artist_name', 'Black Star', 'utf-8'));

    //Add the documents to the Index
    $Index->addDocument($Artist1);
    $Index->addDocument($Artist2);
    $Index->addDocument($Artist3);
    $Index->addDocument($Artist4);
    $Index->addDocument($Artist5);

    echo 'Index created<br/>';
    echo 'Total Documents: '.$Index->maxDoc();

}catch(Zend_Search_Exception $e){

    echo $e->getMessage();

}

//Suppress the view.
$this->_helper->viewRenderer->setNoRender();
}
```

Listing 8-5 demonstrates how to successfully create a field for a document. Creating a field requires the use of the Zend_Search_Lucene_Field class as well as the Zend_Search_Lucene_Document addField() method.

The addField() method accepts a single Zend_Search_Lucene_Field object as a parameter. Each of the $Artist[1-5] objects call the addField() method to create a new field. You then use the Text()method to create a Text field type containing the field name artist_name, the name of the artist as its second parameter, and encoding type. The Text field type enables the user to search for specific words such as "Elton" or "Star" and then receive results. After the fields are created, you can add the document to the index using the Zend_Search_Lucene addDocument() method, as shown in previous examples.

Load the action once more to create the index and overwrite your current index created in our previous examples by loading the URL http://localhost/search/create-index.

---

■ **Note** You'll see lots of sample data in the following examples before moving on to adding real data into the fields. You have to understand the basics of using each field type before looking at how to extract data from the site to add to the index.

---

# Field Type Overview

The Zend_Search_Lucene component contains five field types (refer to Table 8-3), and each type has a different purpose. Let's see how to use each field type.

## Field Type: Keyword

The Keyword field type is used to index specific keywords such as Zend Framework or PHP. It does not tokenize each word and is recommended for use during full keyword content indexing. If users search for "Zend" not "Zend Framework," they won't get a result.

Let's build a Keyword field using the Zend_Search_Lucene_Field class for the search engine, as shown in Listing 8-6.

**Listing 8-6.** *Implementing a Keyword Field Type*

```
/**
 * Create the Index.
 *
 */
public function createIndexAction (){

  try{

    //Create the index.
    $Index = Zend_Search_Lucene:: create('../application/searchindex');

    //Create a Document
```

```
$Artist1 = new Zend_Search_Lucene_Document();
$Artist2 = new Zend_Search_Lucene_Document();
$Artist3 = new Zend_Search_Lucene_Document();
$Artist4 = new Zend_Search_Lucene_Document();
$Artist5 = new Zend_Search_Lucene_Document();

//Add the artist data
$Artist1->addField(Zend_Search_Lucene_Field::
     Text('artist_name', 'Paul Oakenfold', 'utf-8'));
$Artist1->addField(Zend_Search_Lucene_Field::
     Keyword ('genre', 'electronic'));

$Artist2->addField(Zend_Search_Lucene_Field::
     Text('artist_name', 'Christopher Lawrence', 'utf-8'));
$Artist2->addField(Zend_Search_Lucene_Field::
     Keyword ('genre', 'electronic'));

$Artist3->addField(Zend_Search_Lucene_Field::
     Text('artist_name', 'Sting', 'utf-8'));
$Artist3->addField(Zend_Search_Lucene_Field::
     Keyword ('genre', 'rock'));

$Artist4->addField(Zend_Search_Lucene_Field::
     Text('artist_name', 'Elton John', 'utf-8'));
$Artist4->addField(Zend_Search_Lucene_Field::
     Keyword ('genre', 'rock'));

$Artist5->addField(Zend_Search_Lucene_Field::
     Text('artist_name', 'Black Star', 'utf-8'));
$Artist5->addField(Zend_Search_Lucene_Field::
     Keyword ('genre', 'hip hop'));

//Add the documents to the Index
$Index->addDocument($Artist1);
$Index->addDocument($Artist2);
$Index->addDocument($Artist3);
$Index->addDocument($Artist4);
$Index->addDocument($Artist5);

echo 'Index created<br/>';
echo 'Total Documents: '.$Index->maxDoc();
```

```
}catch(Zend_Search_Exception $e){

    echo $e->getMessage();

}

//Suppress the view.
$this->_helper->viewRenderer->setNoRender();

}
```

You add the new field, genre, to the documents using the code shown in Listing 8-6. Begin the action by creating the index file and creating the $Artist[1-5] document objects. As in Listing 8-5, you add the Text fields and expand on that example by creating the Keyword field type, genre, using the Keyword() method. You pass in two required parameters into the method: the new field name and the artist genre. Finally, you add the documents to the index and print out a success message and the total number of documents within the index.

Load the URL http://localhost/search/create-index to add the documents into the index. Once they're loaded, the user can search for the artist name as well as the genre.

## Field Type: UnIndexed

UnIndexed field types contain supplemental information that can be returned to the user along with the search results. This field type does not tokenize, index, or allow users to search within this field type; it simply stores data to accompany user search results.

Storing the created date for the document, saving the date the band was formed, or saving the date the band broke up are good examples of what can be stored in a UnIndexed field type.

Open the SearchController.php file and update the createIndexAction once again. You'll add a new field for each of the documents that contains the date the artist began their career (see Listing 8-7).

**Listing 8-7.** *Creating an UnIndexed Field Type*

```
/**
 * Create Index.
 *
 */
public function createIndexAction (){

    try{

        //Create index.
        $Index = Zend_Search_Lucene::
            create('../application/searchindex');
```

```
//Create a Document
$Artist1 = new Zend_Search_Lucene_Document();
$Artist2 = new Zend_Search_Lucene_Document();
$Artist3 = new Zend_Search_Lucene_Document();
$Artist4 = new Zend_Search_Lucene_Document();
$Artist5 = new Zend_Search_Lucene_Document();

//Add the artist data
$Artist1->addField(Zend_Search_Lucene_Field::
        Text('artist_name', 'Paul Oakenfold', 'utf-8'));
$Artist1->addField(Zend_Search_Lucene_Field::
        Keyword ('genre', 'electronic'));
$Artist1->addField(Zend_Search_Lucene_Field::
        UnIndexed ('date_formed', '1990', 'utf-8'));

$Artist2->addField(Zend_Search_Lucene_Field::
        Text('artist_name', 'Christopher Lawrence', 'utf-8'));
$Artist2->addField(Zend_Search_Lucene_Field::
        Keyword ('genre', 'electronic'));
$Artist2->addField(Zend_Search_Lucene_Field::
        UnIndexed ('date_formed', '1991', 'utf-8'));

$Artist3->addField(Zend_Search_Lucene_Field::
        Text('artist_name', 'Sting', 'utf-8'));
$Artist3->addField(Zend_Search_Lucene_Field::
        Keyword ('genre', 'rock'));
$Artist3->addField(Zend_Search_Lucene_Field::
        UnIndexed ('date_formed', '1982', 'utf-8'));

$Artist4->addField(Zend_Search_Lucene_Field::
        Text('artist_name', 'Elton John', 'utf-8'));
$Artist4->addField(Zend_Search_Lucene_Field::
        Keyword ('genre', 'rock'));
$Artist4->addField(Zend_Search_Lucene_Field::
        UnIndexed ('date_formed', '1970', 'utf-8'));

$Artist5->addField(Zend_Search_Lucene_Field::
        Text('artist_name', 'Black Star', 'utf-8'));
$Artist5->addField(Zend_Search_Lucene_Field::
        Keyword ('genre', 'hip hop'));
$Artist5->addField(Zend_Search_Lucene_Field::
```

```
                UnIndexed ('date_formed', '1999', 'utf-8'));

        //Add the documents to the Index
        $Index->addDocument($Artist1);
        $Index->addDocument($Artist2);
        $Index->addDocument($Artist3);
        $Index->addDocument($Artist4);
        $Index->addDocument($Artist5);

        echo 'Index Updated<br/>';
        echo 'Total Documents: '.$Index->maxDoc();

    }catch(Zend_Search_Exception $e){
        echo $e->getMessage();
    }

    //Suppress the view.
    $this->_helper->viewRenderer->setNoRender();

}
```

Building on the documents, add another field: date_formed. The supplemental field date_formed contains the date the artists began their career (the dates are not accurate; they are used only as an example). Because you don't want the search engine to narrow down potential search results based on the date_formed field yet want to display the data to the user, the UnIndexed field type is perfect.

Listing 8-7 creates a new field type and is basically the same code as shown in Listing 8-6; the only difference being the way you create the UnIndexed date_formed field type. To add the new field, use the Zend_Search_Lucene_Field factory method UnIndexed(). Pass in the three parameters: the initial parameter is the name of the field to create, date_formed; the second is the date the artist was created; and the third is the encoding type you want to use.

Reload the URL http://localhost/search/create-index to add the documents containing three fields.

# Field Type: Binary
The Binary field type stores binary data. Unfortunately, the data can't be searched because it's not indexed or tokenized. The main purpose of the Binary field type is to store supplemental binary data such as images. This field type is ideal to use if you want to save the artist logo that is returned, along with any of the search results the user might receive.

# Field Type: Text
The Text field type allows you to tokenize, index, and store data in the field. It is a great field type if you are required to store the data inside a document and allow the user to search for a specific word. You should use the Text field instead of the Keyword field when you need to support the search of a word within a larger body of text (instead of specific keywords or phrases).

Listing 8-8 demonstrates the updated createIndexAction that adds short descriptions to the documents.

***Listing 8-8.*** *Creating a Text Field Type*

```
/**
 * Create Index.
 *
 */
public function createIndexAction (){

  try{

    //Create an index.
    $Index = Zend_Search_Lucene:: create('../application/searchindex');

    //Create a Document
    $Artist1 = new Zend_Search_Lucene_Document();
    $Artist2 = new Zend_Search_Lucene_Document();
    $Artist3 = new Zend_Search_Lucene_Document();
    $Artist4 = new Zend_Search_Lucene_Document();
    $Artist5 = new Zend_Search_Lucene_Document();

     //Add the artist data
    $Artist1->addField(Zend_Search_Lucene_Field::
          Text('artist_name', 'Paul Oakenfold', 'utf-8'));
    $Artist1->addField(Zend_Search_Lucene_Field::
          Keyword ('genre', 'electronic'));
    $Artist1->addField(Zend_Search_Lucene_Field::
          UnIndexed ('date_formed', '1990'));
    $Artist1->addField(Zend_Search_Lucene_Field::
          Text('description', 'Paul Oakenfold description
             will go here.', 'utf-8'));

      $Artist2->addField(Zend_Search_Lucene_Field::
            Text('artist_name','Christopher Lawrence','utf-8'));
      $Artist2->addField(Zend_Search_Lucene_Field::
            Keyword ('genre', 'electronic'));
      $Artist2->addField(Zend_Search_Lucene_Field::
            UnIndexed ('date_formed', '1991'));
      $Artist2->addField(Zend_Search_Lucene_Field::
            Text('description', 'Christopher Lawrence
```

```
            description will go here.', 'utf-8'));

$Artist3->addField(Zend_Search_Lucene_Field::
        Text('artist_name', 'Sting', 'utf-8'));
$Artist3->addField(Zend_Search_Lucene_Field::
        Keyword ('genre', 'rock'));
$Artist3->addField(Zend_Search_Lucene_Field::
        UnIndexed ('date_formed', '1982'));
$Artist3->addField(Zend_Search_Lucene_Field::
        Text('description', 'Sting description
            will go here.', 'utf-8'));

$Artist4->addField(Zend_Search_Lucene_Field::
        Text('artist_name', 'Elton John', 'utf-8'));
$Artist4->addField(Zend_Search_Lucene_Field::
        Keyword ('genre', 'rock'));
$Artist4->addField(Zend_Search_Lucene_Field::
        UnIndexed ('date_formed', '1970'));
$Artist4->addField(Zend_Search_Lucene_Field::
        Text('description', 'Elton John description
            will go here.', 'utf-8'));

$Artist5->addField(Zend_Search_Lucene_Field::
        Text('artist_name', 'Black Star', 'utf-8'));
$Artist5->addField(Zend_Search_Lucene_Field::
        Keyword ('genre', 'hip hop'));
$Artist5->addField(Zend_Search_Lucene_Field::
        UnIndexed ('date_formed', '1999'));
$Artist5->addField(Zend_Search_Lucene_Field::
        Text('description', 'Black Star description
            will go here.', 'utf-8'));

//Add the documents to the Index
$Index->addDocument($Artist1);
$Index->addDocument($Artist2);
$Index->addDocument($Artist3);
$Index->addDocument($Artist4);
$Index->addDocument($Artist5);

echo 'Index created<br/>';
echo 'Total Documents: '.$Index->maxDoc();
```

```
}catch(Zend_Search_Exception $e){
    echo $e->getMessage();
}
```

```
//Suppress the view.
$this->_helper->viewRenderer->setNoRender();
}
```

Listing 8-8 creates a new field: description. The description field lets users search in the description for a specific word, and display the description to the user. To create the new field type, use the Zend_Search_Lucene_Field class factory method Text() and pass in the three parameters. Set the name of the field, description, in the first parameter; set the text you want to save into the field in the second; and set the third to UTF-8 as the encoding type. Load the URL http://localhost/search/create-index to create the index with five documents, each document containing four fields.

# Field Type: UnStored

The UnStored field type indexes and tokenizes the data, but does not store the content as the Text and Keyword field types do. The UnStored field type keeps the data in memory. The user can search for content in these fields, but the data has to be retrieved from other sources (such as a database or a file) to display to the user.

Listing 8-9 demonstrates an example implementation of this field type by creating two additional fields for each document. The first field, full_profile, contains a very long description of the artist; the second field, artist_id, contains the unique ID given to the artist within a database table.

The user can search within the UnStored field; if there are any matching documents, use the artist_id field to fetch the specific row in a database table.

---

■ **Tip** If you've been following along and building the LoudBite application, these fields do not appear in the database tables; they are used here only as an example.

---

Now open the SearchController.php file and update the createindexAction, as shown in Listing 8-9.

***Listing 8-9.*** *Creating an UnStored Field Type*

```
/**
 * Create Index.
 *
 */
public function createIndexAction (){

    try{
```

```
//Create an index.
$Index =
  Zend_Search_Lucene::create('../application/searchindex');

//Create a Document
$Artist1 = new Zend_Search_Lucene_Document();
$Artist2 = new Zend_Search_Lucene_Document();
$Artist3 = new Zend_Search_Lucene_Document();
$Artist4 = new Zend_Search_Lucene_Document();
$Artist5 = new Zend_Search_Lucene_Document();

//Add the artist data
$Artist1->addField(Zend_Search_Lucene_Field::
        Text('artist_name', 'Paul Oakenfold', 'utf-8'));
$Artist1->addField(Zend_Search_Lucene_Field::
        Keyword ('genre', 'electronic'));
$Artist1->addField(Zend_Search_Lucene_Field::
        UnIndexed ('date_formed', '1990'));
$Artist1->addField(Zend_Search_Lucene_Field::
        Text('description', 'Paul Oakenfold description
            will go here.'));
$Artist1->addField(Zend_Search_Lucene_Field::
        UnIndexed ('artist_id', '1'));
$Artist1->addField(Zend_Search_Lucene_Field::
        UnStored('full_profile', "Paul Oakenfold's
            Full Profile will go here."));

$Artist2->addField(Zend_Search_Lucene_Field::
        Text('artist_name', 'Christopher Lawrence', 'utf-8'));
$Artist2->addField(Zend_Search_Lucene_Field::
        Keyword ('genre', 'electronic'));
$Artist2->addField(Zend_Search_Lucene_Field::
        UnIndexed ('date_formed', '1991'));
$Artist2->addField(Zend_Search_Lucene_Field::
        Text('description', 'Christopher Lawrence description
            will go here.'));
$Artist2->addField(Zend_Search_Lucene_Field::
        UnIndexed ('artist_id', '2'));
$Artist2->addField(Zend_Search_Lucene_Field::
        UnStored('full_profile', "Christopher Lawrence's
```

```
                            Full Profile will go here."));

$Artist3->addField(Zend_Search_Lucene_Field::
        Text('artist_name', 'Sting', 'utf-8'));
$Artist3->addField(Zend_Search_Lucene_Field::
        Keyword ('genre', 'rock'));
$Artist3->addField(Zend_Search_Lucene_Field::
        UnIndexed ('date_formed', '1982'));
$Artist3->addField(Zend_Search_Lucene_Field::
        Text('description', 'Sting description
            will go here.'));
$Artist3->addField(Zend_Search_Lucene_Field::
        UnIndexed ('artist_id', '3'));
$Artist3->addField(Zend_Search_Lucene_Field::
        UnStored('full_profile', "Sting's Full Profile
                will go here."));


$Artist4->addField(Zend_Search_Lucene_Field::
        Text('artist_name', 'Elton John', 'utf-8'));
$Artist4->addField(Zend_Search_Lucene_Field::
        Keyword ('genre', 'rock'));
$Artist4->addField(Zend_Search_Lucene_Field::
        UnIndexed ('date_formed', '1970'));
$Artist4->addField(Zend_Search_Lucene_Field::
        Text('description', 'Elton John description
            will go here.'));
$Artist4->addField(Zend_Search_Lucene_Field::
        UnIndexed ('artist_id', '4'));
$Artist4->addField(Zend_Search_Lucene_Field::
        UnStored('full_profile', "Elton John's Full Profile
                will go here."));


$Artist5->addField(Zend_Search_Lucene_Field::
        Text('artist_name', 'Black Star', 'utf-8'));
$Artist5->addField(Zend_Search_Lucene_Field::
        Keyword ('genre', 'hip hop'));
$Artist5->addField(Zend_Search_Lucene_Field::
        UnIndexed ('date_formed', '1999'));
$Artist5->addField(Zend_Search_Lucene_Field::
        Text('description', 'Black Star description
            will go here.'));
```

```
    $Artist5->addField(Zend_Search_Lucene_Field::
        UnIndexed ('artist_id', '3'));
    $Artist5->addField(Zend_Search_Lucene_Field::
        UnStored('full_profile', "Black Star's Full Profile
            will go here."));

    //Add the documents to the Index
    $Index->addDocument($Artist1);
    $Index->addDocument($Artist2);
    $Index->addDocument($Artist3);
    $Index->addDocument($Artist4);
    $Index->addDocument($Artist5);

    echo 'Index created<br/>';
    echo 'Total Documents: '.$Index->maxDoc();

}catch(Zend_Search_Exception $e){

    echo $e->getMessage();

}


    //Suppress the view.
    $this->_helper->viewRenderer->setNoRender();

}
```

Listing 8-9 shows the final field type, UnStored, which is used the same way as the other four field types. Using the UnStored()factory method, add a new field, full_profile, to the documents. Pass in two parameters: the name of the field and a string that represents a very large profile. You also create an additional field, artist_id, with the UnIndexed field type because it will contain supplemental data that is not searchable. After the new field types are added to the documents, add the documents into the index and print the success message.

Re-create the index by loading the URL http://localhost/search/create-index. The new index will now contain five documents which holds the artist name, genre, a small description of the artist, full profile of the artist, artist ID, and the date the artist began his/her career.

With the structure completed, it's time to look at how you can add data into each field using the built-in parsing classes and how to add string data into the fields.

## Populating Fields with Data

In many cases, populating the fields is as simple as passing in the data as the second parameter to the available field types, as shown in the previous section. Other times this simple approach is not as efficient as indexing HTML documents or Microsoft Word files.

Popular search data is typically found on these types of files so let's go over the built-in functionality that allows you to load the data in such files so the user can search through them.

## Parsing HTML

By default, you can use the Zend_Search_Lucene_Document_Html class to parse the content from the title as well as the body of HTML documents. The only requirement is that the HTML must be either a string or an HTML file stored locally. See Table 8-4.

**Table 8-4.** *Zend_Search_Lucene_Document_HTML Methods*

| Method | Parameter | Description |
|---|---|---|
| getHeaderLinks() | N/A | Returns an array containing all links that appear in the header. |
| loadHTML() | loadHTML(String) | Loads an HTML or XHTML string. |
| loadHTMLFile() | loadHTMLFile(String) | Loads an HTML file from the local file system. |
| highlight() | highlight(String\|Array, String) | Highlights the word(s) found in the loaded HTML with the specified color.<br>Parameter 1: Word or array of words to highlight.<br>Parameter 2: Color used for highlighting (ex #FF0000).<br>Returns a String. |
| getHTML() | N/A | Returns a string containing the HTML to parse. |
| setExcludeNoFollowLinks() | setExcludeNoFollowLinks(Boolean) | Determines whether links with the rel="nofollow" attribute should be excluded.<br>If true, parser excludes links; if false, parser includes links. |
| getExcludeNoFollowLinks() | getExcludedNoFollowLinks() | Determines whether links with the rel="nofollow" attribute should be excluded. |

By default, the Zend_Search_Lucene_Document_Html class saves the parsed document into the index with the following fields:

- title

- content

It also contains all the methods available to you in the Zend_Search_Lucene_Document class shown in Table 8-2 as well as any metadata present in the HTML file in the form of properties. Let's take a look at an example of parsing an HTML document and adding the document to the index.

Open the SearchController.php file and create a new action, parseHtmlAction(). The action will handle parsing HTML, as shown in Listing 8-10.

***Listing 8-10.*** *Parsing HTML Files*

```
/**
 * ParseHtml Action
 *
 */
public function parseHtmlAction(){

  try{

    //Open the Index for updating.
    $Index = Zend_Search_Lucene::open('../application/searchindex');

    //Set Path to the HTML to parse.
    $htmlDocPath = '<PATH TO YOUR FILE>';

    //Check if the file is present
    if(!file_exists($htmlDocPath)){
      throw new Exception("Could not find file $htmlDocPath.");
    }

    //Parse the the HTML file.
    $htmlDoc = Zend_Search_Lucene_Document_Html:: loadHTMLFile ($htmlDocPath);

    //Example of getters and property calls.
    $links       = $htmlDoc->getLinks();
    $headerLinks = $htmlDoc->getHeaderLinks ();
    $title       = $htmlDoc->title;
    $body        = $htmlDoc->body;

    //Add the content to the Index.
    $Index->addDocument($htmlDoc);

    echo 'Successfully parsed HTML file.<br/>';
    echo 'Total Documents:'. $Index->numDocs().'<br/><br/>';
```

```
//Validate parsed links within document
echo "Links Parsed<br/>";
foreach($links as $link){

   echo "$link <br/>";

}

}catch(Zend_Search_Exception $e){

  echo $e->getMessage();

}

//Suppress the view
$this->_helper->viewRenderer->setNoRender();
}
```

The action begins by opening the index for updating; and initializing the $htmlDocPath variable which contains the absolute path to the HTML document. You then verify if the file exists. Since Zend_Search_Lucene_Document does not throw an exception if the file does not exists we add the logic in ourselves. We then call the loadHTMLFile() method and pass in the $htmlDocPath variable to load and parse the data.

Next, you use both methods and properties of the Zend_Search_Lucene_Document object. In this case, you fetch all the header links using getHeaderLinks(), fetch the links in the page using getLinks(), and use the title and body properties to quickly fetch the data within the title and body HTML nodes. Finally, you save the document into the index using the addDocument() method and for verification purposes we print out to the screen all the links that were located and saved.

Let's go ahead and create a simple XHTML file (see Listing 8-11).

***Listing 8-11.*** *Creating an HTML File to Parse*

```
<!DOCTYPE html PUBLIC "-//W3C//DTD XHTML 1.0 Strict//EN"
"http://www.w3.org/TR/xhtml1/DTD/xhtml1-strict.dtd">
<html xmlns="http://www.w3.org/1999/xhtml" xml:lang="en" lang="en">
<head>
<meta http-equiv="Content-Type" content="text/html; charset=UTF-8" />
<title>MyHTML file example</title>
<link rel="stylesheet" href="http://www.loudbite.com/css/style.css" />

<meta name="generator" content="Generator 123" />
<meta name="example_meta" content="Meta Example" />

</head>
```

```
<body>
<p>
This is your first HTML file to parse.

<a href=" http://en.wikipedia.org/wiki/Paul_Oakenfold">Paul Oakenfold</a>
<a href=" http://en.wikipedia.org/wiki/Christopher_Lawrence_(DJ)">
  Christopher Lawrence
</a>
<a href=" http://en.wikipedia.org/wiki/Sting_(musician)">Sting</a>
<a href=" http://en.wikipedia.org/wiki/Black_Star_(hip_hop_group)">Black Star</a>
</p>
</body>
</html>
```

The XHTML shown in Listing 8-11 contains basic information. You have the title, metadata fields, and a small excerpt in the body that contains not only text but also four links.

Save the file as htmlexample.html somewhere in your file system and then update the $htmlDocpath variable in the code shown in Listing 8-10. Load the document into the index now by loading the http://localhost/search/parse-html page. If there were no errors, you should now have the document loaded into your index with the title, generator, body, and example_meta fields. These fields are also available as $htmlDoc object properties.

## Parsing Microsoft .docx Word Documents

It's easy to parse Microsoft Word 2007 documents with the Zend_Search_Lucene_Document_Docx class. The class allows you to parse the title, file name, subject, and document creator. A full list of available data that can be parsed from a Word document is shown in Table 8-5. After the data is parsed, the document can be added to the index using the Zend_Search_Lucene addDocument() method.

**Table 8-5.** *Zend_Search_Lucene_Document_Docx Default Attributes*

| Attribute | Description |
| --- | --- |
| title | Title of the Word 2007 document |
| subject | Subject of the Word 2007 document |
| filename | File name of the Word 2007 document |
| creator | Creator of the Word 2007 document |
| keywords | Keywords of the Word 2007 document |
| description | Description of the Word 2007 document |

| lastModifiedBy | Username of the last user who modified the Word 2007 document |
| --- | --- |
| revision | Current revision of the Word 2007 document |
| modified | Modified date/time of the Word 2007 document |
| created | Created date/time of the Word 2007 document |
| body | Body of the Word 2007 document (comments and revisions are not included) |

To get started, the PHP installation must have the ZipArchive module installed. Without this module, Zend_Search_Lucene_Document_Docx can't parse the data within the document. So take a few seconds to see whether the module is already installed; if it's not, take the time to install it. Because the module is also required for parsing Excel and PowerPoint files, it's a good idea to install it now.

Open the directory in which you installed PHP. Within this directory, there is an ext folder. The folder contains all the extensions PHP currently uses. Open it and see whether the php_zip.dll file (Windows users) or the php_zip.so file (Unix users) is present. If the file is not present, simply download the PHP installation .zip or .tar.gz file again, extract its content, and copy the file to your local directory. The second step is to make a modification to your php.ini file. Open it and uncomment (Windows users):

extension=php_zip.dll

Linux users need to compile PHP and set --enable-zip as a configure option. Restart Apache to finalize the installation.

Now open the SearchController.php file and create a new action, parseWordDocAction(), which will demonstrate the way you can load, parse, and save the document into the index (see Listing 8-12).

**Listing 8-12.** *Parsing Word 2007 Documents*

```
/**
 * Parse Word 2007 File.
 *
 */
public function parseWordDocAction(){

  try{

    //Open the index.
    $Index = Zend_Search_Lucene:: open("../application/searchindex");

    //Initialize Word Document Path
    $wordDocPath = '<PATH TO YOUR Word FILE>';

    //Load and parse the Word Doc.
```

```
$wordDoc = Zend_Search_Lucene_Document_Docx::
        loadDocxFile($wordDocPath, true);

//Example of getters.
$title        = $wordDoc->title;
$createdDate = $wordDoc->created;
$body         = $wordDoc->body;

//Add the Document into the index
$Index->addDocument($wordDoc);

echo 'Successfully parsed Word file.<br/>';
echo 'Total Documents: '.$Index->numDocs().'<br/>';

//Display Word document information
echo "Title of Word document: $title <br/>";
echo "Created Date of Document: $createdDate";

}catch(Zend_Search_Lucene_Exception $e){

echo $e->getMessage();

}

//Suppress the view
$this->_helper->viewRenderer->setNoRender();

}
```

In Listing 8-12, the code demonstrates the complete functionality of how you can load, parse, and save a .docx document into the index. Start by initializing the path to the Word 2007 document in the file system. Keep in mind that a document that is not a Word 2007 file will not parse or index.

Load the document for parsing by using the loadDocxFile() method, which accepts two parameters: the path to the document and a Boolean flag which determines whether you want to store the content of the body. The example sets the flag that stores the body to true. You then issue three calls to the available data that fetches the title of the document, the created date, and the body of the document. These properties are also document fields after they are saved into the index. Finally, store the document into the index by issuing the call to the addDocument() method and passing in the $wordDoc variable.

Create a Word 2007 document now and give it a try by updating $wordDocPath and loading the URL http://localhost/search/parse-word-doc.

## Parsing Other Formats

Other document types, such as PowerPoint and Excel files, are supported by the search feature of Zend Framework

Using the Zend_Search_Lucene_Document_Xlsx class, you can parse and save Excel files into the index. Likewise, with the Zend_Search_Lucene_Document_Pptx class you can parse PowerPoint files. Both file types can be loaded, parsed, and indexed by replacing the Zend_Search_Lucene_Document_Docx references shown in Listing 8-12 with the specific class you want to use. Moreover, the available fields and properties for both files are shown in Table 8-5, the same data used by the Zend_Search_Lucene_Document_Docx class.

Now that you have plenty of data in the index, let's see how to search it.

# Fetching Data

This section covers the way you build a query for the search engine (which identifies the fields that you want to search).

## Text-based Queries

A *text-based query* is a query that contains all the information which the user will search for as a string. Look at the structure of the following query string. It must contain a field to search and must contain the value that the user wants to search for:

<field name>:<field value> [Operator <field name>:<field value>]

The query contains a field followed by a colon (:) and then the value to search for. Using the currently created index, let's perform a search for the artist with the name paul. In this case, the query string is artist_name:paul.

By default, a search is done on all fields available in the index. You can set a default search field by calling the Zend_Search_Lucene method, setDefaultSearchField(), that accepts a single string field name.

## Operators

Boolean operators are also supported in the form of AND, OR, NOT; as well as && and ||. The AND operator joins two or more terms and fetches the documents that contain all occurrences of the string.

Searching for a document that contains the genre rock and the word will in the description, the search query is the following:

genre:rock AND description:will

The above query will return the documents for Sting and Elton John.

The OR operator returns all documents that match one or more search criteria. Using the artist information already stored in the index a search for all artists that belong to the rock electronic genres is as follows:

(genre:rock OR genre:electronic) AND description:will

Or it can be created as follows:

(genre:rock || genre:electronic) && description:will

You can also force the query to match all documents with a specific word by using the + symbol, which forces the search to return all documents containing the term following the symbol. For example, if you want to search within the description field for all documents containing the word Lawrence, the query is the following:

description:+Lawrence

To specify more than one word, surround the words using quotes, as follows:

description:+"Christopher Lawrence"

Likewise, the – symbol forces the search to exclude any document which contains the word preceding the – symbol in the specified field. For example, description:-Star returns all artists except for the artist Black Star because the description contains the word *Star*.

# Wildcards

Wildcard searches are used when the user knows a few bits of information that the document contains, but doesn't know specifics. For example, if you want to search in the description field and don't know the entire spelling of Christopher, you can construct a query as chri* law*, which matches all words with these patterns: christopher lawrence, chri123 law, chritofer lawranse, chris lawense, and so on.

To use wildcard values as a search query, place them in the value portion of the term with at least 3 characters preceding it. With the search index, use this:

description:chris* law*

The result contains only a single document pertaining to Christopher Lawrence.

To search for single missing values, use the ? wildcard symbol. For example, if you want to search for the term Paul Oakenfold, but don't know whether there is a *c* in the artist's last name, you can pass in the ? after the *c*. The query looks like this:

description:Paul Oac?kenfold

# Fuzzy Searches

*Fuzzy searches* help users when they don't know how to spell the word or want similar documents. The fuzzy search is represented by a tilde (~) at the end of the search word and contains a ranking parameter that can be used to narrow down the documents returned:

<search word>~<ranking parameter>

The ranking parameter immediately follows the ~ symbol and contains a float value from 0 to 1. Numbers closer to 1 represent close matches to the word supplied; numbers closer to 0 represent matches that are less similar.

Let's create a term which matches all documents that closely match the word *Pal*. The query is the following:

artist_name:Pal~0.6

The search term created matches Paul, which is probably what the user meant, and returns all documents that closely match the wording supplied.

## Ranges

*Ranges* are used to search for documents that fall between a numerical range and an alpha range. The range function is structured by supplying two values inside a string format:

[lower boundary TO upper boundary]

The first value is the starting boundary value, and the second value represents the upper boundary value.

Using the index created previously, you can search for the all artist names from Paul Oakenfold to Sting by issuing the following range query:

artist_name:[Paul TO Sting]

This query returns all documents that contain values in the range Paul Oakenfold to Sting for the artist_name. You can also search for numerical values much the same way.

## Special Characters

The search functionality of Zend Framework uses many characters that a user can also utilize within a search term. Such characters are the following:

+ - && || ! ( ) { } [ ] ^ " ~ * ? : \

To escape the characters, use the \ character before executing a query containing any of the preceding characters. For example, if you want to query the search engine for the term "This is a test", the string must be escaped as follows before running the search query:

\"This is a test\"

# Displaying Result Sets

All data storage components need a way to display content, and it is no different for the search index. You need a way to display the data that the user has searched for within the index.

The Zend_Search_Lucene class uses the find() method to search through the index. The find() method accepts a query like the ones you've just looked at as its single parameter. Let's search for a few items in the index you've created and display each result.

Open the SearchController.php file and create a resultAction() action. The action will contain all the functionality to search for content, as shown in Listing 8-13.

*Listing 8-13. Displaying Search Results*

```
/**
 * Result.  Fetch the result and display to the user.
 *
 */
```

```php
public function resultAction(){


    //Open the index to search in.
    $Index = Zend_Search_Lucene:: open('../application/searchindex');

    //Set the properties for the Index.
    $Index->setDefaultSearchField('artist_name');

    //Construct Query
    $query = 'paul*';
    //Search.
    $hits = $Index->find($query);

    //Set the view variables
    $this->view->hits = $hits;
}
```

The resultAction() shown in Listing 8-13 creates the Zend_Search_Lucene object, and then uses one of the methods outlined in Table 8-2 to set the default search field as the artist_name. You then construct the query that searches for all documents that match the pattern paul* and then using the find() method we execute the query. The find() method returns a Zend_Search_Lucene_QueryHit object that you save for use in the view.

Let's now create a view for the action. Open the application/views/scripts/search directory, create the result.phtml file, and copy Listing 8-14.

**Listing 8-14.** *Creating a Results View*

```php
<?php echo $this->doctype('XHTML1_STRICT'); ?>
<html xmlns="http://www.w3.org/1999/xhtml" xml:lang="en" lang="en">
<head>
  <?php echo $this->headTitle('LoudBite.com – Search Results'); ?>
</head>
<body>

  <?php echo $this->render("includes/header.phtml"); ?>
    <table border='0' width='600'>
    <tr><td colspan="3"><b>Search Results</b></td></tr>

      <?php foreach($this->hits as $hit){ ?>

      <tr><td><a href='artist/<?php echo $hit->artist_id?>'>
          <?php echo $hit->artist_name; ?></a> -
```

```
    <?php echo $hit->genre;?>
</td></tr>
<tr><td><?php echo $hit->description;?><br><br></td></tr>

    <?php } ?>
```

```
</table>
</body>
</html>
```

The $hits variable can be iterated with a foreach loop. Notice how the individual field names are called. You can call them either by using the property name, as in this example, or by using the getDocument() method that returns a Zend_Search_Lucene_Document object. You can then use the getFieldValue() method to return the value of a specific field in the document. Load http://localhost/search/result to see the page shown in Figure 8-3.

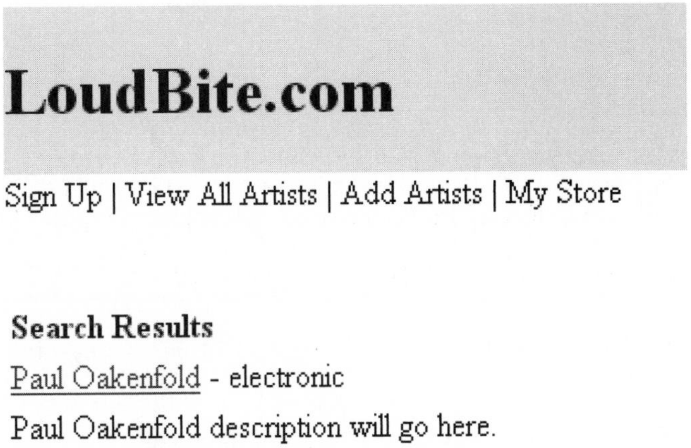

# LoudBite.com

Sign Up | View All Artists | Add Artists | My Store

## Search Results

Paul Oakenfold - electronic

Paul Oakenfold description will go here.

*Figure 8-3. Search results*

The data returned by the search engine can be manipulated to return only a limited number of records and can also be sorted in many different ways. Let's take a look at each method now.

# Limiting Results

Limiting the number of records returned to the user is helpful when dealing with large numbers of search results. Referring to Table 8-2, you can use the method setResultSetLimit() to limit the total number of records to display. This method accepts a single numerical value that represents the number of records to return.

Open the SearchController.php file once more and update the resultAction() to return only the top match for the search term 'genre:rock', as shown in Listing 8-15.

**Listing 8-15.** *Setting the Result Set Limit*

```
/**
 * Result.  Fetch the result and display to the user.
 *
 */
public function resultAction(){

    //Open the index to search in.
    $Index = Zend_Search_Lucene:: open('../application/searchindex');

    //Set the properties for the Index.
    $Index->setDefaultSearchField('artist_name');
    $Index->setResultSetLimit(1);

    //Construct Query
    $query = 'genre:rock';

    //Search.
    $hits = $Index->find($query);

    //Set the view variables
    $this->view->hits = $hits;

}
```

Listing 8-15 is an updated version of the code shown in Listing 8-14—with two slight modifications. The new lines of code (shown in bold to set the total number of records to display) were added, and the search scope to match everything in the rock genre within the index added. In this case, the total number to display is set to 1 which will return the best match that is then displayed in the view. Refresh the view you created by loading the URL http://localhost/search/result again. You should see something similar to Figure 8-4 in your browser.

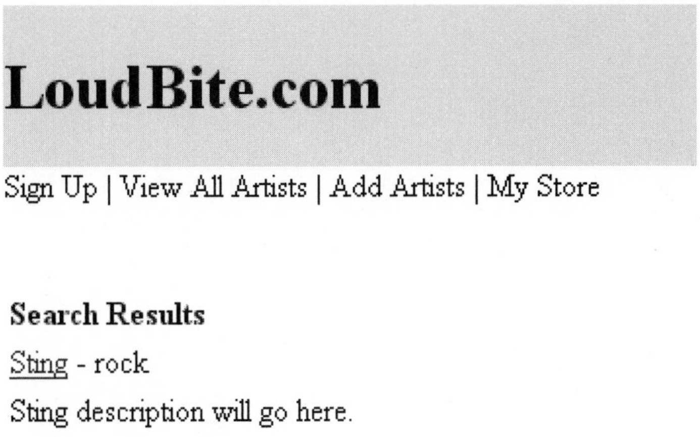

# LoudBite.com

Sign Up | View All Artists | Add Artists | My Store

**Search Results**

Sting - rock

Sting description will go here.

*Figure 8-4. Updated result set*

# Sorting the Search Result

By default, the Zend_Search_Lucene class displays the high-scoring results at the top. It's a score generated for a document in a database and is calculated using the number of times a keyword or phrase appears in the document. Suppose that you search for the keyword cat. A document containing the word 20 times will score higher than another document that contains the word 5 times.

If you don't want to sort the data by the best matching result, you can specify the sort type and sort field from the document using the find() method's additional parameters. The sort field is the second parameter, must be a string, and must exist in the document. This is the field that you want the searches to be sorted by.

The third parameter is the sort type, which identifies the type of sorting you want to do. You can sort the data alphabetically, numerically, or with the regular scoring system. The string parameters that are accepted are shown in Table 8-6.

*Table 8-6. Sort Types*

| Sort Type | Description |
| --- | --- |
| SORT_REGULAR | Regular sorting; based on the scoring system |
| SORT_STRING | Alphabetical sorting |
| SORT_NUMERIC | Numerical sorting |

The fourth parameter identifies the way you want to sort the data. This is similar to DESC and ASC ordering in a database query language. The acceptable values are SORT_DESC and SORT_ASC.

Let's now update the code to sort the data by the title (see Listing 8-16).

***Listing 8-16.*** *Sorting the Search Results*

```
/**
 * Result.  Fetch the result and display to the user.
 *
 */
public function resultAction(){

    //Open the index to search in.
    $Index = new Zend_Search_Lucene('../application/searchindex');

    //Set the properties for the Index.
    $Index->setDefaultSearchField('artist_name');
    $Index->setResultSetLimit(3);

    //Construct Query
    $query = 'genre:rock';

    //Search.
    $hits = $Index->find($query, 'artist_name', SORT_STRING, SORT_ASC);

    //Set the view variables
    $this->view->hits = $hits;
}
```

The code shown in Listing 8-16 uses the find() method to sort the data. The second parameter was used to specify the field to sort by: artist_name. The third parameter was set as SORT_STRING because you're dealing with string data. The fourth parameter was set as SORT_ASC to sort the data alphabetically. Load the URL http://localhost/search/result to see the updated search result.

# Highlight Colors

Search results can be enhanced by highlighting keywords that were used for searching. An additional feature, the Zend_Search_Lucene component, allows you to highlight keywords by using the htmlFragmentHighlightMatches() method.

The htmlFragmentHighlightMatches() method accepts an XHTML string and (depending on the search query) it highlights the matching keywords. Let's take an example with the current search engine, as shown in Listing 8-17.

**Listing 8-17.** *Highlighting Colors*

```
/**
 * Result.  Fetch the result and display to the user.
 *
 */
public function resultAction()
{

  //Open the index to search in.
  $Index = new Zend_Search_Lucene('../application/searchindex');

  //Set the properties for the Index.
  $Index->setDefaultSearchField('artist_name');
  $Index->setResultSetLimit(10);

  //Construct Query
  $query = 'genre:electronic';
  $query = Zend_Search_Lucene_Search_QueryParser::parse($query);

  //Search.
  $hits = $Index->find($query,
               'artist_name',
               SORT_STRING,
               SORT_ASC);

  $text = "";
  foreach($hits as $hit){

    $text .= "<tr><td>
           <a href='artist/'>$hit->artist_name</a>
           $hit->genre
        </td></tr>";

    $text .= "<tr><td>$hit->description<br/><br/></td></tr>";

  }

  //Highlight the words.
  $text = $query->htmlFragmentHighlightMatches($text);
```

```
//Set the view variables
$this->view->text = $text;
}
```

Listing 8-17 demonstrates the updated code that will match all records containing the electronic genre. It runs much like all the other code examples: loading the required classes to create an index, creating the index, setting all the required settings using the setters, and then creating the query. The Zend_Search_Lucene_Search_QueryParser class is utilized by calling its parse() method..

After you search for the matching documents containing the search terms, you iterate over the results and create the XHTML in the action, not in the view. You create the $text variable and add in the XHTML that you require. After the iteration completes, you pass the $text variable into the htmlFragmentHighlightMatches() method that will highlight the matching text located within the XHTML and it will return only the body of the HTML and exclude any HTML headers and body tags so your markup won't look like a dog's dinner . Finally you set the view variable and display it once more in the results page.

Before loading the page, you need to also make an additional change to the result.phtml view. Open the file located at application/views/scripts/search/result.phtml and update the XHTML as shown in Listing 8-18.

**Listing 8-18.** *Showing Highlighted Search Results*

```
<?php echo $this->doctype('XHTML1_STRICT'); ?>
<html xmlns="http://www.w3.org/1999/xhtml" xml:lang="en" lang="en">
<head>
  <?php echo $this->headTitle('LoudBite.com – Search Results'); ?>
</head>
<body>

  <?php echo $this->render("includes/header.phtml"); ?>
  <table border='0' width='600'>
  <tr><td colspan="3"><b>Search Results</b></td></tr>
  <?php echo $this->text; ?>
  </table>


</table>
</body>
</html>
```

The XHTML will use the view variable $text to print out the XHTML for the search results instead of using the foreach loop previously implemented. Now take a look at the resulting view by loading the URL http://localhost/search/result. It will look like Figure 8-5.

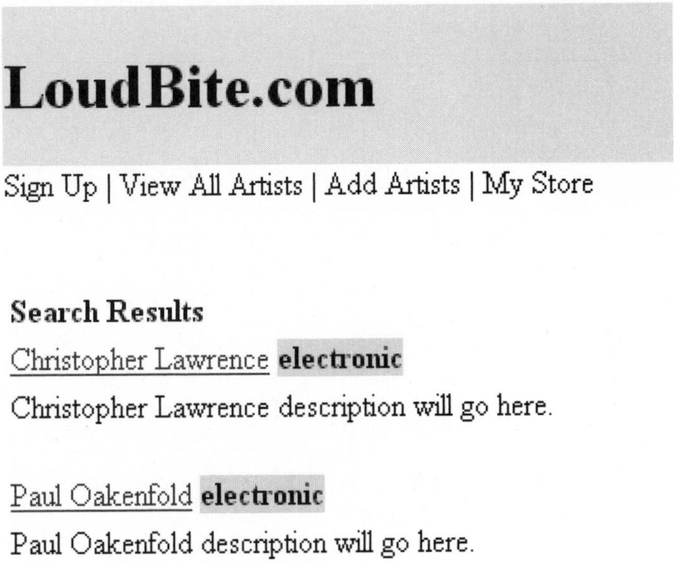

# LoudBite.com

Sign Up | View All Artists | Add Artists | My Store

### Search Results

Christopher Lawrence **electronic**

Christopher Lawrence description will go here.

Paul Oakenfold **electronic**

Paul Oakenfold description will go here.

*Figure 8-5.The keyword is now highlighted.*

You have now concluded the complete implementation of a search engine for any application. Try creating your own search implementation using what you've learned in this chapter for the Loudbite application.

## Summary

The topic of this chapter was search engines: what a search engine is, what it does, the basic terminology, and how Zend Framework supports an out-of-the-box search engine using the Zend_Search_Lucene component.

The chapter continued by giving you a good look at what it takes to create a search engine and all the building blocks that go into it, such as a document and its fields.

You continued by creating and adding fields to the searchable document. The five field types and when and how to use them were illustrated. With the fields you created, you learned how to add content into the search engine. You learned the basic features as well as the methods to add content from an HTML file as well as a Word document.

You learned how to create queries to search for data in the search engine, techniques to display the content, and how the component sorts and ranks search results.

# CHAPTER 9

■■■

# Caching with Zend Framework

*Caching* allows you to decrease the load time for content by reusing content that was previously loaded by a different user. This chapter will cover every step Zend Framework takes to create cached content.

You'll start with a basic introduction to caching: what it is, how it works, and the different tools web applications use to cache data. With an overall understanding of caching, you'll move into Zend Framework and see how it implements caching. You'll take a look at how to cache anything from functions and classes to sections of the web page, and how to delete and group cached items for better cleanup. The chapter ends by integrating the Zend_Cache component with memcached and APC, two of the most widely used caching tools currently in use for PHP.

## Introducing Caching

To get a better understanding of what caching is, let's use a quick example of a user arriving at the home page of a web site. The page contains many images and uses dynamic content derived from a database to populate it. When a user arrives at the page, the server must do a number of things. At a high level, the server must call each of the images from the directory to display, connect to the database, retrieve the data from the database tables, and present the data to the user.

Using the same flow, let's view the process at a granular level: the CPU and memory level. At each of the steps, the data must be converted into bits: ones and zeros. With the bits converted, you present the data to the browser, which then formats the data into a nice web page for the user. The process described is costly compared with reading only from memory. Reading from memory is what caching is.

Taking the example currently in use to the next level, you'll update the code behind the home page to use caching. When a user arrives at the home page, the data must be initially read from disk before it's stored into memory. Requesting this in-memory data during subsequent requests then involves the process of loading the data using an identifier and determining whether there was a hit or a miss.

In cache lingo, a *hit* happens any time the request for the specific piece of cached data marked with the specified ID has been located. When a hit is made, the data is retrieved from the cache and used for processing. If the request does not locate the identified cached data, it is a *miss*. When you encounter a miss, you load the content from disk and place it into the cache for subsequent calls. Zend Framework has a similar approach.

## Caching with Zend Framework

Zend Framework has put together a set of classes that can cache database content, classes, and any general content you might need to cache in order to speed up loading.

To use the caching feature, you need to use the Zend_Cache component, which contains two primary classes. The initial class is Zend_Cache_Frontend, which allows you to cache content such as functions, classes, and general data (see Table 9-1).

**Table 9-1.** *Front-end Cache Types*

| Cache Type | Class | Description |
| --- | --- | --- |
| Core | Zend_Cache_Core | Parent class to all other Zend_Cache_FrontEnd classes; caches general data. |
| Class | Zend_Cache_Frontend_Class | Caches classes (objects) with their methods and properties. |
| File | Zend_Cache_Frontend_File | Caches files that will expire when the file is updated. |
| Function | Zend_Cache_Frontend_Function | Caches function calls. |
| Output | Zend_Cache_Frontend_Output | Caches any content displayed between the Zend_Cache_Frontend_Output methods start() and end(). |
| Page | Zend_Cache_Frontend_Page | Caches an entire page using the Zend_Cache_Frontend_Page start() method at the beginning of the content to cache. Impossible to use end(). |

The Zend_Cache_Core class contains a wide variety of methods to set the data you'll cache and determines how much space is available for caching. Table 9-2 contains the available methods for front-end caching.

**Table 9-2.** *Zend_Cache_Core Methods*

| Method | Description |
| --- | --- |
| setBackend(Zend_Cache_Backend) | Sets the Zend_Cache_Backend object for use; determines how to save the cached data. |
| getBackend() | Returns a Zend_Cache_Backend object. |
| setOption(String, Mixed) | Sets the front-end options. The first parameter is one of the option shown in Table 9-5; the second parameter is the value for the option. |
| getOption(String) | Returns the stored value for the specified option. |
| setLifetime(int) | Sets the lifetime for the front end in seconds. |

| | |
|---|---|
| load(String) | Returns the cached data with the ID specified by the string parameter. |
| test(String) | Determines whether the cache ID specified is available for use. If available, returns true; otherwise, returns false. |
| save(String, String, Array, int, int) | Saves data into the cache. The first parameter is the data to cache. The second parameter is the unique ID for the cached content. The third parameter is an array containing a list of strings for tagging the data. The fourth parameter is the time to keep the content in the cache. The fifth parameter contains the priority of the data, 0–10 (0 = very low; 10 = very high). |
| remove(String) | Removes a specific cached item containing the string ID. Returns true if successfully removed. |
| clean(String) | Removes all cached items specified by the clean mode string. Clean modes are shown in Table 9-8. |
| getIdsMatchingTags(Array) | Returns an array containing all the cache IDs that contain the matching tags. |
| getIdsNotMatchingTags(Array) | Returns an array containing all the cache IDs that do not contain the matching tags. |
| getIds() | Returns an array containing all the IDs cached. |
| getTags() | Returns an array containing all the tags cached. |
| getFillingPercentage() | Returns an int value between 0 and 100 that represents the percent of space taken up by the cache. |
| touch(String, int) | Adds extra life to the cached content containing the specified ID. The first parameter is an ID; the second parameter is the extra time to allocate to the cached content. |

To understand what Zend_Cache_Frontend does, think of it as the class that tells Zend_Cache the type of data you want to cache.

The second component to the Zend_Cache component is Zend_Cache_Backend. If the Zend_Cache_Frontend tells Zend_Cache what you're going to cache, Zend_Cache_Backend identifies how you're going to cache it.

Zend_Cache_Backend contains six class types (see Table 9-3) that range from simple file caching to the ZendPlatform cache.

**Table 9-3.** *Cache Record Types*

| Cache Record Type | Class | Description |
|---|---|---|
| File | Zend_Cache_Backend_File | Caches data onto the local file system. |
| SQLite | Zend_Cache_Backend_Sqlite | Integrates Zend_Cache into SQLite. |
| Memcached | Zend_Cache_Backend_Memcached | Integrates Zend_Cache into memcached. |
| Apc | Zend_Cache_Backend_Apc | Integrates Zend_Cache into APC. |
| Xcache | Zend_Cache_Backend_Xcache | Integrates Zend_Cache into Xcache. |
| ZendPlatform | Zend_Cache_Backend_ZendPlatform | Integrates Zend_Cache into ZendPlatform. |

The Zend_Cache_Backend class is the parent class of each of the classes in Table 9-3 and contains the methods shown in Table 9-4.

**Table 9-4.** *Zend_Cache_Backend Methods*

| Method | Description |
|---|---|
| setDirectives(array) | Sets the front-end directives. Possible values: lifetime, logging, logger. |
| setOption (String, String\|Array) | Sets the specific back-end option. The first parameter is the name of the option to set; the second parameter is the value for the option. |
| getTmpDir() | Returns the systemwide tmp directory. |

With these methods and classes you can now start to create cached records.

# Creating Cached Records

This chapter began by looking at a small home page scenario that loads content from disk and the database. Now, let's expand on that scenario and assume that your traffic has increased. The application takes a total of five seconds to load both static content as well as dynamic content. The static content is composed of images and rarely changes. You also have database-driven, dynamic content. The dynamic content changes periodically from every hour to every day.

One quick way to decrease the load time for the page is to add one or two additional servers along with a load balancer, but that requires money. You can do something much more-cost effective (as in free) by using a cache.

Create a controller, CachingController.php, and place it into your application/controllers directory. The controller will be the main controller for the rest of this chapter and will contain a few actions you'll get to later. For now, create a new action, cacheTextAction(), and copy the code shown in Listing 9-1.

**Listing 9-1.** *Creating the Cache*

```php
<?php
/**
* Caching Controller
*
*/
class CachingController extends Zend_Controller_Action
{

  /**
* Cache Text Action
*
*/
  public function cacheTextAction()
  {

    //Frontend attributes of what we're caching.
    $frontendoption = array('cache_id_prefix' => 'loudbite_',
                'lifetime'      => 900);

    //Backend attributes
    $backendOptions = array('cache_dir' => '../application/tmp');

    //Create Zend_Cache object
    $cache = Zend_Cache::factory('Core', 'File',
                  $frontendoption,
                  $backendOptions);

    //Suppress the view
    $this->_helper->viewRenderer->setNoRender();
  }
}
```

The new action shown in Listing 9-1 demonstrates the basic setup for caching. To use a cache, you need to specify four different parameters to the Zend_Cache::factory() method:

- The initial parameter accepts the type of front-end caching you will do.

- The second parameter is the type of record you want to generate.

- The third parameter shows the front-end settings.

- The fourth parameter shows the back-end settings.

The front-end settings options are shown in Table 9-5. Listing 9-1 set the lifetime during which the item in cache should be valid. You set the lifetime from the default of 1 hour to 15 minutes, which means that the cached data will be cleared every 900 seconds (15 minutes), and an updated item will be stored on the first request for that data. The next option you set is the cache_id_prefix, which is the cache's namespace. Add the text loudbite_ as the prefix that will be added to the front of the every ID you create.

***Table 9-5.*** *Available Front-end Options*

| Option | Description | Default |
|---|---|---|
| write_control | When turned on, the cache is tested for corruption after data is written to it.<br>Slows down writing only. | true |
| caching | Enables/disables caching. | true |
| cache_id_prefix | Places a prefix string on every cached ID item. | null |
| automatic_serialization | Saves nonstring data. | false |
| automatic_cleaning_factor | Destroys old cached files after the total number of reads specified is reached (0 = never). | 10 |
| lifetime | Lifetime of a cached item in seconds. | 3600 |
| logging | Enables/disables logging. When on, performance is slower. | false |
| ignore_user_abort | Limits cache corruption when turned on (true). | false |

The next step is to set the back-end settings, which allow the cache to determine how the content is saved. Referring to Table 9-6, you used only the cache_dir option and set the cache directory to application/tmp. The directory must be present before you issue the cache call, so go ahead and create the directory now. Zend Framework uses the directory specified here to house all your cached data.

**Table 9-6.** *Available Back-end Options: File Type Only*

| Option | Description | Default |
|---|---|---|
| cache_dir | Location where the cached files will reside. | /tmp/ |
| file_locking | Reduces risk of cache corruption when turned on (true). Does not work in multithreaded web servers. | true |
| read_control | When enabled, the control key is saved in cache. After reading, the control key is compared to the one in cache. | true |
| read_control_type | Encryption type for read_control (when enabled). Values: md5, crc32, adler32, strlen. | crc32 |
| hashed_directory_level | Identifies hashed directory structure level. Used when there are many cached files.<br>0 = no hashed directory structure<br>1 = one level of directory<br>2 = two levels | 0 |
| hashed_directory_umask | Sets the umask for the hashed directory structure. | 0700 |
| file_name_prefix | Sets the prefix for the cache files. | zend_cache |
| cache_file_umask | Sets the umask for the cache file. | 0700 |
| metadatas_array_max_size | Sets the maximum size for the metadatas array. | 100 |

Load the cache by opening the URL http://localhost/caching/cache-text. Don't worry if nothing appears; you haven't created the data to cache yet. Let's go through each cacheable item from the basic text string to the advanced database result set.

## Caching Basic Text

Basic content such as static text is one of the first things you want to cache long term. There are two important methods that you need to use to determine whether you need to cache the content and to actually cache the content.

To determine whether you need to cache the content, use the Zend_Cache_Core load() method. This method requires a string parameter, which is the unique identifier of the cached content. If the ID is found, the load() method returns the data; otherwise it returns empty.

The second method which is required is the Zend_Cache_Core save() method. It accepts five parameters:

- The first parameter is the data you want to cache.

- The second parameter is the ID you want to set for the cached item.

- The third parameter is an array of tags you want to associate to the cached item.

- The fourth parameter is a specific lifetime.

- The fifth parameter is an int parameter representing the cached item's priority.

Open the CachingController.php file. You'll modify the cacheTextAction() method a bit more. First, determine whether you need to cache a piece of specific text; if you do, you'll cache it, as shown in Listing 9-2.

***Listing 9-2.*** *Adding Text Content to the Cache (Updated Action)*

```
/**
 * Cache simple text
 *
 */
public function cacheTextAction()
{

  //Frontend attributes of what we're caching.
  $frontendoption = array('cache_id_prefix' => 'loudbite_',
                'lifetime'      => 900);

  //Backend attributes
  $backendOptions = array('cache_dir' => '../application/tmp');

  //Create Zend_Cache object
  $cache = Zend_Cache::factory('Core',
                  'File',
                  $frontendoption,
                  $backendOptions);

  //Create the content to cache.
  $time = date('Y-m-d h:m:s');

  //Check if we want to retrieve from cache or not.
  if(!$myTime = $cache->load('mytime')){

    //If the time is not cached cache it.
```

```
    $cache->save($time, 'mytime');
    $myTime = $time;

}else{

    echo "Reading from cache<br>";

}

echo "Current Time: ".$myTime;

//Suppress the view
$this->_helper->viewRenderer->setNoRender();

}
```

The code shown in Listing 9-2 places the current date-time string value into the cache. First, the code is created to generate the date-time using the PHP date() function. The function generates the current time on your server and places it into the $time variable. With the content to cache set, load the caching classes using Zend_Loader and pass in the caching options into the factory() method. You then reach the important sections of the code, determining whether the content has been cached or not. You do this by calling load() with the ID of the cached content. If the content is not present, create it by issuing a call to save(), passing in a cache ID of mytime. If the content is there, read the time from memory (the result of the load() call). Load the action into your browser by visiting the URL http://localhost/caching/cache-text.

On the initial visit, you see the current time read from the results of the date function. During this initial visit, the if-else statement enters into the if portion and stores the time for any subsequent visits. Reload the page and notice that the time does not change. It is now reading from cache.

## Caching Files

Caching data and automatically expiring the content using the lifetime front-end option is beneficial, but you can also automatically trigger cache clearing of a specific data as soon as the source has been updated by using the Zend_Cache_Frontend_File class. This method of caching is recommended if you store important data in an XML file such as user permission settings or configuration parameters. You can even use it for something as simple as an FAQ HTML page, which requires the cache to be updated when updates are made to it.

To demonstrate this feature, you need to create an About page to contain a small excerpt of data. Create the new HTML file called aboutus.html anywhere in your file system and copy the HTML shown in Listing 9-3. I saved it in the public folder.

***Listing 9-3.*** *About Us HTML*

```
<h2>About Us</h2>
LoudBite is a music mashup application that aggregates content from
```

a wide variety of sources that include YouTube, Amazon, and del.icio.us.

Open the CachingController.php file and create a new action, cacheFileAction, which will determine whether you have currently cached the document and whether the cached document is out of date. If the cached document is out of date or if the ID is not found, you can create the cached item. The process is shown in Listing 9-4.

*Listing 9-4. Caching a File – cacheFileAction()*

```
/**
* Cache data from file.
*
*/
public function cacheFileAction()
{

  try{
    //Initialize file path
    $filePath = "../public/aboutus.html";

    //Frontend attributes of what we're caching.
    $frontendOption = array('cache_id_prefix' => 'loudbite_',
                'lifetime'      => 900,
                'master_file'   => $filePath);

    //Backend attributes
    $backendOptions = array('cache_dir' => '../application/tmp');

    //Create Zend_Cache object
    $cache = Zend_Cache::factory('File',
                 'File',
                 $frontendOption,
                 $backendOptions);

    //Check if we want to retrieve from cache or not.
    if(!$myContent = $cache->load('aboutuscontent')){

      //Retrieve data from file.
      $content = file_get_contents($filePath);

      //If the document is not cached cache it.
```

```
        $cache->save($content, 'aboutuscontent');
        $myContent = $content;

    }else{

      echo "Reading from cache<br>";

    }

      echo $myContent;


    }catch(Zend_Cache_Exception $e){

      echo $e->getMessage();

    }

    //Suppress the view
    $this->_helper->viewRenderer->setNoRender();




}
```

The cachefileAction() starts by initializing the $filePath variable. The variable contains the relative path to the file, aboutus.html, located in the public directory. The file contains the data to cache and is also the source or master file that needs to be updated. You then load the required class, Zend_Cache, using Zend_ Loader and start setting the front-end as well as the back-end options. At this point, take a look at the new option that you pass into the front-end array. The new option, master_file, is unique to this type of caching. The master_file option identifies the file to cache.

After the front-end and back-end options are set, pass the data into the Zend_Cache:: factory() method with the initial parameter set to File to indicate the cache type. With the cache object instantiated, you can check for the existence of the data using the load() method as well as the if-else statement. If the data with cache ID, aboutuscontent, is present, print out the cached content. Otherwise, use the PHP file_get_contents() internal function to retrieve the file contents. Finally, save the content into cache with the aboutuscontent ID.

Load the URL http://localhost/caching/cache-file to see the initial HTML directly read from the file, which means that its content is cached. Now reload the page; you should see a statement onscreen, verifying that you are no longer reading straight from the file.

Open the aboutus.html page once more and change About Us to About LoudBite.com. Save the file and reload the URL. The cache will clear the old content, cache the updated content, and present the aboutus.html file to you.

# Caching Classes

Zend_Cache allows developers to also cache class methods using the Zend_Cache_Frontend_Class class. The benefits of caching classes are apparent when using expensive methods within the class or when the process of instantiating the object is resource-intensive.

The Zend_Cache_Frontend_Class class contains additional options you can supply to the front end (see Table 9-7).

**Table 9-7.** *Zend_Cache_Frontend_Class Options*

| Option | Description |
| --- | --- |
| cached_entity | Caches either all the class methods when passing in an object or caches an abstract class when the class name is specified. |
| cache_by_default | If set to true, all calls to the specified class will be cached. |
| cached_methods | Caches only specific methods that are identified in an array. |
| non_cached_methods | Identifies all the methods that will not be cached in an array. |

Using the previous options, create a new action, cacheClassAction, in the CachingController.php file as well as a new class in a new directory, models/Misc, called Misc.php.

**Listing 9-5.** *Caching Classes*

```
/**
 * Cache Class
 *
 */
public function cacheClassAction()
{

  require "Misc/Misc.php";

  try{

    //Frontend attributes of what we're caching.
    $frontendoption = array('cache_id_prefix' => 'loudbite_',
                'lifetime'       => 900,
```

```
                    'cached_entity'  => new Misc_Misc(),
                    'cached_methods' => array("add"));


    //Backend attributes
    $backendOptions = array('cache_dir' => '../application/tmp');

    //Create Zend_Cache object
    $cache = Zend_Cache::factory('Class',
                    'File',
                    $frontendoption,
                    $backendOptions);

    echo $cache->add(1,4);

    //Suppress the view
    $this->_helper->viewRenderer->setNoRender();

}catch(Zend_Cache_Exception $e){

    echo $e->getMessage();

}

}
```

Listing 9-5 contains two additional front-end options: cached_entity and cached_methods. The cached_entity option allows you to specify either an object to cache or a string containing the class name. By providing the object instead of a string, you cache every method within the class. Providing the name of the class as a string, on the other hand, caches only abstract methods, and you must use static calls.

The next option, cached_methods, identifies the methods to cache within the class. In this example, you pass in the array containing the add string. Finally, you cache the class by simply calling the Zend_Cache::factory() method, passing in the Class type as well as the additional parameters, and print the returned sum from the cached add() method onto the screen.

Before you load the example on the browser, you need to create the Misc_Misc class, as shown in Listing 9-6.

**Listing 9-6.** *Misc.php*

```
<?php
/**
 * Misc class file.
 */
```

```
class Misc_Misc
{

  public function add($a, $b)
  {

    return $a+$b;

  }
}
```

The class contains only a single method, add(), which takes in two int parameters, adds them, and then returns the sum. After you copy the code shown in Listing 9-6, load the URL http://localhost/caching/cache-class in your browser. You will see the sum 5 display. At this point, the class is now cached. The internal logic within the method is cached, and any calls to the add() method will use the cached logic, but not the original parameters passed into the method. To verify that you are using the cached logic, change the numbers used previously in the add() method call in the cacheClassAction from 1 and 4 to **5** and **5**. Reload the URL and notice that the method returns the correct sum.

To be absolutely sure that you are using the cached logic, make a change to the add() class method. Update the return statement to read as follows:

```
return $a+$b+2;
```

Refresh the page and notice that the resulting data has not been changed. The new value does not show up until the lifetime has been reached.

## Caching Database Data

It's very expensive to open a connection to the database, run a query on the database, and then return the data. It's much more efficient to run through the process once and reuse the output when called subsequent times.

Caching database records can be done much like caching text. The initial request for the data will result in connecting to the database and retrieving the data. The data will be saved into cache for any subsequent requests. The process will then repeat itself after the data's lifetime has been met or you clean the cache.

In the next example, you'll use the database you created in Chapter 2. Open the CachingController.php file and create a new action, cacheDatabaseAction, as shown in Listing 9-7.

***Listing 9-7.*** *Caching Database Content*

```
/**
 * Cache Database content.
 *
 */
public function cacheDatabaseAction()
{
```

```php
try{

    //Frontend attributes of what we're caching.
    $frontendoption = array('cache_id_prefix'      => 'loudbite_',
                    'lifetime'            => 900,
                    'automatic_serialization'=> true);

    //Backend attributes
    $backendOptions = array('cache_dir' => '../application/tmp');

    //Create Zend_Cache object
    $cache = Zend_Cache::factory('Core', 'File',
                    $frontendoption,
                    $backendOptions);

    //Check if data exists in cache.
    if(!$records = $cache->load('databasecontent')){

        require_once ('Db/Db.php');

        //If the data is not cached cache it.
        $db = Db_Db::conn();

        $query   = "SELECT * FROM artists";
        $records = $db->fetchAll($query);

        //Cache the Array.
        $cache->save($records,'databasecontent');

        echo "Caching Content from DB.";

    }else{

        echo "Reading from cache<br>";

    }

    //Display the records
    foreach($records as $row){
```

```
        echo $row['artist_name'].'<br>';

    }

}catch(Zend_Cache_Exception $cacheError){

    echo $cacheError->getMessage();

}catch(Zend_Db_Exception $dbError){

    echo $dbError->getMessage();

}

//Suppress the view
$this->_helper->viewRenderer->setNoRender();

}
```

Database result sets are cached using the same process as other forms of caching. The only difference is the additional parameter to the front-end options and the connection to the database, as shown in Listing 9-7.

Listing 9-7 begins by loading the required Zend_Cache class, which is where it differs from all other examples you've seen. Instead of only two initial options, add an additional option: automatic_serialization. This option will convert an array into a serialized string. This setting is necessary when saving the result set returned by the Zend_Db_Statement fetchAll() method.

After the front-end options are set, create the back-end options and the Zend_Cache_Core object. You can then use an if-else statement; if the cached data can be loaded using the unique ID databasecontent, place the content from cache into the $records variable and use it as you would any other Zend_Db fetchAll() result set. This example uses a foreach loop to display the artist name. If the content is not present, a database connection is created, the data is retrieved using the fetchAll() method, and it is then saved into cache.

The fetchAll()method returns an associated array instead of a PHP Data Object (PDO) that can't be serialized. This is an important tip when caching database result sets. Now print one of the two success messages.

Open the URL http://localhost/caching/cache-database and load the data into cache.

# Grouping Cached Data (Tags)

With the skills to create cached content fresh in your mind, you'll now learn how to group related cached data by implementing tags. *Tags* are keywords that describe content within the text. For example, a paragraph pertaining to Tears for Fears, a 1980s rock band, might contain these keywords/tags: rock,80-music. These tags then allow you to associate the paragraph to other pieces of content containing one of the two tags. The same concept can be used in caching.

Tagging can be accomplished by using the third parameter of the Zend_Cache_Core save() method. The third parameter accepts an array that contains strings, representing the tags to associate with the data to cache.

The next example demonstrates how to place content into groups using tag functionality. Let's say you have data to cache that can be tagged with indexcontent, artistcontent, and/or usercontent. The indexcontent tag contains all content that will display in the index page, artistcontent contains content that will display within the artist sections of the site, and usercontent contains content that will display within the user sections of the site.

Open the CachingController.php file once more and create a new action, cacheTagsAction, as shown in Listing 9-8.

**Listing 9-8.** *Implementing Tags*

```
/**
 * Cache data using tags
 *
 */
public function cacheTagsAction()
{

  try{

    //Frontend attributes of what we're caching.
    $frontendoption = array('cache_id_prefix' => 'loudbite_',
                'lifetime'       => 900);

    //Backend attributes
    $backendOptions = array('cache_dir' => '../application/tmp');

    //Create Zend_Cache object
    $cache = Zend_Cache::factory('Core', 'File',
                  $frontendoption, $backendOptions);

    //Create 7 pairs of cached content.
    $cache->save("index content 1",
          "data_1",
          array("indexcontent"));
    $cache->save("index content 2",
          "data_2",
          array("indexcontent"));
    $cache->save("index content 3",
          "data_3",
          array("indexcontent"));
    $cache->save("artist content 1",
          "data_4",
          array("artistcontent"));
```

```
    $cache->save("artist content 2",
            "data_5",
            array("artistcontent"));
    $cache->save("user content 1",
            "data_6",
            array("usercontent"));
    $cache->save("general content 1",
            "data_7",
            array("artistcontent", "usercontent"));
    echo "Successfully cached data";

}catch(Zend_Cache_Exception $e){

    echo $e->getMessage();

}


//Suppress the view
$this->_helper->viewRenderer->setNoRender();


}
```

Listing 9-8 demonstrates two ways to add tags to cacheable content. The initial six items to cache contain only a single tag, whereas the general content 1 item contains two tags that identify it with two groups: artistcontent and usercontent. By adding two tags to the cached content, you associate the content with both groups.

Before you retrieve the data based on tags, you need to load it into the cache. Load the cached data by loading the URL http://localhost/caching/cache-tags. After you finish, update the cacheTagsAction() action, as shown in Listing 9-9.

**Listing 9-9.** *Retrieving Cached IDs Based on Tags*

```
/**
 * Cache data using tags
 *
 */
public function cacheTagsAction()
{

  try{

    //Frontend attributes of what we're caching.
```

```
            $frontendoption = array('cache_id_prefix' => 'loudbite_',
                       'lifetime'      => 900);

            //Backend attributes
            $backendOptions = array('cache_dir' => '../application/tmp');

            //Create Zend_Cache object
            $cache = Zend_Cache::factory('Core', 'File',
                       $frontendoption, $backendOptions);

            //Create 7 pairs of cached content.
            $cache->save("index content 1",
                   "data_1",
                   array("indexcontent"));
            $cache->save("index content 2",
                   "data_2",
                   array("indexcontent"));
            $cache->save("index content 3",
                   "data_3",
                   array("indexcontent"));
            $cache->save("artist content 1",
                   "data_4",
                   array("artistcontent"));
            $cache->save("artist content 2",
                   "data_5",
                   array("artistcontent"));
            $cache->save("user content 1",
                   "data_6",
                   array("usercontent"));
            $cache->save("general content 1",
                   "data_7",
                   array("artistcontent", "usercontent"));
echo "Successfully cached data<br>";
echo "Cached Content Ids with tag 'artistcontent'<br>";
$ids = $cache->getIdsMatchingTags(array("artistcontent"));
foreach($ids as $id){
  echo $id."<br>";
}
```

```
        }catch(Zend_Cache_Exception $e){

            echo $e->getMessage();

        }

        //Suppress the view
        $this->_helper->viewRenderer->setNoRender();

    }
```

To retrieve the content by tag, use the Zend_Cache_Core getIdsMatchingTags() method (refer to Table 9-2). Listing 9-9 demonstrates its use by retrieving all the cache IDs that contain the artistcontent tag. Call getIdsMatchingTags() and iterate through the array using a foreach loop. From the data cached in the action, you know that there should be three IDs with a positive match: 4, 5, and 7. Reload the URL http://localhost/caching/cache-tags and see the IDs print onscreen.

# Deleting Cached Records

With a few pieces of cached data in memory, you might now need to remove some of the data. The Zend_Cache_Core class provides the remove() method for testing purposes or if you're trying to remove the data by force.

The remove() method allows you to remove individual items from the cache by passing in the ID of the cached item as its first parameter.

Let's take a look at how to delete a cached record. Open the CachingController.php file and create a new action: deleteCacheAction(). The new action in Listing 9-10 expands on the example shown in Listing 9-2, which caches the current time.

**Listing 9-10.** *Deleting Cached Records with remove()*

```
/**
 * Remove Cached Item.
 *
 */
public function deleteCacheAction()
{

    //Frontend attributes of what were caching.
    $frontendoption = array('cache_id_prefix' => 'loudbite_',
                'lifetime'      => 900);

    //Backend attributes
    $backendOptions = array('cache_dir' => '../application/tmp');
```

```
//Create Zend_Cache object
$cache = Zend_Cache::factory('Core','File',
                $frontendoption,
                $backendOptions);

$time = date('Y-m-d h:m:s');

if(!$myTime = $cache->load('mytime')){

  //If the time is not cached cache it.
  echo "ADDING TO CACHE <br>";
  $cache->save($time, 'mytime');
  $myTime = $time;

}else{

  echo "FROM CACHE: ".$myTime."<br>";
  echo "REMOVING CACHED TIME <br>";
  $cache->remove('mytime');
  $myTime = $time;

}

echo $myTime;

//Suppress the View
$this->_helper->viewRenderer->setNoRender();

}
```

The action sets the front- and back-end options, creates a Zend_Cache object, and initializes the data to cache in the $time variable. You then see whether the data is currently present in the cache by attempting to load the data using the load() method and the mytime ID. If the cache ID is not present, you can create the cache data and then display it onscreen. If the ID is located, you can print out the cached time, remove the data from cache using the remove() method, and print the noncached time.

Open the URL http://localhost/caching /delete-cache. The initial load displays the cached time that has been added into memory. The next load shows the message indicating that you have removed it. Reload the page to add the date back into the cache.

# Deleting Cached Sets

In previous sections of this chapter, you cached data by using tags, which enabled you to group cached data based on relevancy. The Zend_Cache_Core class allows you to remove cached items based on these tags with the clean() method.

The clean() method accepts two parameters: the initial parameter is one of the cleaning modes outlined in Table 9-8, and the second optional parameter is an array type. The array must contain string values representing the individual tags. Specifying tags narrows down the removal of the cached data.

Let's use the clean() method to clear all the items with the indexcontent tag. Update the CachingController.php file and add a new action, deleteTagsCacheAction(), as shown in Listing 9-11.

**Listing 9-11.** *Clearing Cached Data*

```
/**
 * Remove data by tags.
 *
 */
public function deleteTagsCacheAction()
{

    //Frontend attributes of what we're caching.
    $frontendoption = array('cache_id_prefix' => 'loudbite_',
                'lifetime'      => 900);

    //Backend attributes
    $backendOptions = array('cache_dir' => '../application/tmp');

    //Create Zend_Cache object
    $cache = Zend_Cache::factory('Core','File',$frontendoption,
                    $backendOptions);

    //Clear the cache
    $cache->clean(Zend_Cache::CLEANING_MODE_MATCHING_TAG,
            array('indexcontent'));

    //Suppress the View
    $this->_helper->viewRenderer->setNoRender();

}
```

The action shown in Listing 9-11 demonstrates the use of the clean() method and how you can use one of the cleaning modes shown in Table 9-8 to remove cached data containing the indexcontent tag. The action begins by setting the required options and creating an instance of the Zend_Cache_Core class.

Using the object, call the clean() method, pass in the clean mode
Zend_Cache::CLEANING_MODE_MATCHING_TAG, and pass the second array parameter with the
indexcontent element. With the clean mode CLEANING_MODE_MATCHING_TAG, the clean() method
narrows down its removal of cached data to only those cached items that contain the indexcontent tag.
Load the URL http://localhost/caching/delete-tags-cache to remove all cached data containing the indexcontent
tag. To confirm that the cached content was removed successfully open the application/tmp directory and
notice that the files zend_cache_loudbite_data_[1-3] as well as the files zend_cache_internal-
metadatas_loudbite_data_[1-3] have been removed. These files contained your cached data before running
the action.
    Let's now clear out all the data currently stored in cache by using the clean mode
CLEANING_MODE_ALL. Update the deleteTagsCacheAction action, as shown in Listing 9-12.

***Listing 9-12.*** *Clearing All Data from Cache*

```
/**
 * Remove data by tags.
 *
 */
public function deleteTagsCacheAction()
{

  //Frontend attributes of what we're caching.
  $frontendoption = array('cache_id_prefix' => 'loudbite_',
              'lifetime'      => 900);


  //Backend attributes
  $backendOptions = array('cache_dir' => '../application/tmp');


  //Create Zend_Cache object
  $cache = Zend_Cache::factory('Core','File',$frontendoption, $backendOptions);


  //Clear the cache
  $cache->clean(Zend_Cache::CLEANING_MODE_ALL);


  //Suppress the View
  $this->_helper->viewRenderer->setNoRender();


}
```

**Table 9-8.** *Cleaning Modes*

| Cleaning Mode | Description |
| --- | --- |
| CLEANING_MODE_ALL | Removes all data from cache regardless of status. |
| CLEANING_MODE_OLD | Removes old data that has passed its specified lifetime. |
| CLEANING_MODE_MATCHING_TAG | Removes all data that matches the tags supplied. The data must contain all the tags supplied. |
| CLEANING_MODE_NOT_MATCHING_TAG | Removes all data that does not have tags that match the tags supplied. |
| CLEANING_MODE_MATCHING_ANY_TAG | Removes all data that contains any of the tags supplied. |

The updated action shown in Listing 9-12 clears out the entire cache by using the clean mode CLEANING_MODE_ALL. The action contains the same code as Listing 9-10 and can be called using the same URL as before: http://localhost/caching/delete-tags-cache. Like the previous example, open the application/tmp directory and verify that all the files within this directory are not removed.

You now know how to create and remove cached data within a file system, but the Zend_Cache component contains much more functionality. Let's see how you can use the built-in support for a few of the most widely used caching tools.

# Integrating Zend_Cache and Third-Party Tools

The Zend_Cache component can be used to cache data by using third-party caching software. The back end can currently be integrated into the following:

- APC: http://pecl.php.net/package/APC

- memcached: http://pecl.php.net/package/memcache

- SQLite: http://www.sqlite.org/

- XCache: http://xcache.lighttpd.net/

- ZendPlatform: http://www.zend.com/products/platform/

Each of the listed caching software contains a unique Zend_Cache_Backend class (as outlined in Table 9-2) that contains specific options you can pass into Zend_Cache.

To use any of the software, it must be installed on your local file system, and the proper cache core type (refer to Table 9-3) must be identified when calling the Zend_Cache::factory() method.

This book demonstrates only the initialization of a Zend_Cache object using one of the classes. The remaining classes can be initialized in the same way, but each class contains its own unique set of front- and back-end options. (These options are outlined in the tables that follow.)

The action shown in Listing 9-13 is a template to use when caching content into third-party caching tools such as memcached or SQLite. The differences among the types are the front- and back-end options and the second parameter of the Zend_Cache::factory() method.

**Listing 9-13.** *Implementing Third-Party Caching: memcached*

```
/**
 * Caching items into memcached
 *
 */
public function cacheMemcachedAction()
{


    //Set Frontend Options
    $frontendOptions = array("cache_id_prefix" => "loudbite_",
                    "lifetime"      => 900,
                    "server"        =>
                    array(array('host' => 'HOST',
                            'post' => 'PORT NUMBER',
                            'persistence' => true)));

    //Backend attributes
    $backendOptions = array('cache_dir' => '../application/tmp');

    $cache = Zend_Cache::factory('Core',
                    'Memcached',
                    $frontendOptions,
                    $backendOptions);

    //CACHE THE SAME WAY AS BEFORE

    //Suppress the view
    $this->_helper->viewRenderer->setNoRender();


}
```

The example uses the Zend_Cache_Backend_Memcached class and options to save data. You can load the required file and set the front-end option with a unique option, server, which identifies the memcached servers containing the cache. Using this option you can identify more than one server at a time by adding an additional array into the array value. If you use SQLite, you can use the options shown in Table 9-10.

When it's time to cache, you do it the same way you cached using non-third-party caching. Take a look at the following tables for additional options required by each caching tool. Neither Zend_Cache_Backend_Apc nor Zend_Cache_Backend_ZendPlatform contains any special options.

*Table 9-9.* Zend_Cache_Backend_memcached *Options*

| Option | Description |
| --- | --- |
| servers | Sets the memcached servers to use in an associated array. Each array identifies a server. Format: array(array('host' => 'HOST', 'port' => PORT , 'persistence' => PERS). |
| compression | Enables/disables compression; default is false. |

*Table 9-10.* Zend_Cache_Backend_SQLite *Options*

| Option | Description |
| --- | --- |
| cache_db_complete_path | Sets the complete path to the SQLite database. |
| automatic_vacuum_factor | Defragments the database file.<br>0 = no automatic defragment.<br>1 = defragment only when clean() and delete() called.<br>x = defragments database file after x cleans/deletes have been called. |

*Table 9-11.* Zend_Cache_Backend_XCache *Options*

| Option | Description |
| --- | --- |
| User | Sets string user; format: xcache.admin.user. |
| password | Sets string password; format: xcache.admin.pass. |

# Summary

You reached the end of the book. Instead of giving you a short summery of this chapter, I decided to provide an overall summary of the book with this chapter's summary.

In Chapter 1, you began the book by learning how to set up your environment, setting up Apache, MySQL, PHP, and Zend_Tool (which you later used to create not only your first application but also controllers and actions throughout the course of the book).

Chapter 2 discussed in detail the application you went on to build using Zend Framework.

Chapters 3 and 4 covered how to use Zend_Controller and Zend_Controller_Action to give your web application life. You also learned about views_what they are, what they contain, and how each controller-action pair can contain one. You also learned how to create, validate, and filter forms using the Zend_Form , Zend_Validate, and Zend_Filter components of the framework.

Chapter 5 covered how to interact with different databases using its adaptors. You learned about its built-in CRUD support and created object-oriented statements that you later applied while using Zend_Paginator to paginate through many result sets.

You created and sent e-mail and added attachments to e-mail in Chapter 6. You learned about web services and RSS feeds in Chapter 7, and you learned about how to set up a search engine using Zend_Search_Lucene in Chapter 8.

Finally, this chapter focused on caching content—saving data into memory to quickly retrieve and process the content for the user instead of fetching the content from the disk. It covered what caching is, why you need it, and how Zend Framework has implemented support for it with the Zend_Cache component.

You learned how to create cached items that originate from the database, cache functions, cache complete classes and its methods, and delete and group cached items. You then discovered how you can easily integrate with third-party caching software such as memcached and APC using Zend_Cache.

I hope this book is useful to you as a reference. You can use the tables outlined throughout the book for specific Zend Framework components.

# Index

# C